When they came to the place that is called The Skull, they crucified Jesus there with the criminals, one on the right and one on his left.

LUKE 23:33 (NRSV)

GOOD PUNISHMENT?

Christian Moral Practice and U.S. Imprisonment

James Samuel Logan

WILLIAM B. EERDMANS PUBLISHING COMPANY
GRAND RAPIDS, MICHIGAN / CAMBRIDGE, U.K.

Published 2008 by
Wm. B. Eerdmans Publishing Co.
2140 Oak Industrial Drive N.E., Grand Rapids, Michigan 49505 /
P.O. Box 163, Cambridge CB3 9PU U.K.

Printed in the United States of America

12 11 10 09 08   7 6 5 4 3 2 1

Library of Congress Cataloging-in-Publication Data

Logan, James Samuel.
    Good punishment? : Christian moral practice and U.S. imprisonment /
James Samuel Logan.
        p.   cm.
    ISBN 978-0-8028-6324-9 (pbk.: alk. paper)
    1. Imprisonment — United States. 2. Prisons — United States.
    3. Punishment — United States. 4. Punishment — Religious aspects —
Christianity. 5. Christian ethics.   I. Title.

HV9471.L64   2008
261.8'336 — dc22
                                                    2007028195

www.eerdmans.com

For Alice Eugenia Jones:
mother, friend, oracle

Contents

Acknowledgments

The production of this book required sufficient communal support. Family, friends, colleagues, and mentors far too numerous to mention here kept me energized and sane throughout the process of its writing. I am especially indebted to my Princeton Seminary doctoral advisors, Mark Lewis Taylor, Peter Paris, and Cornel West. It was especially in the work of Mark Taylor that the idea for this book came to life. Taylor's brilliant guidance has significantly aided my academic progress from my first days as a doctoral candidate. Taylor, Paris, and West have helped me to see clearly that the life of the mind is like an empty vessel if what one learns has no love-inspired bearing on the lives of those whom Sly and the Family Stone called everyday people.

I want to thank my mother, Alice Jones, from whom I inherited the strength to press on against some of life's longest odds. I am also supremely indebted to my wife Sarah, and to our two young sons, Davis Ogima and Isaiah Bemidji, who never let me forget the miracle of life's joys in the midst of writing about the anguish of crime and imprisonment in the United States. Gratitude is due as well to my sisters (Wendy, Debra, Loretta, and Tanya), my brothers (Ivan Corey and Michael), and my in-laws (Sylvia and Marvin Reimer), all of whom have given so much of their time and resources in support of my work.

I am also indebted to, and give thanks for, the many other Princeton Seminary and Princeton University teacher-scholars, colleagues, and friends who with their friendship, conversation, and support have played an important part in sustaining me through this book project. A hopelessly partial list of these folk include Kevin Reilly, Marlene Fox, Mary Ann Rodriguez, Brian K. and Sharon Blount, Anaida Pascual and Luis Rivera-Pagán, Carrie and Geddes Hanson, Nancy Duff and David Mertz, Richard Fenn, Adrienne Daniels Paris, Abiola and Adrian Backus, Inn Sook and Sang Hyun Lee, Annie and David Willis, Max Stackhouse, Elsie Anne McKee, Scott Hendrix, Daniel Migliore, George Hunsinger, Wentzel van Huyssteen, Ross Wagner, James Deming, Bruce McCormack, Charles Bartow, Cleo LaRue, Kristin Saldine, Jeff Stout, Robert Wuthnow, Al Raboteau, Noliwe Rooks, John Gager, Eddie Glaude Jr., Kenyatta and Allison Gilbert, Jonathan and Cecily Walton, Nyasha Junior, Heather White, Lisa Serrano-Dodd and Dylan Dodd, Rita and Moses Biney, Melody and Jacob Cherian, Mieko and Tomu Sakon, Ajit and Daisy Prasadam, Alice Yafeh, Kenneth Ngwa, Dion LaPoint and Ray Owens, Sandra and Joe Scrivner, Karen and David Miller, Regina Langley, Sharon Stewart, Maureen F. Reed Sumners, Sylvie and Kossi Ayedze, Atola Longkumer, Yuki Shimada, JianGuo Wang, Ronda Rhone, Bridgett Green, Annie Lockhart, Aisha and Carl Brooks-Lytle, Erin Epp and Todd Cioffi, Carla Jones, Jeremy Schipper, Jana Strukova and Doug Hume, Chad Mullet Bauman, Sun Young Kim, Noreen Santos, Cynthia and Anthony Rivera, Jill and James McCullough, Mati Moros and John Taylor, Julie Claassens, Rachel Baard, Anna Johnson, Amy Marga, Rebecca and Cress Darwin, Carol and Tom Hasting, Charmaine and Retief Mueller, Toby Sanders, Dwight Davis, Greg Ellison, Audrey Thompson, Cedric Johnson, Mereides Delgado, Dawn and Mark Wilhelm, Kim Strange-Shanks, Dante and Monica Quick, Antonia Brown, Patrick Daymond, La-Tonia Middleton, Shenell Smith, AnneMarie Mingo, Touré Marshall, Eustacia Moffett, Lerone Martin, Erin Hayes, William Heard Jr., Maria Norales, Carol McCleary, Eun Hyey Park, Armand Collins, Akilah and Simeon Banister, Janette Ok, Amaury Tanon-Santos, Keon Gerow, Nicole Massie, Imani and Colin Jones, Michael Hegeman, Theresa Latini, Sang Uk Lee, La Sang Dingrin, Pangernungba, Bruno Linhares, Shang Jen Chen, Yun Hui Kim, Raimundo Barreto Jr., Greg Walter, Ron Choong, Matt Lundberg, Ronald Hinton Jr., Scott Collins-Jones, Lisa Powell, Laura Thelander, Edip Aydin, Chi Yi Chen, Theo Cornish, Tommy Ayala Casarez, Martin Tel, Larry Stratton, Paul Kim, Graeme Wilson, Anita Kline, Elliot Raztman, Andrea Jones, Larraine Fuhrmann, Pat Bogdziewicz, Kerry Smith, Paul Koop, Kevin Osterloh, and Mark Rowe.

I also extend much gratitude to the significant groups of other Princeton folk who continually feed and lifted my spirits on many a tough writing day: ARAMARK food service workers (especially Lonnie Kirk,

Dorothy Kirk, Aaron Kirk, Tina Moore, Theresa Carmichael, Ceceline Perry, Guillermo Ramon, and Amy Ehlin); security guards (particularly Juanito Pierre, Charlie Buttaci, Ernest Burford, and Juan Garcia); Association of Black Seminarians; Hispanic Theological Initiative (particularly its director Joann Rodriguez); Association of Latino/Hispanic American Seminarians; Asian Association at PTS; International Student Association; Gay, Lesbian and Bi-Sexual Association of Seminary Students; Princeton University's Women's Center (especially Amada Sandoval); Princeton University's African American Studies Program (particularly Jean Washington and Hattie Black); Princeton United Methodist Church (especially Peggy Fullman); various office workers, administrators, and staff (especially Teresa Reed, Carol Belles, Manuel Alvarez, Betty Angelucci, Susan Pope, Chester Polk, Victor Aloyo Jr., Kate Skrebutenas, Julie Dawson, Brenda Hermanson, Mack Swain Jr., Felicia Sparrow-Ricks, Doreen Warble, Bill Milton, and Bobby Marshall). Thanks also to the Fund for Theological Education (particularly Sharon Fluker) for supporting my work over the years. A word of thanks is also due for the thoughtful and patient professionalism of the staff at Eerdmans Publishing.

I have been grateful for the support of my colleagues and teaching assistants in the religion department and in the African & African American Studies Program at Earlham College (as well as at Earlham School of Religion and Bethany Theological Seminary) — Lyn Miller, Mary Garman, Michael Birkel, John Newman, Phyllis Boanes, Tanya Beam, Bonita Washington-Lacey, Shenita Piper, Trayce Perterson, Anupama Arora, Joann Quiñones, Karim Sagna, Steve Butler, Carol and Bob Hunter, Aletha Stahl, Kevin Miles, Charles Watson, Charles Holmond, Margaret Hampton, Deb NcNish, Steve Angell, and Scott Holland. In addition to the aforementioned faculty, I extend a note of thanks to other faculty colleagues who have supported my work through their strong advocacy and/or support for my researh and writing as inextricably tied to my vocation of teaching: Ferit Güven and Marya Bower (in the Philosophy Department), Jo Ann Martin (Anthropology), Christine Larson and Neal Baker (Reference Librarians), and (now retired Academic Dean) Len Clark. Finally, I must thank my teaching assistants who continuously inspire and challenge me with fresh perspectives on the politics of justice and love — Tulani Zakiya Foy, Ginger Leigh, and Monica Fleetwood Black.

Introduction: The Problem
of Imprisonment in the United States

. . . here was the house of the living dead, a life like none other
on earth, and people who were special, set apart. It is this special corner that I am setting out to describe.

Fyodor Dostoyevsky, *House of the Dead*

The Problem of Imprisonment in the United States

Today over 2.3 million persons occupy America's various federal, state, and
local prisons and jails. This number represents the highest per capita incarceration rate in U.S. history; currently more than 700 per 100,000 U.S.
residents are incarcerated.[1] Writing for the National Criminal Justice
Commission, Steven Donziger has reported that, "Since 1980, the United
States has engaged in the largest and most frenetic correctional buildup of
any country in the history of the world."[2] Indeed, with just 6 percent of the
world's population, the United States now holds 25 percent of its prisoners
at a cost of about $50 billion per year to process and house inmates.

If one were also to consider, in addition to the $50 billion annual cost
of direct administration and maintenance of prisons and jails, the profits
now routinely enjoyed by companies that employ prison labor, the annual

1. *New York Times*, April 9, 2003.
2. Steven R. Donziger, ed., *The Real War on Crime: The National Report of the National Criminal Justice Commission* (New York: HarperPerennial, 1996), p. 31.

1

economic activity surrounding the U.S. prison system approaches or exceeds $100 billion. Companies that utilize prison labor include Honda, Victoria's Secret, (the now-defunct) TWA, Microsoft, Procter & Gamble, Helene Curtis, and AT&T. Indeed, for the aforementioned companies (along with a host of others) prison cells have come to symbolize "bars of gold."[3] With regard to the merger of punishment and profit, Pulitzer Prize-winning journalist Joseph Hallinan has observed during his travels to various U.S. prisons that

> Prisons are tremendous public works projects, throwing off money as a wet dog throws off water. When I began my travels, I had no idea of the amount of money to be made from prisons, no idea that a single pay phone inside a prison could earn its owner $12,000 a year, or that a warden, if he played his cards right, could make himself a millionaire. But corporate America did.[4]

The financial incentive to increase the numbers of those imprisoned is not limited to the pursuit of corporate profit. Over the past two decades many economically depressed communities in the United States have come to support the boom in prisons as a way out of financial distress. A recent *New York Times* article reporting on a study conducted by the Urban Institute noted that "some counties in the United States now have more than 30 percent of their residents behind bars." The study also found that nearly a third of United States counties now have at least one prison. (This includes the county where I now teach college, Wayne County in Indiana.) The contemporary network of new prisons and jails aids the survival of struggling local businesses. Moreover, new prison and jail construction attracts new businesses to economically depressed communities and creates new jobs for construction workers and prison guards. Since prisoners are counted as residents of the counties in which

---

3. See the essay by behavioral scientist Anne Larson Schneider, "Public-Private Partnership in the U.S. Prison System," and news columns by Joseph T. Hallinan, "Private Prisons Not Saving Strapped Company Closing Three in Texas," and Cait Murphy, "Crime and Punishment." These pieces all appear under the subheading "Bars of Gold: Prison Economics" in Peter G. Herman, ed., *The American Prison System* (New York: H. W. Wilson, 2001), pp. 85-115. See also Joseph T. Hallinan, *Going Up the River: Travels in Prison Nation* (New York: Random House, 2003), p. xiv.

4. Hallinan, *Going Up the River*, p. xiv.

they are incarcerated, an added benefit of a community's willingness to accommodate a new prison or jail is more federal and state funding, as well as greater political representation.

A significant and obvious question in all this is, *at what social cost do we build and fill more prisons?* According to Jeremy Travis, a senior fellow at the Urban Institute and one of the authors of the aforementioned study, a significant societal concern was the study's finding that "the prison network is now deeply intertwined with American life, deeply integrated into the physical and economic infrastructure of a large number of American counties."[5] One of the most significant aspects of the prison boom phenomenon is the overt public bigotry of anti-Black White racism that it fosters. In a discussion of the connection between what he describes as "correctional Keynesianism" and "the new racism," Paul Street, the director of research at the Chicago Urban League, argues that

The ultimate policy irony at the heart of America's passion for prisons can be summarized by what I call "correctional Keynesianism;" the prison construction boom fed by the rising "market" of black offenders is a job and tax-base creator for predominately white communities that are generally far removed from urban minority concentrations. Those communities, often recently hollowed out by the deindustrializing and family farm-destroying gales of the "free market" system, have become part of a prison-industry lobby that presses for harsher sentences and tougher laws, seeking to protect and expand their economic base even as crime rates continue to fall. With good reason: the prison building boom serves as what British sociologist David Ladipo calls "a latter-day Keynesian infrastructural investment program for [often] blight-struck communities. Indeed, it has been phenomenally successful in terms of creating relatively secure, decent paid, and often unionized jobs."[6]

5. Fox Butterfield, "Study Tracks Boom in Prisons and Notes Impact on Counties," *New York Times*, March 4, 2004: A19. Also see the Urban Institute study by Sarah Lawrence and Jeremy Travis, "The New Landscape of Imprisonment: Mapping America's Prison Expansion," (Washington, D.C.: Urban Institute, 2004).

6. Paul Street, "Color Blind: Prisons and the New American Racism," in *Prison Nation: The Warehousing of America's Poor*, ed. Tara Herivel and Paul White (New York: Routledge, 2003), p. 36. See also David Ladipo, "The Rise of America's Prison Industrial Complex," *New Left Review* 7 (January/February 2001): 109-23.

Indeed, prison expansion — not even counting local jails — has been phenomenal over the last eighty or so years. The United States had just 61 federal and state prisons in 1923; by 1974 there were 592 prisons. This number grew to 1,023 by the year 2000. Currently there are an estimated half-million more people incarcerated in the United States than in Communist China, a nation some three and a half times more populous than the U.S. Like China, the United States is commonly cited by various international human rights organizations as a major contributor to social misery related to the treatment of prisoners.

The basic reasons for the increase in the number of U.S. residents being imprisoned appear to be (at least) four: (1) the development of legislation since the 1970s requiring mandatory long-term sentencing as a cornerstone of corrections public policy; (2) the nationwide declaration of a "war on crime," specifically the "War on Drugs," since the 1980s; (3) an ever-increasing social policy commitment to prison incarceration as a control solution geared toward containing and regulating the frustrations of the nation's most exploited residents, those who must perpetually confront society's most entrenched social ills (e.g., economic exploitation, substandard education and housing, and various other social consequences of poverty); and (4) the economic profit generated by increased imprisonment. Taken as an interrelated whole, these causes are said by some to have produced a "prison-industrial complex," that is, a set of bureaucratic, economic, and political interests which encourage increased spending on incarceration.

Perhaps it is true that most prison officials today, as well as perhaps most of the general public, would not condone "old school" practices such as chaining prisoners in dungeons or pits as a useful form of therapeutic rehabilitation — a practice once employed, for example, at the notorious San Quentin State Prison in California. Nonetheless, the numbers of prison officials and legislators who may have once considered it the job of the criminal justice system to approach punishment as an effort to correct behaviors attributable to psychological and social forces has steadily declined. David Sheff, writing for *The New York Times Magazine*, reported in 2004 that

The ranks of wardens who believe that even felons convicted of the most unspeakable crimes can change for the better, given enough instruction, counseling and . . . maternal admonishing, have thinned in the last few decades. Most wardens strive only to control and house their share of the nation's growing prison population, which, in the last 20-odd years, has quadrupled, to 2.1 million people. In California, the word "rehabilitation" was expunged from the penal code's mission statement in 1976. Since then, prison officials have been exhorted to punish, and they have fulfilled that mandate in new, highly secure prisons, devoid of anything that could lead to accusations of pampering inmates.[7]

One could lament a past era in which an alleged nobler mission of the prison was to reform or restore prisoners to some semblance of civility and cultured humanity. But we would do well to interrogate even this perhaps wishful myth. David Cayley, drawing on social commentary from eighteenth-century prison observers, argues that

> The prison has always been a doubtful instrument of correction. "In a prison," Samuel Johnson wrote in *The Idler* in 1759, "the awe of public eye is lost, and the power of the law is spent, there are few fears, there are no blushes. The lewd inflame the lewd; the audacious harden the audacious." Johnson's contemporary, Henry Fielding, the novelist and magistrate, made a similar observation. Speaking of the "houses of correction" of his time, he pointed out that "whatever these houses were designed to be, or whatever they at first were, the fact is that they are at present . . . no other than schools of vice, seminaries of idleness, and common bearers of nastiness and disease."[8]

Even of the well-intended, supposedly humane, and reformative conditions of solitary confinement modeled after the nineteenth-century Quaker-influenced Eastern Penitentiary in Pennsylvania, Charles Dickens once wrote,

> I believe that very few men are capable of estimating the immense amount of torture and agony which this dreadful punishment, prolonged for years, inflicts upon the suffers; and in guessing at it myself,

---

7. David Sheff, "The Good Jailer," *New York Times Magazine*, March 14, 2004, pp. 44-47.

8. David Cayley, *The Expanding Prison: The Crisis in Crime and Punishment and the Search for Alternatives* (Cleveland: Pilgrim Press, 1998), p. 1.

and in reasoning from what I have seen written upon their faces, and what to my certain knowledge they feel within, I am only the more convinced that there is a depth of terrible endurance in it which none but the sufferers themselves can fathom, and which no man has a right to inflict on his fellow-creature. I hold this slow and daily tampering with the mysteries of the brain, to be immeasurably worse than any torture of the body: and because its ghastly signs and tokens are not so palpable to the eye and sense of touch as scars upon the flesh; because its wounds are not upon the surface, and it exhorts few cries human ears can hear; therefore I the more denounce it, as a secret punishment which slumbering humanity is not roused up to stay.[9]

Indeed, there appears to be reasonable doubt about whether the actual social function of the prison has ever been fashioned for serious reform.

Contemporary prisoner rights advocates Marc Mauer and Meda Chesney-Lind, writing for the Sentencing Project, have recently observed that over the past thirty years "a social policy that can only be described as mass imprisonment" has significantly transformed the nation's family and community dynamics.[10] The increased scale of incarceration today has an impact that extends far broader than just individual prisoners and their families. The collateral consequences of society's reliance on large-scale incarceration as a primary means of achieving "criminal justice" include the exacerbation of racial divisions, broad-scale economic hardship, and economic and social risk for the most vulnerable of the nation's residents, particularly children. In addition, incarceration on such a large scale poses fundamental questions of justice, fairness, and citizenship in a democratic society.

Echoing a 1955 United Nations document entitled "Standard Minimum Rules for the Treatment of Prisoners," the 1976 U.N.-sponsored "International Covenant on Civil and Political Rights" (ICCPR) imagines a world where some 185 nations would adhere to the prescription that the "penitentiary system shall comprise treatment of prisoners the essential aim of which shall be their reformation and social rehabilitation" (Article

9. Charles Dickens, *American Notes and Pictures from Italy* (London: Chapman and Hall, 1906), pp. 83-84.

10. Marc Mauer and Meda Chesney-Lind, eds., *Invisible Punishment: The Collateral Consequences of Mass Imprisonment* (New York: New Press, 2002), pp. 1-2.

10). 150 nations ratified the ICCPR. The United States, which ratified the covenant on June 8, 1992, ostensibly put it in full force on September 8, 1992. International human rights advocate Robert Drinan, a Jesuit priest and former U.S. congressman, argues that the philosophy advanced in Article 10 of ICCPR "appears to be really at odds with the dominant approach of federal and most state officials in the United States; their aim is to penalize and punish rather than to reform or rehabilitate them."[11]

Day by day the nation bears witness to the devastating effects of U.S. prisons and jails that deal "in the currency of lost human connections," as it was aptly put by *Newsweek* journalist Ellis Cose. These lost human connections are particularly acute in communities like the one in which I was raised in the South Bronx and in a multitude of other poor communities, particularly those "of color." The U.S. penal system now fosters "a nation of jailers" in which more money is spent on building and maintaining prisons than on public schools.[12] We have also created a situation where some "[t]wo percent of America's children must now visit prison to see mom or dad."[13] Because of my own connection to many of the social consequences of imprisonment, my analyses and arguments in this book will make occasional reference to friends and family in the South Bronx. Some of the experiences of ordinary people in my life are representative of the devastation effected by prisons in the lives of millions of U.S. residents.

Christians and United States Imprisonment

A serious concern related to the problem of imprisonment in the United States (all too briefly summarized above) has been the general lack of systematic and constructive critical investigation on the parts of Christian theologians and ethicists with regard to the social costs of imprisonment on such a large scale. Part of the significance of my efforts in this book is

11. Robert F. Drinan, *The Mobilization of Shame: A World View of Human Rights* (New Haven: Yale University Press, 2001), p. 27.

12. In 1985 Jonathan Kozol reported that New York City spent $58,000 yearly on each adult inmate and $70,000 on each juvenile inmate, "nearly ten times what it spends to educate a child in its public schools." See Jonathan Kozol, *Amazing Grace: The Lives of Children and the Conscience of a Nation* (New York: Harper Perennial, 1985), p. 142. I suspect that this spending disparity is worse now than it was then.

13. Ellis Cose, "The Prison Paradox," *Newsweek*, November 13, 2000, p. 43.

related to this lacuna. Notwithstanding the specifically Christian lacuna that I flag for concern, the rapid swelling of the nation's prisons and jails over the past three decades or so has prompted vast amounts of scholarship and journalistic commentary concerning the social function of criminal punishment in the United States. Since the mid-1980s, numerous sociopolitical studies related specifically to the social function of large-scale incarceration have emerged.

Simultaneously, Christian theologians, ethicists, pastors, and laypersons have published works on various issues related to criminal punishment. In more recent years such works have included Lee Griffith's *The Fall of the Prison: Biblical Perspectives on Prison Abolition* (1999), Christopher Marshall's *Beyond Retribution: A New Testament Vision for Justice, Crime, and Punishment* (2001), T. Richard Snyder's *The Protestant Ethic and the Spirit of Punishment* (2001), *The Spiritual Roots of Restorative Justice* (2001) edited by Michael Hadley, and Mark Lewis Taylor's *The Executed God: The Way of the Cross in Lockdown America* (2001). What has not been done, however, is a Christian social ethics of punishment that focuses specific attention on the devastating social function of punitive large-scale imprisonment as a social practice. A distinctive contribution and significance of this book lies in its bringing to bear a constructive theological ethics of (perhaps oxymoronic) "good punishment" on social problems associated with contemporary large-scale imprisonment.[14] This effort brings together an examination of salient empirical data and social theory related to the contemporary U.S. practice of imprisonment with a constructive theological ethics of Christian praxis.

It must be said that Christians who have been wrestling with problems associated with society's fixation on punishment and imprisonment as significant, if not primary, means of social control have done some very important and admirable work. Given this truth, the "lacuna" I cite in the collective work of others is not to be taken as self-righteous criticism of what others have failed to do. This notwithstanding, I will not always agree with others or they me. My work simply adds to the voices of those Chris-

---

14. It is widely assumed that a well-functioning prison system is essential to a good society, or at least a necessary feature of such a society. This study will show, however, that the system of retributive degradation and "mass incarceration" that U.S. prisons have become constitute a general departure from any kind of punishment (i.e., infliction of harm, unpleasantness, suffering, etc.) that might be called "good."

tians who lament, wrestle, and hope over the manner in which society deals with those viewed as its criminals. With this in mind, the work herein represents, imperfectly but earnestly, a contribution to the larger collective struggle on the parts of Christians to imagine and construct a better church and societal response to crime. I recognize that this is a work of love and justice that is always in a state of becoming.

In light of the problem that I have only summarized above, this book will suggest that a Christian social ethics of "good punishment" focused on the contemporary United States practice of imprisonment can be developed through a re/constructive critique of the "Anabaptist Methodist" Stanley Hauerwas's theological ethics of punishment. To focus Christian social ethics on the contemporary United States practice of imprisonment, which is now employed on an unprecedented scale, is to foreground a major obstacle to the transformation and restoration of offenders in community as well as society at large. An assumption underlying the effort that follows is that incapacitating and controlling socially destructive persons is a legitimate social aim for any society wishing to preserve itself. Indeed, it would be naïve to deny that in a highly complex society at least some minimum system of justice is necessary. This includes police, courts, and other institutions set up to adjudicate justice claims whenever some fair distribution of goods and/or rights has been "criminally" disrupted. In addition, society must continually secure effective ways of addressing criminal breaches of responsibility that threaten the cohesion of the nation. Central to Christian perspectives on criminal justice is the requirement of discerning the difference Jesus makes for Christian participation in society's understanding and carrying out of punishment. Christians must continually struggle with how best to embrace the praxis of criminal justice while demonstrating a politics of better hope for society. This better hope should connect the Christian worship of God to a radically reconfigured reality of justice ushered into human history by God's self-unveiled love and justice in the person of Jesus Christ.

Overview of the Argument

This book generally proceeds from an inquiry into the social function and consequences of U.S. imprisonment and concludes with movement toward a constructive Christian social ethics of "good punishment" that may be practically applied to the problem of imprisonment and its collateral social consequences. My intention is to be highly critical of practices of "criminal" punishment that leave individuals, communities, and society-at-large less able to realize the expansion and enhancement of flourishing communities with justice. Flourishing communities (and the individuals that sustain them) are the foundation of a stable society.

Chapters One through Three are interrelated and draw on materials from among social history, sociology, anthropology, law and penal theory, current affairs, theology, social ethics, philosophy of religion, and critical race theory. In Chapter One I argue that the current punitive practice of imprisonment as an ostensible means of reducing criminality plays a significant social role, on the contrary, in the maintenance and promotion of criminality and associated social consequences, and these in the service of what many today call a "prison-industrial complex." I will suggest that a significant social function of contemporary punishment has been to mete out what I will call "retributive degradation."[15] Retributive degradation refers to the punitive practice of (authorized) social vengeance and status humiliation carried out on those convicted of crime. Retributive degradation re/produces criminality, even when this is not the motive that lies behind punishment in this form. Although a significant function of large-scale incarceration is retributive degradation, incarceration also serves a number of other interrelated social functions, such as the following:

1. alleviating widespread public anxiety and fear of crime;
2. providing economic stimulus and profit to local and state governments and private corporate investors involved in various ventures

---

15. While the term "retributive degradation" may seem prematurely or inappropriately value-laden, there is a history of usage for naming empirical practices of degradation and retribution (to avenge) as opposed to the laudable function of "chastisement" (to correct) more routinely practiced in Europe. James Q. Whitman and others demonstrate the establishment of such terms as part of the phenomenon of imprisonment and punishment in the U.S. See, for example, in Whitman's book *Harsh Justice* (Oxford: Oxford University Press, 2003), his analysis of the empirical harshness and degrading character of U.S. imprisonment in comparison to European imprisonment practices. In comparison to Europe, the U.S. criminalizes a far greater number of moral offenses, enforces its standing laws more frequently, is more willing to subject classes of persons to criminal liability, and is less open to adjusting punishments in light of mitigating circumstances. And the divide between Europe and the U.S. on the matter continues to widen.

that have become dependent on the promotion and expansion of prisons;

3. insuring the political relevance and survival of politicians who feel a need to be responsive to the concerns just mentioned;
4. providing a control and management solution geared toward containing and regulating the frustrations of the nation's most exploited residents.

I will contend that retributive degradation is compounded and worsened by the continual pursuit of these goals, which, working together, constitute a "prison-industrial complex," i.e., an "array of relationships linking corporations, government, correctional communities, and media," in the words of social philosopher and activist Angela Y. Davis.

In Chapter Two I will argue that the unprecedented growth in the sanction of imprisonment has issued in a variety of collateral social consequences, which undermine communal and societal well-being. In this chapter I will offer salient examples of the collateral social consequences of large-scale vengeful and status-humiliating incarceration, which exacerbates the stigmatization of "people of color" (particularly Black people), overburdens women, children, and poor and working-class communities, erodes necessary social unity, and undermines civil liberty and regard for others.

Chapter Three contends that the prison system's retributive degradation function as well as the numerous collateral social consequences tied to imprisonment reinforce human alienation. I define "alienation" as humans' basic and tragic tendency to turn away from their mutual affections for one another, to participate in both neglectful indifference toward and the most virulent oppression of persons and groups. In this chapter I will start by briefly discussing some salient forms of alienation that inform the contemporary practice of criminal punishment in the United States: the atomization of individuals, community, and society at large; and the role of individualism (with support from religion). My brief discussion of the aforementioned (mutually reinforcing) dimensions of alienation provides the backdrop against which I move into a more substantial examination of anti-Black White racism and the conception of the "Black criminal." In general, my analysis in Chapter Three serves to help demonstrate the relationship between current prison practices and social corrosion. Various dimensions of alienation, including widespread anti-Black White racism, are key problems which a Christian ethics of punishment will need to address.

Informed by my examination of the problem of imprisonment in Chapters One through Three, I then turn in Chapter Four to an explication of Stanley Hauerwas's Christian ethics of punishment. Specifically, I will explore Hauerwas's understanding of Christian punishment as a possible resource and way forward in the Christian discernment regarding better social responses to imprisonment and its social consequences. In this chapter I suggest that Hauerwas is arguably one of the exemplary Christian theologians of our time advocating for a recovery of the moral skills (or virtues) that enable a proper understanding of social reality and practice from the perspective of the Christian narrative of Israel as Jesus Christ presents it.

Moreover, my rationale for critical engagement with Hauerwas rather than with someone else around the issue of criminal punishment and imprisonment relates, for one thing, to his publication of a provocative essay on the issue entitled "Punishing Christians."[16] Furthermore, I make particular appeal to Hauerwas rather than to others who are also doing important work around issues of imprisonment and punishment not only because of the Anabaptist pacifist sensibilities he as a Methodist shares with my Mennonite faith, but also because, arguably, no other contemporary Christian theologian or ethicist has secured quite as extensive a church-wide and public hearing on various contemporary peace and justice issues. With regard to social arrangements related to the issue of punishment, Hauerwas, as we shall see, views forgiveness and reconciliation as the *telos* of Christian "good punishment."

In Chapters Five and Six I will continue the constructive movement, begun in Chapter Four, toward a transformative and restorative Christian moral vision of punishment. In Chapter Five, I will critically assess the usefulness of Hauerwas's vision of "good punishment" as "excommunication." Excommunication is the name Hauerwas gives to the Christian process of penance, forgiveness, and reconciliation. Hauerwas calls this process a "politics of healing memories." I will flesh out the implications and usefulness of Hauerwas's ethics of punishment for Christians wishing to confront more publicly the problem of U.S. imprisonment practices and the attending collateral social consequences.

16. This essay has now been published in Stanley Hauerwas's recent book *Performing the Faith: Bonhoeffer and the Practice of Nonviolence* (Grand Rapids, Mich.: Brazos Press, 2004).

Finally in Chapter Six I suggest a *telos* of the transformative politics of healing memories, namely, restoration envisioned as a "politics of ontological intimacy." Ontological intimacy refers to the binding and dynamic way of being-there-with-and-for-others that should characterize a Christian faith seeking to participate in the being of God, as modeled for Christians in God's self-revelation in Jesus Christ. In this final chapter, in some continued conversation with Hauerwas's work, I develop the significance of a Christian understanding of "ontological intimacy" as a "politics." Here I invite readers to imagine how this expression of radical human bondedness amidst difference might be developed to take Christians to a fuller, more dynamic, and more socially responsible practice of good punishment. Since racism is one of the most intractable features of U.S. imprisonment practice, I will also give significant attention to the problem of racism and imprisonment in the context of ontological intimacy. In addition to considering the problem of racism and imprisonment, the social relevance of a politics of ontological intimacy will also be demonstrated in a review of representative social practices where signs of such a politics in the making are already apparent, namely, restorative justice and systemic alternatives. I conclude by offering an assessment of what peaceable Christians might learn from "the liberals" in the service of their social participation in "good punishment."

Imprisonment as a Concern for Christian Ethics

Christian ethics (as an intellectual discipline) can be defined as the practical science (or even art) of moral inquiry, reasoning, and practice guided by careful reflection on, and obedience to, what we more or less come to agree God is doing in the world. Put differently, ethics (in general) can be understood as the study of the reasons and justifications that lay behind moral belief and practice. A focus on the practice of imprisonment in the United States has important implications for the study of Christian ethics because a central role of "Christian" ethics ought to be that of aiding in the production and promotion of particular moral communities. Moreover, Christian ethics is concerned that particular moral communities work together in unity and justice with one another for the sake of society's well-being as a whole. Christian ethics is concerned with the building of a diverse yet common society. A focus on contemporary imprisonment is a relevant focus for Christian ethics because, generally speaking, the practice of imprisonment undermines the best of the Christian impulse to foster the good of others, and therefore of all of us.

The scale of U.S. incarceration in particular hurts the nation's ability to create and maintain communities and a society at large in which individuals and groups agree to work out the trials, tribulations, hopes, and dreams of unavoidable human association in ways which invite us to be mutually vulnerable, accountable, and in covenant with one another. The current ethos of the U.S. prison system, and by extension a critical mass of U.S. residents, is to lock people up at excessive rates and (for a prescribed period of time) throw away the key — if not execute them. This state of affairs produces and reproduces an environment where it is less likely that residents will choose to do the good of the other despite real human differences, disagreements, and even assaults upon one another.

Because vengeful and status-humiliating imprisonment is now so widely employed a means of domestic security, punitive large-scale imprisonment has emerged as a powerful cultural force in itself. The massive resources put into jailing wrongdoers makes it far more difficult to apply needed resources to other, more hopeful means of securing societal well-being (e.g., education, critical material and medical resources, civic habituation, and education in positive virtues or excellences).

Human associations of goodwill and justice are harmed by the alienating factionalism encouraged by our national reliance on imprisonment. This harm is apparent as residents of African American, Latina/o, Native American, low-income, and working class communities are disproportionately incarcerated and executed, while, increasingly, the rich and powerful retreat to gated communities of nonassociation with "the masses."

Christian social ethics, precisely because it is "Christian," cannot avoid commenting on the quality of human relationships. Yet, as Christians attempt to affirm the expansion of positive moral communities across society, moral hegemony and repressive dogmas must be resisted as we attend to the task of constructing just relations amongst diverse peoples. It seems reasonable to expect that people from a wide diversity of backgrounds, religious and otherwise, would care that the U.S. prison system, albeit an admittedly legitimate social institution, routinely re/produces illegitimate social consequences.

My suggestion that not only does the prison have criminogenic properties, but also that the large-scale use of incarceration exacerbates crime, seems implausible to many U.S. residents. I concur with the criminologist Todd Clear's assertion: "Americans are so accustomed to thinking of prison as a last-ditch means of controlling crime, the proposal that it may increase crime strikes us as almost absurd."[17] Yet isn't it worth all of us considering the provocative sociological tradition supporting investigations into the actual social effects of what is supposed to constitute crime control and prevention? The late social philosopher Michel Foucault argued that prison invented delinquency, "in the sense that the intellectual language underlying the concept of the individual criminal was one of the products of the formation of the prison."[18] Foucault went on to suggest that it is essential to its own self-survival as a prominent social institution that the prison fails in its ostensible task of controlling criminality.[19]

Even if one resists adopting Foucault's perspective on the prison, perhaps the "reflective analysis" of Pierre Bourdieu might offer a useful platform for considering the social function of the prison and its growth. Bourdieu's analytical perspective situates prison within human experience and within social life in the United States. Borrowing from the Durkheimian tradition of analyzing the social function of deviance, interactionalist theorists like Bourdieu, as well as others like Armand Mauss and Kai Erikson, help us to see that prisons inevitably produce certain effects on individuals and communities inside and outside its walls. Clear correctly points out that "these effects change the way people on the outside understand the social significance of prison. In short, one sees prison as influencing groups other than prisoners."[20] We should care about putting to the test, in light of our current situation, the possibility that the carceral matrix does not merely cast society's criminal offenders into a confused world of retributive degradation physically separated from

17. Todd Clear, "Backfire," in *The Unintended Consequences of Incarceration: Conference Papers*, ed. Karen Fulbright (New York: Vera Institute of Justice, 1996), p. 7. Note that the words *America* and *Americans* used in this work are synonyms for the United States and its peoples.

18. Clear, "Backfire," p. 7.

19. Michel Foucault, *Discipline and Punish: The Birth of the Prison*, trans. Alan Sheridan (New York: Vintage Books, 1995), pp. 293-308.

20. Clear, "Backfire," p. 7. See also Pierre Bourdieu and Loïc J. D. Wacquant, *An Invitation to Reflexive Sociology* (Chicago: University of Chicago Press, 1992); Armand Mauss, *Social Problems as Social Movements* (Philadelphia: Lippincott, 1975); and Kai T. Erikson, *Wayward Puritans: A Study of the Sociology of Deviance* (New York: Wiley, 1966).

the "outside world," but also intensifies Foucault's contention that the delinquent can be a product of the prison and that no one is outside the carceral archipelago.[21]

An additional important aim of this book is to advance a Christian social ethics of good punishment against large-scale imprisonment while at the same time avoiding the imposition of a metaphysical, necessary, and absolute Christian cultural hegemony on others. It is hoped that a view of large-scale imprisonment as socially corrosive is a human concern that all residents of the U.S. can view as a threat to common social flourishing.

An examination of alienating human relationships vis-à-vis certain dimensions of punishment, although informed by my Christian faith, extends beyond it to a level of concern that can be embraced by peoples of other religious traditions or by people with more secular understandings of human association. My assumption here is that attention to the quality of human relationships is a human interest, which is not uniquely Christian, but which a Christian vision of good punishment can positively inform.

21. Foucault, *Discipline and Punish*, p. 301.

1. Re/producing Criminality and the Prison-Industrial Complex

The Problem

In the United States today, the current practice of imprisonment as a means of reducing criminality and securing public safety in fact does just the opposite, maintaining and even promoting criminality. If this is so, as I will argue, prisons and jails cannot, in general, play an effective role in preserving and promoting individual transformation and community flourishing.

Punitive practices associated with incarceration undermine the individual transformation of wrongdoers and the well-being of communities in two significant and interrelated ways. First, and most directly, the inner workings of so-called "correctional facilities" are rife with practices of violence and degradation. Since violence breeds violence, prisons and jails can therefore hardly avoid their current social function as preservers and producers of violence. Second, prisons and jails have entered into arrangements in recent decades that place considerable social, political, and economic pressure on them to put ever-greater numbers of offenders behind bars. This pressure comes from a number of sources: (1) an intensified fear of crime among the general populace; (2) a political need to redress perceptions about crime run amok; (3) the pursuit of profits by big business and economic stability for distressed communities; and (4) the need to regulate and control the frustrations of significant populations of U.S. residents who feel exploited and denied access to the American dream of "life, liberty, and the pursuit of happiness." Working together, these interrelated forces create significant institutional pressure to lock more people up.

And, just like the internal workings of today's prisons, they also serve to re/produce criminality.

Penitence, Retribution, and the Persistence of Crime

The perceived social function of prisons, by both prison administrators and the public, has changed over time. Michel Foucault's influential *Discipline and Punish*, published in 1977, documented a major shift in eighteenth-century penology away from humiliating forms of bodily retribution and toward the beginnings of the modern prison bureaucracy. Ostensibly this was seen as a move in the direction of more "humane" (i.e., rational, almost clinical) methods of punishment.[1]

In the United States, the prevailing philosophy gradually shifted from the notion of deterrence (in which punishments were modeled on British codes) just after the colonial period, to that of rehabilitation during the era of Andrew Jackson (1829-1837). Marc Mauer, assistant director of the Sentencing Project, explains that the rehabilitative approach to criminal corrections "assumes — based on sociological, psychological, or moral beliefs — that an offender is someone who has erred but is capable of change, and that the period of incarceration can be viewed as a time to effect interventions that may bring about more law-abiding behavior."[2] Although there was some fluctuation, rehabilitation was arguably the prevalent guiding principle of the U.S. penal system well into the twentieth century.

The early history of moral-rehabilitative penal institutions in the United States was associated with the Quakers in eighteenth-century Pennsylvania. It was under Quaker influence that Philadelphia's Eastern State Penitentiary, arguably the first modern American prison, was opened in 1829.[3] Earlier Quakers, who were "anxious to find an effective substitute

---

1. Michel Foucault, *Discipline and Punish: The Birth of the Prison*, trans. Alan Sheridan (New York: Vintage Books, 1995); See also Don Sabo, Terry A. Kupers, and Willie London, eds., *Prison Masculinities* (Philadelphia: Temple University Press, 2001), p. 19.

2. Marc Mauer, *Race to Incarcerate* (New York: New Press, 1999), p. 42.

3. Modern detention facilities whose purpose it was to punish convicts while simultaneously serving as occasions for penitence and reform already had established a presence by the time Eastern Penitentiary was opened for occupancy. Already in 1796, Pennsylvania's Walnut Street Jail became the first "penitentiary-house" in the United States to experiment with solitary confinement. Angela Y. Davis points out that "Walnut street's austere regime

for brutal flogging and the lopping off of ears . . . instituted the solitary confinement plan."[4] They believed that places of detention and penitence should replace those of unchristian retributive punishment. Since the redemption of a criminal's soul was critical, and since Quaker theology viewed no one as beyond the possibility of redemption, Quakers saw penitence as the way to reform those convicted of crime; hence places designated for reform came to be called "penitentiaries." The penitentiary was the place "where the offender could ponder his sins in solitude, and then reform as he did penance."[5] The idea proved popular. The New Jersey state prison system was founded in 1797 (or 1798) at Lamberton, with the following inscription engraved over the main door: "Labor, Silence, Penitence — That those who are feared for their crimes may learn to fear the laws, and be useful."[6]

Although the penitentiary was conceived of by the Quakers in a "hu-

---

— total isolation in single cells where prisoners lived, ate, worked, and read the Bible (if, indeed, they were literate), and supposedly reflected and repented — came to be known as the Pennsylvania system." Another major Pennsylvania-style prison named Western State Penitentiary opened in 1826, thus also predating Eastern State by three years. But the prison was completely abandoned seven years later in 1833 because its circular, panoptical design allowed inmates to communicate with each other. The one major rival to the Pennsylvania system was the "Auburn system" (or corporate/congregate system). The first "corporate" prison opened in Auburn, New York, in 1817. In the words of theologian Muriel Schmid, inmates confined under the corporate system "were kept in individual tiny cells at night and worked together during the day under a strict rule of silence. . . ." The corporate system "became the dominant alternative to the Pennsylvania system. For decades, the two systems were held in opposition in the United States and wherever new prison systems were studied." See Muriel Schmid, "The Eye of God: Religious Beliefs and Punishment in Early Nineteenth-Century Prison Reform," *Theology Today* 59:4 (January 2003): 546-558. From Davis's point of view, the philosophical basis of the two "rival" models did not differ substantively: "The Pennsylvania model, which eventually crystallized in the Eastern State Penitentiary in Cherry Hill — the plans for which were approved in 1821 — emphasized total isolation, silence, and solitude, whereas the Auburn model called for solitary cells but labor in common. This mode of prison labor, which was called congregate, was supposed to unfold in total silence. Because of its more efficient labor practices, Auburn eventually became the dominant model for both the United States and Europe." See Angela Y. Davis, *Are Prisons Obsolete?* (New York: Seven Stories Press, 2003), p. 47. Eastern State remained open until 1971.

4. Fred T. Wilkinson, *The Realities of Crime and Punishment: A Prison Administrator's Testament* (Springfield, Mo.: Mycroft Press, 1972), p. 12.

5. Wilkinson, *The Realities of Crime and Punishment*, p. 12.

6. Wilkinson, *The Realities of Crime and Punishment*, p. 12.

mane and religious spirit," the plan did not work, "as is true of many of to-day's idealistic reform proposals," according to Fred Wilkinson, former Director of the Missouri State Department of Corrections.[7] Wanting to move away from the goal of penitence for crimes committed, Dr. Benjamin Rush of Pennsylvania, a signer of the Declaration of Independence, insisted that prison officials provide harsher oversight of the so-called houses of repentance: "Let all the officers be strictly forbidden to discover [i.e., exhibit] any sign of mirth or even levity, in the presence of the criminals. To increase the horror of this abode of discipline and misery, let it be called by some name that shall import its design."[8]

Over the course of American history, penal philosophy has cycled back and forth between these two approaches; penitence/reform (rehabilitation) versus harsher retributive oversight. Today, the pendulum has swung in the direction of harsher forms of punishment. Sociologist Don Sabo, writing with Terry Kupers, a psychiatrist, and Willie London, an inmate at Eastern Corrections and editor of the prison publication *Elite Expressions*, has pointed out that

> From the late thirties to the late seventies a large number of politicians and prison administrators favored the rehabilitative model of incarceration. By now, however, most have switched to harsh punishment, claiming that rehabilitation and all efforts to correct are useless because prisoners are incorrigible. Efforts to rehabilitate prisoners have been curtailed or at least downsized considerably. Today, the conservative law-and-order lobby urges us to deny prisoners educational opportunities and even to remove the exercise weights from the prison yards.[9]

Henry N. Pontell, an assistant professor of social ecology at the University of California–Irvine, concurs, pointing out that, "[Most] experts today would agree that the criminal justice system does little, if anything, to 'reform' criminals."[10] Pontell argues that the original aim of reforming the

7. Wilkinson, *The Realities of Crime and Punishment*, p. 12.

8. Quoted by Negley K. Teeters in "Prison Architecture of the 19th Century," *Germantown Crier*, Summer 1969. Quoted also in Wilkinson, *The Realities of Crime and Punishment*, p. 12.

9. Sabo et al., *Prison Masculinities*, p. 19.

10. Henry N. Pontell, *A Capacity to Punish: The Ecology of Crime and Punishment* (Bloomington, Ind.: Indiana University Press, 1984), p. 3.

criminal in the U.S. has not triumphed in practice. This is not to say that reform can never work, "but only that past attempts and methods have not
succeeded."[11] The original goal of U.S. penology, that is, the penitence of
the wrongdoer, has been displaced by a number of other, competing goals,
"including retribution ('just deserts'), incapacitation (mere detention), and
deterrence (curtailing crime through the fear of punishment)."[12] We will
look at each of these briefly.

The retributive justification of punishment is believed by most legal
theorists to be necessary, at least to some degree, because it is "the only one
that contains the elements of justice and reciprocity in sanctioning criminals."[13] Indeed, many (if not most) legal experts today contend that retribution should be the major purpose of punishment because it offers the
"strongest rationale, given the paucity of evidence on the effectiveness of
other purposes of punishments."[14] Technically speaking, the term "retribution" (from the Latin *retribuere*) means repayment, in other words, giving
back to someone what he or she deserves either in terms of rewards or punishments. Today the term is used primarily "in the negative sense of punitive
recompense for wicked deeds rather than positive rewards for good deeds."[15]

Incapacitation refers to the mere restraining effects of the prison:
while incarcerated, an individual cannot be out on the street committing
crime(s). According to Alfred Blumstein, a criminologist at Carnegie-
Mellon University, the well-established penal theory of incapacitation dic-
tates that "if a guy's committing ten crimes a year and you lock him up for
two years, you've prevented twenty crimes."[16] Blumstein goes on to point

11. Pontell, *A Capacity to Punish*, p. 3.

12. Pontell, *A Capacity to Punish*, p. 3.

13. Pontell, *A Capacity to Punish*, p. 3.

14. Pontell, *A Capacity to Punish*, p. 4. Cf. E. van den Haag's very good discussion of
issues related to criminal punishment, and retribution in particular, in *Punishing Criminals:
Concerning a Very Old and Painful Question* (New York: Basic Books, 1975). Also see John B.
Braithwaite, "Challenging Just Deserts: Punishing White Collar Criminals," *Journal of Crim-
inal Law and Criminology* 73 (1982): 723-63; and E. van den Haag, "The Criminal Law as a
Threat System," *Journal of Criminal Law and Criminology* 73 (1982): 769-85. Finally, also see
Andrew von Hirsch, *Doing Justice: The Choice of Punishments* (New York: Hill and Wang,
1976).

15. Christopher D. Marshall, *Beyond Retribution: A New Testament Vision for Justice,
Crime, and Punishment* (Grand Rapids, Mich.: William B. Eerdmans, 2001), p. 109.

16. Quoted in Scott Shane, "Locked Up in the Land of the Free," *Baltimore Sun*, June 1,
2003: A2.

out the shortcomings of incapacitation theory in the context of the "War on Drugs." While incapacitation may succeed in reducing the numbers of rapes and robberies, "locking up drug dealers does not necessarily reduce their number, because new recruits quickly take their place . . . with drugs there's a resilient market out there. The incarceration of drug offenders is an exercise in futility."[17]

The doctrine of criminal deterrence is wedded to the utilitarian thinking of what is known as the "classical school of criminality." Two notable works in this school are Jeremy Bentham's *An Introduction to the Principles of Morals and Legislation* (first published in 1789) and Cesare Beccaria's essay *On Crimes and Punishments* (first published anonymously in 1764 under fear of political backlash). While there are many different forms of deterrence theory, two stand out most in the social scientific literature: (1) "specific" or "individual" deterrence; and (2) "general" deterrence. Individual deterrence has to do with the "preventive effect that punishment has on an individual who is punished."[18] The idea is that a person who experiences the unpleasantness of punishment will not want to engage in criminal conduct again. General deterrence, on the other hand, refers to the effects of punishment on those who are contemplating criminal acts, causing them to "think again." Here the aim of punishment is to offer up an "example" of punishment that will produce conformity in the general population.[19] Given today's rapidly increasing prison population (including those sentenced to execution), it seems apparent that neither individual nor general deterrence is very effective.

In a recent study focused on the divide between American and European criminal justice practices, James Q. Whitman, a professor of comparative and foreign law at Yale University, asserted that "the most important Anglo-American movement of the last forty years or so [is] the great philosophical revival of retributivism."[20] Led by contemporary philoso-

---

17. Quoted in Shane, "Locked Up."

18. Pontell, *A Capacity to Punish*, p. 4.

19. Pontell, *A Capacity to Punish*, p. 4.

20. James Q. Whitman, *Harsh Justice: Criminal Justice and the Widening Divide between America and Europe* (Oxford: Oxford University Press, 2003), pp. 23-24. Also see, e.g., Elizabeth Lane Beardsley, "A Plea for Deserts," *American Philosophical Quarterly* 6 (1969): 36; Joseph Weiler, "Why Do We Punish?: The Case for Retributive Justice," *University of British Columbia Law Review* 12 (1978): 310-16; Sidney Gendin, "A Plausible Theory of Retribution," *Journal of Value Inquiry* 5 (1970): 1; John Finnis, "The Restoration of Retributivism," *Analysis*

phers like Andrew von Hirsch, Jeffrie Murphy, and Jean Hampton, the rise of retributive justice as the primary goal of criminal corrections aims, in Whitman's words, "to reintroduce ideas of moral agency and moral responsibility into the criminal law, abandoning the brute therapeutic psychologism of the mid-twentieth century."[21]

In addition to retribution, Whitman has noted that degradation is one of the most obvious aspects of punishment as well as one of the least studied by philosophers and sociologists of punishment. He argues that offenders feel punished in part because they feel degraded. The criminal justice system's primary goal of retributive punishment routinely carries with it an urge to degrade offenders; therefore, any analysis of punishment is undermined if the issue of degradation is neglected.

The Degradation of Offenders

In the contemporary United States, it is impossible to fully understand the harshness of retributive punishment without understanding degradation and its function. We should begin by noting that "degradation" is a term widely used in the field of law, particularly in the area of human rights. It is a practice that is expressly forbidden by important international conventions. In the 1972 human rights case *Denmark v. Greece,* for example, "the European Commission defined 'degrading treatment' for purposes of Ar-

---

32 (1972): 131; Andrew von Hirsch, *Censure and Sanctions* (New York: Oxford University Press, 1993).

21. Whitman, *Harsh Justice,* p. 24. Note that "abandoning the brute therapeutic psychologism of the mid-twentieth century" refers to a basic rejection of viewing the primary aim of criminal justice in terms of various rehabilitative strategies. In general, rehabilitative theories of criminal justice view crime as a disease, and the criminal as a sick person in need of cure, not punishment. Here "therapy, not torture," is the motto. Proponents of this view include B. F. Skinner and Carl Menninger. Punishment, on this view, is considered a prescientific response to antisocial behavior. Louis P. Pojman and Jeffrey Reiman point out that, "At best punishment temporarily suppresses adverse behavior, but if left untreated, [as] Skinner argues, it will resurface again as though the punishment never occurred." Indeed rehabilitationists generally charge that retributivists are guilty of holding an antiquated notion of human beings as possessing free wills and being responsible for their behavior. We are all products of our heredity and, especially, our environment according to this view. See Louis P. Pojman and Jeffery Reiman, *The Death Penalty: For and Against* (New York: Rowman & Littlefield, 1998), p. 24.

ticle 3 of the Convention for the Protection of Human Rights and Fundamental Freedoms as treatment that 'grossly humiliates' an individual, or forces him to act against his will or conscience."[22] If this is a somewhat vague definition, it is worth noting that other conventions have used the term without defining it at all; Whitman points out that, "The Convention Against Torture and Other Cruel, Inhumane or Degrading Treatment [ratified by the United Nations on June 26, 1987] does not undertake to define 'degradation.'"[23]

So while "degradation" has indeed been forbidden in much international law, "it is not a term that has been carefully defined in the legal literature."[24] Whitman argues, in the service of offering a working definition of degradation, that the term "is not coterminous with either violence or torture. Degrading acts are not necessarily violent, nor are they 'torture' in its technical sense: harsh treatment intended to coerce persons to cooperate or confess."[25] Of course torture, in this technical sense, can be degrading, but, as Whitman correctly notes, "there is plenty of degrading treatment that has nothing to do with coercing cooperation or confession; [hence] torture and degradation are not the same thing."[26]

Whitman suggests that degradation "is treatment of others that makes them feel inferior, lessened, lowered."[27] The relationship between punishment and degradation makes sense if one acknowledges that "some quality of inferiority clings to punishment."[28] As the late sociologist Heinrich Popitz pointed out, "When somebody inflicts pain on us, we never experience it as 'merely physical.' . . . When you are subjected to physical punishment, you feel that you must submit to the power of your punisher. You feel that you are being subjugated in every aspect of your being."[29] Everyday life and history offer innumerable examples of degrading language and practices in the name of punishment: the prone posture of those being punished; the bared buttocks of a person being spanked or caned. Whit-

22. Whitman, *Harsh Justice*, p. 212, n. 2.
23. Whitman, *Harsh Justice*, p. 212, n. 2.
24. Whitman, *Harsh Justice*, p. 20.
25. Whitman, *Harsh Justice*, p. 20.
26. Whitman, *Harsh Justice*, p. 20.
27. Whitman, *Harsh Justice*, p. 20.
28. Whitman, *Harsh Justice*, p. 20.
29. Heinrich Popitz, *Phänomene der Macht*, 2d ed. (Tübingen: Mohr Siebeck, 1992), pp. 45-46; quoted in Whitman, *Harsh Justice*, p. 20.

man points out that the very language of criminal justice has sometimes given vent to an astonishing vocabulary of disgust when describing offenders: "filth," "dirt," "slime," "scum," "excrement," "pieces of shit," "diseased," "contagious," "wreckage," "debris," "monsters," etc.

Such words highlight the fact that an important element of retributive punishment, and especially a dimension of the process of degradation, includes the powerful metaphor of criminals as filth. A consequence of this metaphor is that prison authorities (and often many in the general public) often wish to imprison criminals in places that are thought to be as suitably filthy and malodorous as the criminal is conceived to be.[30] Whitman argues that it is critical to understand that degradation is not simply some incidental by-product of punishment. A number of thoughtful social scientists and philosophers have argued that degradation is, in fact, essential to punishment, because authorities often feel that "punishment only works if it succeeds in making the punished person feel like an inferior."[31]

A number of scholars have pointed out that punishment is viewed as effective when it diminishes or demeans the offender.[32] The sociologist Harold Garfinkel argues that criminal trials amount to "degradation ceremonies," which aim to ritually (i.e., performatively and communicatively) demean the offender.[33] Erving Goffman's *Asylum* traced the practice of a similar form of degradation in the routine daily life of prisoners with mental illness and others.[34] Anthropologist Mary Douglas has observed that low-status persons in societies are polluted persons.[35] Metaphorically transformed to the status of filth, "dirty" and "polluted" criminals are

30. For an insightful and provocative discussion of the metaphor of filth in Western criminal justice see Martha Grace Duncan, *Romantic Outlaws, Beloved Prisons: The Unconscious Meanings of Crime and Punishment* (New York: New York University Press, 1996), pp. 121-87. Duncan is a professor of law at Emory University. Cf. Mark Lewis Taylor, *The Executed God: The Way of the Cross in Lockdown America* (Minneapolis: Fortress Press, 2001), p. 57, and Lorna A. Rhodes, *Total Confinement: Madness and Reason in the Maximum Security Prison* (Berkeley: University of California Press, 2004), pp. 163-190.

31. Whitman, *Harsh Justice*, p. 20.

32. Whitman, *Harsh Justice*, p. 20.

33. Harold Garfinkel, "Conditions of Successful Degradation Ceremonies," *American Journal of Sociology* 61 (1956): 420-24.

34. Erving Goffman, *Asylums: Essays on the Social Situation of Mental Patients and Other Inmates* (Garden City, N.Y.: Anchor Books, 1961), pp. 14-74.

35. See Mary Douglas, *Purity and Danger: An Analysis of Concepts of Pollution and Taboo* (London: Routledge & Kegan Paul), 1978.

freighted with unacceptable levels of risk to society. Hence, according to Whitman, "it is wholly unsurprising that criminal punishment should ritually degrade them. Punishment works by assigning the offender to the status of an inferior."

Albert Wright Jr., a fifty-year-old African American man doing time at the Western Illinois Correction Center, affirms the work of these scholars when he says that "there is seldom a positive response to the cries for help in combating the inhuman treatment that we are subjected to daily. Few of you know what the treatment is like. What prison administrators tell you is not anything near the truth." Wright goes on to plead: "We are still people. We just happen to be in prison."[36]

It should be no surprise, then, that prison populations can be generally distinguished by their routine designation as social inferiors. Yet for the overwhelming majority of prisoners, inferior social status was apparent even prior to incarceration. Disproportionately, persons who are imprisoned are the poor, "peoples of color," and the relatively outcast among us. This fact had already been observed long ago by the nineteenth-century French political philosopher Alexis de Tocqueville (1805-1859), whose *Democracy in America* (1835/1840) is considered by many scholars to be among the best examinations and commentaries on the sociopolitical workings of democracy in the United States.

Tocqueville observed that America's civil and criminal laws "appear drafted in a spirit opposed to the dominant spirit of American legislation; these mores seem contrary to the sum of the social state."[37] He noted that American civil and criminal legislation recognized only two means of action against alleged offenders: prison or bail. And since the first act of a court proceeding consisted in securing bail from the defendant, the poor were at a very serious disadvantage, lacking the financial resources that would prevent them from being incarcerated on the spot. Consequently, these low-status persons ended up disproportionately imprisoned. Re-

36. Quoted in Angela Y. Davis, "Race, Gender, and Prison History: From the Convict Lease System to the Supermax Prison," in Sabo et al., *Prison Masculinities*, p. 35. The primary source is Albert Wright Jr., "Young Inmates Need Help, from Inside and Out," *Emerge Magazine*, October 1997, p. 80.

37. Alexis de Tocqueville, *Democracy in America*, trans. and ed. Harvey C. Mansfield and Delba Winthorp (Chicago: University of Chicago Press, 2000), p. 44. The dominant spirit to which Tocqueville refers is the democratic notions of equal rights and principles of true freedom.

garding the nineteenth-century Anglo-American "prison or bail" system, Tocqueville maintained that

> It is evident that such legislation is directed against the poor and favors the rich. The poor man does not always find bail, even in civil matters, and if he is constrained to go await justice in prison, his forced inaction soon reduces him to misery. The rich man, on the contrary, always succeeds in escaping imprisonment in civil matters; even more, should he have committed a punishable offense, he easily escapes the punishment that ought to reach him: after having furnished bail, he disappears. One can say that for him, all penalties that the law inflicts are reduced to fines. What is more aristocratic than that?[38]

Tocqueville does acknowledge that "there are doubtless crimes for which one does not receive bail, but they are very few in number."[39] From Tocqueville's point of view, penal legislation was one important area in which beneath the American democratic exterior the old colors of Anglo-European aristocracy showed through.

Social scientists and legal scholars have not been alone in analyzing the negative social dimensions of what passes for criminal justice. Modern and ancient philosophers have commented on the distinctively Christian dimensions of degrading punishment, which reduces wrongdoers to the status of inferiors. Whitman describes Friedrich Nietzsche's disturbing account of the function of horrific punishment in the Christian afterlife: "What Aquinas and Tertullian promised individual Christians, according to Nietzsche, was the immense satisfaction of witnessing the torments of the damned, and being thereby confirmed in their own blessed superiority. Punishment, as Nietzsche presented it, thus had to do partly with lording it over others, and indeed with the sheer pleasure of lording it over others."[40]

38. Tocqueville, *Democracy in America*, pp. 44-45.
39. Tocqueville, *Democracy in America*, p. 45, n. 42.
40. Whitman, *Harsh Justice*, p. 21. Nietzsche, summarizing Aquinas on the issue of punishment, declares, "The blessed in the kingdom of heaven will see the punishments of the damned, *in order that their bliss be more delightful for them.*" In order to be more precise, Nietzsche then quotes Aquinas directly from *Summa Theologiae*, III, Supplementum, Q. 94, Art. l: "In order that the bliss of the saints may be more delightful for them and that they may render more copious thanks to God for it, it is given to them to see perfectly the punishment of the damned." See Friedrich Nietzsche, *On the Genealogy of Morals*, ed. and trans. Walter Kaufmann (New York: Vintage Books, 1969), pp. 49-50, nn. 1, 2.

In Nietzsche's view, degrading retributive punishment is an important component of the "eternal bliss" of a Christian paradise populated by people created, he maintained, not by eternal love, but by eternal hate. Hence the gateway to the Christian Paradise, for Nietzsche, is "the gateway to a lie!"[41] Whatever we may think of this assessment, Nietzsche's account of the heightened feeling of superiority that accompanies the gaze of the saved upon the damned correlates with a similar reality today. One component of the human drive to degrade those we punish is the heightening of our own sense of superiority, thus reminding ourselves again and again of what providence has spared us from becoming — namely, socially polluted.

Philosophers have not always regarded this kind of treatment of offenders as a necessarily bad thing. The American political philosopher Jean Hampton concurs with Nietzsche that punishment lessens or lowers the offender. But Hampton argues that this is a very appropriate consequence for an offender who has improperly put him- or herself in a superior position of oppressive power over another. Hampton declares, "By victimizing me, the wrongdoer has declared himself elevated with respect to me, acting as a superior who is permitted to use me for his purposes."[42] Thus punishing an offender as an inferior serves the valid social purpose of expressing the wrongness of a criminal claim of superiority: "the retributive motive for inflicting suffering is to annul or counter the appearance of the wrongdoer's superiority and thus affirm the victim's real value."[43] In Hampton's view there is nothing inherently wrong with treating offenders as inferiors. Here the retributive motive for punishment is viewed as an indispensable practice that aims at "resubjugating the subjugator."[44]

Some early Greek philosophers and Christians also believed that the goal of punishment was to bring wrongdoers down a peg or two. But, argues Whitman, the critical distinction to be made between the early Greek practice of punishment and the contemporary American practice lies in the difference between viewing the function of punishment as "chastise-

41. Nietzsche, *On the Genealogy of Morals*, p. 49.

42. Jean Hampton and Jeffrie G. Murphy, *Forgiveness and Mercy* (Cambridge: Cambridge University Press, 1988), p. 125; quoted in Whitman, *Harsh Justice*, p. 21.

43. Hampton and Murphy, *Forgiveness and Mercy*, p. 130; quoted in Whitman, *Harsh Justice*, p. 21.

44. Jean Hampton, "An Expressive Theory of Retribution," in *Retributivism and Its Critics*, ed. Wesley Cragg (Stuttgart: F. Steiner, 1992), pp. 14, 16; quoted in Whitman, *Harsh Justice*, p. 21.

ment," which is laudable, and viewing punishment as vengeance, which is not to be commended:

> For many ancient Greek authors, punishment was intended to penalize hubris — "the failure to behave as befits one's position in the social hierarchy." Correspondingly, the Greeks often spoke of punishment as serving in part the laudable function of *kolasis*, the function of "teach[ing] people their proper place" in that hierarchy. *Kolasis* is often translated as "chastisement," and that translation nicely captures its sense. As K. J. Dover observes in an elegant essay on Greek attitudes, chastisement is the kind of corrective punishment that schoolteachers mete out to their pupils, or that masters mete out to their slaves or their dogs: it is punishment such as one inflicts on "an animal, slave, child, employee or subordinate." For Aristotle and many other Greek authors, such chastisement was one of the two prime purposes of punishment, standing alongside vengeance or retribution *(timoria)*. What distinguished these two faces of punishment, to Greek sensibilities, was particularly their emotional tenor. Vengeance or retribution typically involved some sense of rancor or grievance. In administering chastisement, by contrast, well-bred superiors remained serene, being careful not to lose their temper. Such chastisement, calmly dealt out by superiors to inferiors, seemed to many ancient authors a very good thing indeed. Plato arguably picked up on this tradition in this account of the educative function of punishment: for Plato, too, punishment was an exercise in the serene correction of those who had erred.[45]

In contrast to the abovementioned portrait of vengeful Christian punishment offered by Nietzsche, Whitman notes that some early Christians also embraced chastisement rather than retribution as the rightful function of punishment.

> The idea appealed to the early Christians as well. The gospel of Matthew described God's punishment as *kolasis*, chastisement. The third-century church father Clement of Alexandria embraced this concept, asserting that God was not a vengeful God, but a chastising God, a God

---

45. Whitman, *Harsh Justice*, pp. 21-22.

who "put people in their place." And Saint Augustine adopted the same traditional distinction in his own account of Christian justice. Christian judges, Augustine wrote, should chastise, in the unruffled way that good fathers chastised their sons; they should not seek vengeance.[46]

This distinction between retribution and chastisement is worth considering. But while it does appear that a case can be made that criminal punishment over the years has traditionally aimed to put wrongdoers in their place, it is important to point out that societal authorities over the ages have generally failed to realize, and react against, what Whitman refers to as "the drama of the ways in which punishers can lose themselves in the intoxication of the sense of their own superiority." History shows time and time again that the retributive practice of putting people in their place can and does bring out the worst in us. The routinized meting out of punishment, especially when it becomes a large-scale social phenomenon, helps foster a sense of systemic sadism within the prison. And its effects are wide-ranging, resulting in a widespread loss of what some call "human feeling." The lessening and/or loss of the capacity for human feeling by persons handing down and administering punishment has ugly effects not only on the person punished, but also on the person doing the punishing and on society at large. Even well-intended chastisement for wrongdoing often degenerates into degradation.

Whitman's argument is useful in helping us to understand that a core problem of what I term "retributive degradation" is the intoxicating effect on those administering punishment. Policymakers generally view themselves as fashioning punishments that further the noble goals of deterrence, incapacitation, rehabilitation, or expressive moral condemnation, in addition to retribution. Certainly these goals are not always viewed as involving the motive or prospect of degradation. Indeed, many of the contemporary social scientists and philosophers mentioned above who advocate retribution are clearly against degradation.[47]

Unfortunately, the fact that some contemporary philosophers do

46. Whitman, *Harsh Justice*, p. 22.
47. See, for example, Andrew von Hirsch and Uma Narayan, "Degradingness and Intrusiveness," in *Censure and Sanctions*, pp. 80-87; Jeffrie G. Murphy, "Cruel and Unusual Punishment," in *Retribution, Justice and Therapy* (Dordrecht: D. Reidel, 1979), pp. 233-249. See also Immanuel Kant, *The Metaphysical Elements of Justice*, trans. John Ladd (New York: Macmillan, 1985), pp. 100-102.

forthrightly declare the importance of avoiding degradation in punishment is not adequate, according to Whitman:

> None of them finds much to say about how degradation happens, and consequently none of them can give any account of how particular societies manage to avoid degrading offenders. Certainly none of them can give an account of how contemporary America acquired its spectacularly harsh and degrading brand of retributivism, a system of sentences measured in multiple decades served in an atmosphere of humiliation and despair.[48]

Even the nation's "sober policy goals" tend to invite degrading behavior whenever we authorize punishment. Whitman points out that the nineteenth-century English philosopher and legal and social reformer Jeremy Bentham knew well the dangers of authorizing punishment: "Legislators and men in general are naturally inclined" to excessive harshness, since "antipathy, or a want of compassion for individuals who are represented as dangerous and vile, pushes them onward to an undue severity."[49]

Whitman implies that whatever our legislation may want to claim as the true reforming goals of contemporary punishment, "we do indeed tend to regard offenders as vile: and a certain urge to degrade may indeed take over every time an individual punisher — a prison guard or police officer — punishes an individual offender."[50] And the issue is not only about the attitude of the personnel who actually inflict the punishment, but the general public as well. The strong tendency in the general public is to treat the fact of punishment as "an invitation to view criminal offenders as status-inferiors."[51] This cultural value of "interpersonal degradation" typically clings to punishment and, as Whitman rightly asserts, has important repercussions for the social dynamic of criminal legislation.

In a society claiming to be civilized (i.e., refined and enlightened), retributive degradation devalues crime victims' lives by concentrating

---

48. Whitman, *Harsh Justice*, p. 24.

49. Quoted in Whitman, *Harsh Justice*, p. 23. See also Jeremy Bentham, *Principles of Penal Law*, in *The Works of Jeremy Bentham*, ed. J. Bowring, 2 vols. (Edinburgh: William Tait, 1843), vol. 1, p. 401.

50. Whitman, *Harsh Justice*, p. 23.

51. Whitman, *Harsh Justice*, p. 23.

more on inflicting vengeance and status humiliation on those who commit such crimes than on the physical and social needs of victims, their families, and their communities. In addition, there is the problem of the sorts of values we as a "civilized" society wish to instill even in those individuals, families, and communities wounded by crime. Indeed, as much as I would like to see the rapists and murderers of some of my family's best friends mercilessly punished, I recognize that the passion with which we pursue retributive degradation tears apart the bonds of social affection. Unfortunately, too many contemporary philosophers, social scientists, and theologians in the United States routinely ignore the wider social dynamics related to punishment and imprisonment.

Retributive Degradation and Crime

Whitman's view that chastisement is a legitimate function of punishment is a helpful one. Equally helpful, however, is his caution that chastisement often degenerates into degradation, and that degradation affects the whole society in which it is practiced. He contends that "the analysis of punishment cannot limit itself to what offenders deserve; the way we punish can have momentous social and interpersonal consequences that have nothing to do with the deserts of the person punished."[52] This is particularly true in an era of large-scale imprisonment, in which the "invisible" collateral consequences of such a social practice are scarcely acknowledged.

Of course, those commentators who claim that the problem of imprisonment lies less with the prison bureaucracy than with those individuals who decide to commit crimes are not completely wrong.

Wilkinson lists a number of personal attributes that can predispose persons to commit crimes: a lack of prudence and foresight; an inability to see one's own faults; an inability to learn from experience; the absence of the moral sense; an unwillingness to assume personal responsibility; a desire to escape from reality; genetic deficiencies; an uncontrolled risk-taking attitude; suicidal inclinations (which I would argue are often tied to homicidal ones); revolutionary passions; and so on.[53] He comments that

52. Whitman, *Harsh Justice*, p. 30. See also David Garland, "Philosophical Argument and Ideological Effect: An Essay Review," *Contemporary Crises* 7 (1983): 79-85.
53. Wilkinson, *The Realities of Crime and Punishment*, p. 37.

Behind as well as outside the walls, we have the highly intelligent and the ignorant, a few geniuses and a larger number of feeble-minded. I have known men such as George McCoy convicted of murder, with an Intelligence Quotient of 61. Sam Shockley, executed in California for murdering an officer while attempting an escape, was very inferior in intelligence. John Richard Bayless, bank robber and tough Alcatraz case, registered an I.Q. of 133. William Remington, espionage agent, convicted of perjury, had a Master's degree from Columbia University and had completed qualifying for his Ph.D. when he was arrested and convicted.[54]

Describing his own experience with prisoners, Wilkinson points out, "Intelligence is one thing and character another. . . . Behind the walls we have all vocations from laborer to professor, from soldier to Congressman. While I was Warden at Atlanta we had at one time 25 bankers and 16 preachers (mostly self-ordained)." He concludes correctly that "the prison community, like any other, has its race problem, its sex episodes, its greedy acquisitives, its smoldering hates, its fanatics, its hypochondriacs, its agitators. In short, the prison with its selective population still reflects the human comedy being played out on the outside."

Unfortunately, Wilkinson fails to mention that U.S. prisons, while indeed representative of most every social, racial, psychological, and economic background, are populated overwhelmingly by society's social inferiors: the poor, the weak, the homeless, the drug addicted, the non-White, and so forth. And although there is some truth in Wilkinson's report of the social and moral deficiencies of many inmates, if a significant social function of punishment itself is retributive degradation, then it follows that most prisoners stand much less than an even chance at transforming their lives for the better. Later in this book I will argue that a principal goal of punishment, regardless of whether one wants to call it chastisement, ought to involve incapacitating socially destructive offenders in a way that *transforms* them to social life and health without degrading them or overtaxing society at large. But because a principal social function of contemporary imprisonment is retributive degradation, prisons and jails tend to preserve and re/produce delinquency. In an atmosphere of retributive degradation, inmates must endure the imposition of

54. Wilkinson, *The Realities of Crime and Punishment*, p. 37.

a community not fit for the potential production or actualization of decent human beings in community and society.

Ex-offender David Lewis, president and co-founder of the California-based outreach program Free at Last, maintains that, "prison is a school and violence is the curriculum."[55] Sabo, Kupers, and London have observed that 75 percent of new admissions to prison are for nonviolent crimes, yet violence is omnipresent in the prison. Only a significant minority has been imprisoned for crimes considered violent. "Other prisoners become violent, or at least act as though they are capable of violence, only after being jailed." The specter of violence in prison is for many inmates just a continuation of a lifelong theme and pattern that began with their own victimization by family and community violence as children.[56]

The degradation to which prisoners are subjected today relies heavily on routinized, hierarchical violence, both physical and psychical.

As with male-dominated institutions in general, relations among men in prison are hierarchical. Prison hierarchies extend beyond male prisoners and guards themselves and also include women prisoners and various civil authorities beyond the prison walls. Sabo, Kupers, and London argue that

> Male hierarchies abound, and their day-to-day operation makes prison life work. There are the administrative hierarchies and the chain of command among prison guards. The legitimacy and operation of prison hierarchies stretch well beyond prison walls to include city officials, county executives, state governors, and the federal government. The prison system is extremely male dominated, and male overrepresentation increases with each step up the status ladder. Women and prisoners hold the lowest positions in the pecking order, with women guards and professionals a notch above prisoners themselves. Status differences are also carefully regulated among prisoners, with violence-prone men at the top and feminized males at the bottom.[57]

55. Free at Last Community Recovery & Rehabilitation has been at the forefront of providing community-based substance abuse treatment services in East Palo Alto, California, and its surrounding areas in innovative ways since 1994. The following words by Martin Luther King Jr. are the organization's guiding motto: "Whatever affects one directly, affects all indirectly."

56. Sabo et al., *Prison Masculinities*, p. 8.

57. Sabo et al., *Prison Masculinities*, p. 8; see also pp. 9-10.

In order to maintain this hierarchy, violent forms of degradation are perpetuated by prisoners via the threat and practice of sexual and other forms of physical assault. Guards rule with the threat or application of violence, "keeping their batons in hand and more lethal weapons at the ready."[58] A tendency by many guards to "view prisoners as scum for whom incarceration itself is not sufficient punishment,"[59] as well as the racism of some guards and prisoners, make problems of hate and aggression even worse. Criminality is preserved and produced in such fortresses of consistent violence, degradation, and despair.

The prison also produces delinquency by routinely imposing violent constraints on inmates, either by guards or other inmates. For example, all prisoners must live under the humiliating social control produced by the continuous threat of being "punked out," i.e., becoming the sexual slave ("bitch") of another inmate, or inmates, by force. In describing U.S. prisons as "punk factories" Christian Parenti explains the significance of rape as a form of social control:

> Rape is both absolutely central to, and yet largely invisible within, the politics of incarceration. Hundreds of thousands of men and women alike suffer this most horrible of physical and emotional tortures as an unwritten part of their sentences. And unlike most rape on the outside, rape in prison is usually not a one-time event; instead the victim is often forced to live with and serve their tormentor for years on end. In that respect prison rape is more akin to child sexual abuse or slavery. Women . . . are routinely raped by male guards, while male prisoners are generally raped by other convicts.
>
> In male prisons sexual slavery most often starts in two ways. In one, a younger inmate might be taken under the wing of an older inmate; once debt and dependence are established the older inmate will rape and "turn out" the young prisoner. The other method is simple gang rape in which a weaker inmate is attacked with overwhelming numbers and "punked" by a crew of prisoners, who then announce their control to the general population, which in turn cements the deal through their tacit or active approval of the victim's new status. Once

58. Sabo et al., *Prison Masculinities*, p. 8.

59. David Gilbert, "These Criminals Have No Respect for Human Life," *Social Justice* 18, no 3 (1991): 78; quoted in Sabo et al., *Prison Masculinities*, p. 8.

"turned out," a punk is vulnerable to assault from all sides as the prison grapevine informs everyone of his subordinate status. In the interest of survival, a newly minted punk will usually choose one inmate as their "Man," "daddy," or "husband." In exchange for usufruct of the punk, the Man offers protection against other aggressors. Yet although the "wolves" and "booty bandits" have sex with other men, they, in the hyper-macho cosmology of prison, are not homosexual because they are not sexually penetrated. The cult of "Manhood" — and the struggle to defend, defile, and define it — is the axis around which the prison sex system turns.

The subordinate "gender" in male prisons includes the so-called "punks," straight or gay men forced into a submissive sexual role, as well as "queens," gay men and transsexuals who may embrace homosexual sex and their gendered role as the sexual submissive. Queens may suffer as sexual slaves and rape victims, but very often they use their sexual powers to play stronger inmates off against one another or to find a husband of their own liking. Punks and queens, like women in the straight world, are forced into roles that range from nurturing, mothering wife, to denigrated, over-worked "whore." . . .

Inmate-on-inmate rape also occurs in women's prisons and jails, but a far greater problem for female convicts is the sexual depravity of their male (and sometimes female) keepers. From coast to coast, guards routinely rape women prisoners with near-total impunity.[60]

Even aside from this hierarchy of violence, prisoners are treated like the filth corrections authorities and much of the general public often take them to be. Many prisoners are routinely isolated in dark (often damp) solitary confinement as well as in cold, dirty, and oppressively overcrowded general confinement. They are given jobs that are mainly useless in terms of finding employment when and if they get out. They rarely receive adequate comprehensive drug addiction treatment or psychological or medical assistance if needed. As a pariah population, they receive far too few opportunities for adequate education and habituation in meaningful vocations or societal virtues.

Indeed, prison life can be horrific; yet I am not advocating simply

---

60. Christian Parenti, *Lockdown America: Police and Prisons in the Age of Crisis* (New York: Verso, 1999), pp. 184-185, 190.

throwing the prison doors open and setting every inmate free, especially those who commit the most heinous crimes. I realize, for example, that tolerating open-air crack markets on street corners devastates neighborhoods, and that rape and murder are horrendous crimes against humanity. But placing nonviolent drug addicts in prisons by the thousands does not help. I am willing to concede that there may be some inmates who arguably pose too great a public risk to return to the streets. But within the confines of the prison even such *persons* as these should not be given up on for life as less than human, as persons devoid of any possibility of contributing something positive to even the community of prisoners.

Again, given the harsh conditions that most inmates face while in prison and the increasing collapse of moral community and lack of material and psychological resources both inside and outside the prison, it should be a surprise to no one that criminal recidivism in the U.S. is so high. John Jay College criminologist Todd Clear argues that lack of services inside and outside prison contributes to the high rate of recidivism in the United States, a rate currently estimated to be about 75 percent within three years of release. With regard to prison life itself, Sabo, Kupers, and London point out that, "Many criminologists have pointed toward the irony that the creation of harsher prison conditions and the 'war on crime' may actually be creating more criminals."[61] In the retributive attempt to put wrongdoers in their place, "it is easy to forget how badly awry such treatment can go," in Whitman's words.[62]

While it is true that crime takes root as a result of many social causes — inadequate minimum wage protection; high unemployment in poor communities; poor formal education; poor habituation in positive, community-enhancing virtues — it is particularly ironic when prisons amount to significant social preservers and re/producers of criminality. Yet as long as a significant social function of imprisonment today is retributive degradation, the current practice of punishment in the United States cannot avoid its social function, however unintended it may be, as preserver and re/producer of criminality.

61. Sabo et al., *Prison Masculinities*, p. 7.
62. Whitman, *Harsh Justice*, p. 22.

Origins and History of the Prison-Industrial Complex

If one current social function of imprisonment is to mete out retributive degradation, others are tied to an intense interrelationship among fear, politics, and economic profit. The contemporary interconnectedness of these factors creates institutional pressure to consistently increase imprisonment. This is taking place in a social environment where the bifurcation of wealth and class is increasingly exacerbated: in the last two decades of the twentieth century, the United States experienced a more rapid growth of wage inequality than any other nation in the Western world.[63] Sustaining such inequality naturally results in increasing populations of people who are worn down and worn out, who feel that no matter how much they work, substandard employment, housing, medical care, and education leave them barely holding it together.

Mark Lewis Taylor, a professor of theology and culture at Princeton Seminary, suggests that the nation's unprecedented bifurcation of wealth and class creates social wreckage or debris "that has to be managed, cleaned up, or dispensed with. This wreckage makes up the surplus populations that our economic system of production has to manage and that the United States controls today to a growing extent by systems of punishment and confinement."[64] Such *human beings,* many of whom are simultaneously needed as workers to be exploited as well as persons who are in the way of the nation's economic progress, are, like most inmates, marked as (often threatening) social inferiors, that is, as "social junk," and "social dynamite," who are in constant need of regulation and control. Drawing on the work of criminologist Steve Spitzer, Taylor distinguishes "social junk" and "social dynamite":

> [*Social junk*] includes the mentally ill, drug addicts, lonely and frayed drifters, alcoholics, and cast-off, and impoverished elders. When an economic order no longer structures itself to care for such as these, then the officials must find mechanisms to get them out of the way. [As Spitzer notes], "They must be driven away from the beaches, malls, and tony shopping areas of resort towns and financial districts, and

---

63. William Julius Wilson, *The Bridge over the Racial Divide: Rising Inequality and Coalition Politics,* Wildavsky Forum Series 2 (Berkeley: University of California Press, 1999), p. 27.

64. Mark Lewis Taylor, *The Executed God,* p. 56.

the pleasure zones of theme park cities. . . ." Those who make up Spitzer's category of social junk rarely unite to orchestrate a potent resistance to the social forces that grind them down or to the legalized vigilante men that chase them around. . . .

Social dynamite names that sector of the population left behind by economic production who do pose the threat of social explosion. These often play a role in creating nongovernable spaces. Included here are the impoverished low-wage, working-class, and unemployed youth who often do not appear in statistical summaries of the economy. These youthful spirits are often not bowed and crushed by their disadvantage, and so they fight to be included in the social order. They are called social dynamite because they are, or can be, perceived as a major threat to the functioning of the economic order.[65]

Employing punishment and confinement as strategies to control and manage such groups is a practice that should be cause for concern in any case, but especially when it is tied together with the exploitation of prison labor by private corporations. And tied to this exploitation of prison labor are an "array of relationships linking corporations, government, correctional communities, and media." These relationships constitute what is now commonly referred to as a "prison-industrial complex."[66] Angela Y. Davis offers the best summary to date of the origins of the term:

The term "prison-industrial complex" was introduced by activists and scholars to contest the prevailing beliefs that increased levels of crime were the root cause of mounting prison populations. Instead, they argued, prison construction and the attendant drive to fill these new structures with human bodies have been driven by ideologies of racism and the pursuit of profit. Social historian Mike Davis first used the term in relation to California's penal system, which, he observed, already had begun in the 1990s to rival agribusiness and land development as a major economic and political force.[67]

---

65. Taylor, *The Executed God*, p. 57. See Steven Spitzer's "Toward a Marxist Theory of Deviance," *Social Problems* 22 (1975): 638-51 and Christian Parenti's *Lockdown America: Prison in the Age of Crisis*, pp. 45-46.

66. Angela Y. Davis, *Are Prisons Obsolete?* (New York: Seven Stories Press, 2003), p. 84.

67. Angela Y. Davis, *Are Prisons Obsolete?* pp. 84-85. See also Mike Davis, "Hell Factory in the Field: A Prison Industrial Complex," *The Nation* 260:7 (February 20, 1995): 229.

Other terms that have been associated with the prison-industrial complex include "Lockdown America," "Gulag America," "Big House Nation," and "Prison Nation." Drawing on a 1994 article by Paulette Thomas in the *Wall Street Journal*, Steven Donziger has suggested that the prison-industrial complex "is based on an 'iron triangle' between government bureaucracy, private industry, and politicians. The three entities create interlocking financial and political interests to push for a particular policy . . . [for example] the expansion of the criminal justice system."[68]

In 1998, Eric Schlosser, writing for the *Atlantic Monthly*, defined the prison-industrial complex as "a set of bureaucratic, political, and economic interests that encourage increased spending on imprisonment, regardless of the actual need."[69] Schlosser went on to explain that

> The prison-industrial complex is not a conspiracy, guiding the nation's criminal-justice policy behind closed doors. It is a confluence of special interests that has given prison construction in the United States a seemingly unstoppable momentum. It is composed of politicians, both liberal and conservative, who have used the fear of crime to gain votes; impoverished rural areas where prisons have become a cornerstone of economic development; private companies that regard the roughly $35 billion [now closer to $50 billion] spent each year on corrections not as a burden on American taxpayers but as a lucrative market; and government officials whose fiefdoms have expanded along with the inmate population. . . . The raw material of the prison-industrial complex is its inmates: the poor, the homeless, and the mentally ill; drug dealers, drug addicts, alcoholics, and a wide assortment of violent sociopaths.
>
> The prison-industrial complex is not only a set of interest groups and institutions. It is also a state of mind. The lure of big money is corrupting the nation's criminal-justice system, replacing notions of public service with a drive for higher profits. The eagerness of elected officials to pass "tough-on-crime" legislation — combined with their

68. Donziger, *The Real War on Crime*, p. 87. Also see Paulette Thomas, "Making Crime Pay: Triangle of Interests Creates Infrastructure to Fight Lawlessness," *Wall Street Journal*, May 12, 1994, p. A1.

69. See Eric Schlosser, "The Prison-Industrial Complex," *Atlantic Monthly*, December 1998. Available online (subscription required) at http://www.theatlantic.com/issues/98dec/prisons.htm.

unwillingness to disclose the true costs of these laws — has encouraged all sorts of financial improprieties. The inner workings of the prison-industrial complex can be observed in the state of New York, where the prison boom started, transforming the economy of an entire region; in Texas and Tennessee, where private prison companies have thrived; and in California, where the correctional trends of the past two decades have converged and reached extremes. In the realm of psychology a complex is an overreaction to some perceived threat.[70]

Here again we see the threefold social function of increased imprisonment: to alleviate the pain associated with widespread psychological anxiety and fear of crime, to produce desirable political outcomes for public servants, and to produce economic profitability. Angela Davis expands the influence and reach of the prison-industrial complex beyond the United States' borders as she laments its global dimensions:

> Since the 1980s, the prison system has become increasingly ensconced in the economic, political, and ideological life of the United States and the transnational trafficking in U.S. commodities, culture, and ideas. Thus, the prison industrial complex is much more than the sum of all the jails and prisons in the country. It is a set of symbiotic relationships among correctional communities, transnational corporations, media conglomerates, guards' unions, and legislative and court agendas.[71]

The contemporary political roots of longer, harsher, and more widespread imprisonment can be traced back to a critical date in the origins of the prison-industrial complex: January 3, 1973, the day "Nelson Rockefeller, then the governor of New York, gave a State of the State address demanding that every illegal-drug dealer be punished with a mandatory prison sentence of life without parole."[72] In support of policies being promoted by "tough on crime" partisans, Rockefeller's call for harsher, fixed prison terms resulted in the passage of the so-called Rockefeller Drug Laws.[73]

70. Schlosser, "The Prison-Industrial Complex," pp. 4-5.
71. Angela Y. Davis, *Are Prisons Obsolete?* p. 107.
72. Schlosser, "The Prison-Industrial Complex," p. 6. Also see Marc Mauer, *Race to Incarcerate*, p. 57, and Peter G. Herman, ed., *The American Prison System* (New York: H. W. Wilson, 2001), p. vii.
73. Marc Mauer, *Race to Incarcerate*, p. 57.

Two years earlier, in 1971, Rockefeller had already begun to establish his commitment to a "get tough" approach to law and order by decisively crushing the prison rebellion that had taken place at upstate New York's Attica Correctional Facility. The Rockefeller legislation seemed a logical political evolution, building as it did upon Senator Barry Goldwater's appeal to a widespread fear of crime to attract White, middle-class voters a decade earlier, and Richard Nixon's revival of the same theme during the 1968 presidential campaign.[74]

It should be noted that, at the time, Goldwater and Nixon's political use of public fear-of-crime-anxieties drew little in the way of public demands for law and order justice. "On the contrary," reports Schlosser,

> Congress voted decisively in 1970 to eliminate almost all federal mandatory-minimum sentences for drug offenders. Leading members of both political parties applauded the move. Mainstream opinion considered drug addiction to be largely a public-health problem, not an issue for the criminal courts. The Federal Bureau of Prisons was preparing to close large penitentiaries in Georgia, Kansas, and Washington. From 1963 to 1972 the number of inmates in California had declined by more than a fourth, despite the state's growing population. The number of inmates in New York had fallen to its lowest level since at least 1950. Prisons were widely viewed as a barbaric and ineffective means of controlling deviant behavior.[75]

Yet this view was soon to change. In 1973 the Rockefeller Laws were the harshest narcotics laws in the nation, but other states would follow suit over the next years and decades as war was declared on crime. Many states passed laws that set strict mandatory minimum sentences for certain offenses, mostly gun- and drug-related. As a consequence of the harsh sentences now being handed down for selling and possessing illegal drugs, along with new limits on plea bargaining, the number of state prisons doubled during the 1980s and 1990s. As new prisons sprung up, new jobs began to be created and local economies were spurred.[76]

As economies grew, so did the fear of crime. Cait Murphy, writing for

74. Schlosser, "The Prison-Industrial Complex," p. 6.

75. Schlosser, "The Prison-Industrial Complex," pp. 4-5.

76. Herman, *The American Prison System*, p. vii.

Fortune magazine, has pointed out that the legislative push for harsher punishment for crime was due to an increase in crime and the subsequent widespread public fear and anger that followed. Murphy argues that, "Fundamentally, America's prison population grew because people got sick of feeling scared and elected politicians . . . promised to deliver freedom from that fear. Moreover, it could be argued that America had some catching up to do: From the early 1960s to the early 1970s, the violent-crime rate rose sharply while the incarceration rate actually fell. Those trends probably helped to spawn the 'tough on crime' mentality that has reigned since."[77] With regard to the cause of the initial increase in imprisonment during the 1970s, Marc Mauer concurs with Murphy: "The initial rise in prison populations in the 1970s was not itself a result of newly implemented 'get tough' policies . . . the population increase primarily resulted from the rise in crime rates."[78] In general, the trend in the 1980s was toward lawmakers delivering mandatory minimums, while "three-strike" laws (designed to target repeat felons), truth-in-sentencing legislation, and the abolition of parole in many states were a product of the 1990s.[79]

Criminologist Henry Pontell's work has also tied the political causes of increased incarceration to a social climate of suspicion, anxiety, and fear:

> Ours is a society marked by increasing suspicion, anxiety, and paranoia over the fear of being criminally victimized. This is true especially for the elderly and the poor, the most vulnerable portions of the population, who must bear the brunt of the ugliest crimes. Our fears are brought about through reported crime rates, which are themselves partially created by official agencies. Ironically, our response to the perceived crime problem is to further increase resources, which keeps the cycle intact.
>
> What became known in the 1960s as the war against crime continues into the 1980s, although the nature of the movement has changed significantly. The liberal vision of reducing crime by attacking its social causes, the so-called roots of crime, was replaced in the 1970s by a

77. Cait Murphy, "Crime and Punishment," in Herman, *The American Prison System*, p. 109.

78. Murphy, "Crime and Punishment," p. 109. Cf. Marc Mauer, *Race to Incarcerate*, p. 56. Also see John Irwin and James Austin, *It's About Time: America's Imprisonment Binge* (Belmont, Calif.: Wadsworth, 1994), p. 5.

79. Murphy, "Crime and Punishment," p. 109.

more "pragmatic" and conservative ideology that aimed at punishing criminals and largely ignored the role of the social system in generating crime. The all-out "war" was transformed into a battle between the forces of good and evil.[80]

Pontell goes on to explain that

Social programs designed to attack the social roots of crime and to rehabilitate offenders did not produce conclusive results in the eyes of some researchers and policy makers. Increased expenditures in criminal justice and the community were accompanied by higher reported crime, leading many to question the effectiveness of community-based programs designed to prevent criminal activity. As far as rehabilitation is concerned, however, 'what works' remains an open question.[81]

Christian Parenti, meanwhile, ties the social function of increased imprisonment to the more dubious political strategy to halt widespread social unrest and to get the public's mind off of a stagnant economy:

Beginning in the late sixties U.S. capitalism hit a dual social and economic crisis, and it was in response to this crisis that the criminal justice buildup of today began. After a surge of expansion in the late sixties the growth of criminal justice plateaued in the late seventies, only to resume in earnest during the early and mid eighties with Reagan's war on drugs. Since then we've been on a steady path toward ever more state repression and surveillance. Initially this buildup was in response to racial upheaval and political rebellion. The second part was/is more a response to the vicious economic restructuring of the Reagan era. This restructuring was itself a right-wing strategy for addressing the economic crisis which first appeared in the mid and late sixties. To restore sagging business profits, the welfare of working people had to be sacrificed. Thus the second phase of the criminal justice crackdown has become, intentionally or otherwise, a way to manage rising inequality and surplus populations. Throughout this process of economic restructuring the poor have suffered, particularly poor people

80. Pontell, *A Capacity to Punish*, p. 2.
81. Pontell, *A Capacity to Punish*, p. 2.

of color. Thus it is poor people of color who make up the bulk of American prisoners.[82]

Crime and the Mass Media

No account of the prison-industrial complex would be complete without an assessment of the role of the mass media. Over the past two decades the role of the media has been an important factor in influencing a heightened public fear of crime, which in turn fuels pressure to increase imprisonment. "The media" represents a broad and complex array of competing interests: the *New York Times,* the *National Inquirer, Newsweek;* CNN, National Public Radio, MTV; various "reality" crime shows like *COPS, America's Most Wanted, Court TV;* a feast of crime dramas, and countless other outlets of crime-based information and entertainment. The list is virtually endless, and I concur with the observation of Marc Mauer of the Sentencing Project, who has suggested that today's complex array of media "have converged to shape public perceptions of crime, offenders, and incarceration policy in ways that are often misleading."

While some print media in recent years have criticized mandatory sentencing (notable examples include the *New York Times,* the *Washington Post,* the *Los Angeles Times,* and *Emerge Magazine*), their statements have not made much of a dent in the political and public calls for more mandatory sentencing. This is because the call to repeal mandatory minimums, even when made by powerful print media conglomerates, cannot compete with the overwhelming and steady diet of graphic print, radio, and television depictions of crime, death, and tragedy available to U.S. residents twenty-four hours a day, seven days a week. A flood of images continually

---

82. Parenti, *Lockdown America,* p. xii. A particularly disturbing aspect of the "racialization" of criminal punishment can be seen in the application of the death penalty. Mark Lewis Taylor correctly notes that "the racial bias of the death penalty continues to be confirmed in study after study. In state systems, although 12 percent of the U.S. population is African-American, 40 percent of the death row population is African-American. In some states, like Pennsylvania, 60 percent of the death row population is African-American. On the death row of the Federal system, over 75 percent are minorities. On military's death row, 87.5 percent are minorities." See Taylor, *The Executed God,* p. 69. The primary source is United States Senator Russ Feingold, "Statement on the Federal Death Penalty Abolition Act of 1999," U.S. Congressional Record (November 10, 1999).

communicates to the public and to policymakers the prudence of feeling anxiety and fear about crime-gone-wild in America. And this intensified anxiety and fear "serves to overwhelm any intelligent or informative discussion of the issues."[83] Further, it has become increasingly apparent that the influence of print media, which often presents a more informed, less sensationalized approach, continues to be eroded by electronic media, by television in particular. Mauer maintains that, "Fewer people read newspapers or rely on them for their main source of news; television, on the other hand, with its seemingly endless supply of news channels, has become the primary medium for information. And its power lies in the images it presents on the screen."[84]

Television offers a bountiful buffet of crime and punishment, stoking the fires of anxiety, fear, and widespread social outrage, which, in turn, fuel an intensified public appetite for more and harsher prison terms for offenders. Mauer, citing a published report by the Center for Media and Public Affairs, reports that general crime stories on network television doubled from 1992 to 1993. Murder stories tripled during the same period. By 1993, one of every eight evening network news stories featured a crime. Citing data from Media Monitor, Mauer reports that by 1995 networks featured more than 2,500 crime stories on the evening news, 52 percent more than the previous high in 1993. Even if one excludes the O. J. Simpson trial, which accounted for a third of this increase, murder stories still "rose by 369 percent from 80 stories in 1990 to 375 by 1995, a period in which actual murder rates had declined by 13 percent."[85]

The most heavily watched news programs are late local news shows. In virtually every city in the country, crime stories dominate ten- and eleven o'clock news coverage. In Philadelphia, for example, late night news programs report crime stories almost one third of the time, with three quarters (76 percent) of the crime stories being featured in the first segment of the programs. Some studies have shown that television news violence has had a distorting impact on public and policymaker attitudes to-

83. Mauer, *Race to Incarcerate*, p. 171.

84. Mauer, *Race to Incarcerate*, p. 171. Provocative research has been done by Harvard University public policy professor Robert D. Putnam on the effects of electronic media, above all television, as a serious threat to social connectedness. See Putnam's chapter on "Technology and the Mass Media" in his *Bowling Alone: The Collapse and Revival of American Community* (New York: Touchstone, 2000), pp. 216-46.

85. Mauer, *Race to Incarcerate*, p. 172.

ward crime. For example, Mauer, summarizing a study by the Berkeley Media Studies Group, reports that news stories in California involving youth violence were aired at a frequency far exceeding the actual rate of violence committed by youth:

> The Berkeley Media Studies Group examined news content of a week of local news broadcasts on 26 stations throughout California. The researchers found that violence was the single most frequent story topic featured and that more than one half (55 percent) of the stories on youth involved violence, while more than two thirds (68 percent) of the stories on violence involved youth. This is in contrast to FBI data showing that juveniles represent less than 20 percent of arrests for violence; young people are portrayed as contributing far more to the problem of violence than they actually do.[86]

This lack of proportion is widespread. According to the Dutch Ministry of Justice international surveys on criminal victimization in eleven industrialized countries, when one considers the relationship between fear of crime and the actual risks of being victimized, there is a "lack of much relationship between the level of anxiety and risks of street crime." Rather, the surveys indicate that a significant level of fear of street crime "may be determined by specific 'cultural' pressures such as media influences."[87]

Media images related to crime are indeed powerful. In 1997, political scientists at UCLA, in order to demonstrate the phenomenon of "script-based reasoning," conducted an experiment in which subjects viewed television newscasts of crime stories. In some of the stories a perpetrator was identified, in others none was identified. In a summary of the results of this experiment, Mauer reports that, "Even in instances in which no specific reference was made to a suspect, 42 percent of the viewers recalled having seen one. In two thirds of these cases, they recalled the suspect as being African American."[88] In this study and others like it, one sees the

---

86. Mauer, *Race to Incarcerate*, pp. 173-74.

87. Mauer, *Race to Incarcerate*, p. 174. See also Pat Mayhew and Jan J. M. van Dijk, *Criminal Victimisation in Eleven Industrialised Countries* (Den Haag: Ministry of Justice, 1997), p. 6. Also see summary report of recent surveys by J. N. van Kesteren, Pat Mayhew, and P. Nieuwbeerta, *Criminal Victimisation in Seventeen Industrialised Countries: Key-findings from the 2000 International Crime Victims Survey* (Den Haag: Ministry of Justice, 2000).

88. Marc Mauer, *Race to Incarcerate*, p. 174.

powerful relationship among anxiety, fear, and the media's (especially racialized) representations of crime.

Crime as Big Business

Filling prisons and jails with lawbreakers is also big business. The United States' nearly $50 billion per year correctional spending benefits a host of companies that supply a variety of goods and services to prisons and jails. This boon for big businesses tends to intensify pressure to increase investment in prison construction and services. This, in turn, creates institutional pressure to increase the number of prisoners, which then leads to even more prison construction and contracts for services. At a point, these interests produce a self-preserving cycle of bureaucracy and profit independent of actual crime rates.

Various kinds of businesses contribute to the pressure to keep a steady stream of prisoners coming. Among the most influential are private, for-profit prison management corporations that are paid, predominantly by state governments, to house inmates in an effort to relieve administrative pressure on a chronically overcrowded and economically inefficient prison bureaucracy. In addition to these, major companies — including Microsoft, Honda, Victoria's Secret, and (the now defunct) TWA — "employ prison labor, a practice that has provoked complaints from job seekers about lost opportunities and unfair competition," according to Peter G. Herman, editor of *The American Prison System*.[89] Finally, many communities and counties, mostly in rural areas, feel that by petitioning for prison construction they can stimulate struggling or failing economies.

New York State's North Country (the northernmost region of the state) provides a salient example of how a predominantly economic decision to administer a prison produces institutional pressure to guarantee an adequate supply of prisoners. Here, approximately one out of every twenty people is serving time.[90] Consider the economic repercussions if suddenly 50 percent fewer people were being convicted of crimes requiring incarceration. Clearly officials have a vested interest in being vigilant about finding wrongdoers.

89. Herman, *The American Prison System*, p. 83.
90. Herman, *The American Prison System*, p. 83.

New York is not alone. Many municipalities across the nation are seeking cash from the burgeoning prison system. Civic leaders in Bowling Green, Missouri, successfully lobbied their state capital against twelve other Missouri communities for one of three new state prisons in 1996. The new $79 million, 1,975-bed facility brought hundreds of jobs to Bowling Green, a town once in tremendous economic decline. Because inmates are counted as residents when calculating the distribution of state revenues, the prison will bring $150,000 a year in new state funds, not to mention a new housing subdivision, a Super 8 Motel, and a McDonald's.[91] Elsewhere, the state of Florida has "promoted [its] prison-building spree with a color brochure claiming that a 1,100-bed prison is worth $25 million a year and 350 jobs to a community." According to Eric Lotke, writing for the *Multinational Monitor,* towns are responding to the economic promise of the new prison economy by "lining up for the chance at such bounty."[92] Lotke reports that, "Students in one Sunday school class in Texas actually got on their knees and prayed that a new prison would open in their neighborhood."[93] This is a far cry from the days when communities greeted suggestions of prisons with chants of "Not in my backyard!"

Public-private partnerships in the operations of prisons are nothing new in America. They have existed from the colonial period to the present, through a convergence of interests among reformers, public officials, and local businesses. Anne Larason Schneider, writing for *The American Behavioral Scientist,* explains that

Humanitarian reformers believed that prisons would be more humane than common forms of punishment in the American colonies — and later in the western frontier — which were death, branding, torture, or other physical punishment. The role of reformers was evident in the founding of the first prison in the Quaker colony of William Penn when the great law of 1682 banned the death penalty for everything except premeditated murder. This prison was a 5 feet by 7 feet cell. Later, the colony rented space from local businesses (Walker, 1980). Public officials from the colonial period to the early 1900s believed that pris-

---

91. Eric Lotke, "New Growth Industries: The Prison Industrial Complex," *Multinational Monitor* 17:11 (November 1996). Available online at http://www.multinationalmonitor.org/hyper/mm1196.06.html.

92. Lotke, "New Growth Industries."

93. Lotke, "New Growth Industries."

ons could be self-supporting or even profitable for the state, and businesses were interested in sharing in those profits. Some states permitted a private individual or firm to build, manage, and handle the day-to-day operation of the prison itself, a system similar to the ones that have generated such intense debate in the 1980s and 1990s.[94]

According to Schneider, by the nineteenth century the many different forms of public-private partnerships "eventually generated serious problems that produced opposition from business, labor, and humanitarian reformers." She reports that in certain states "prisoners rioted or protested to such an extent that [many] partnerships were ended . . . [and] by the beginning of World War II, public-private partnerships in prisons were virtually nonexistent."[95]

However, a dramatic reemergence of public-private partnerships in prison administration has taken place since the 1980s. According to the National Institute of Corrections (NIC), the term "privatization of corrections" has (in general) three contemporary meanings or models:

1. Private *Management.* In this arrangement, private firms have total responsibility for the operation of a facility. This is the most common use of the term "privatization" — and the most controversial aspect of the private sector's involvement in corrections.
2. Private *Sector Development.* Here, the private sector develops, designs, and finances or arranges for the financing of facilities. This often involves owning the facility and leasing it back to the jurisdiction through a lease/purchase contract, which serves as an alternative to a public bond issue or outright tax expenditure.
3. Private *Services Provision.* This refers to the common practice of jails contracting with private vendors to run medical, food, training, educational, transportation, and other programs. Provision for child care for incarcerated mothers is the oldest and most familiar privatization model.[96]

94. A. L. Schneider, "Public-Private Partnership in the U.S. Prison System," *The American Behavioral Scientist* 43:1 (1999), p. 86.

95. Schneider, "Public-Private Partnership in the U.S. Prison System," pp. 86-88.

96. National Institute of Corrections Information Center, "Briefing Paper: Trends in Jail Privatization," February 1992. Available online at http://www.nicic.org/pubs/1992/010043.pdf.

The first of these is the one referred to most often in privatization debates today. NIC summarizes that

> The movement to involve the private sector in the operation of correctional facilities began in the early 1980s, but it gained no real momentum until the middle of the decade. A Council of State Governments report noted only a "handful of activity" by 1983. At that time, four states (Arizona, California, Colorado, and Texas) had privately-run detention facilities, all of which were under contract to the U.S. Immigration and Naturalization Service or the Bureau of Prisons. Tennessee was in the planning process for a facility to house local offenders.[97]

As the 1980s went on, however, they ushered in a new era of direct supervision of inmates by private prison firms. The Sentencing Project has summarized the development of modern "prison privatization" as follows:

> With a burgeoning prison population resulting from the "war on drugs" and increased use of incarceration, prison overcrowding and rising costs became increasingly problematic for local, state, and federal governments. In response to this expanding criminal justice system, private business interests saw an opportunity for expansion, and consequently, private-sector involvement in prisons moved from the simple contracting of services to contracting for the complete management and operation of entire prisons.
>
> Today, the privatization of prisons refers both to the takeover of existing public facilities by private operators and to the building of new and additional prisons by for-profit prison companies. (Many of the new prisons, furthermore, are built to house out-of-state inmates.) Depending on the jurisdiction, the local, state, or federal government is then charged a per diem or monthly rate for each prisoner.[98]

Today, private prison management represents one of the fastest-growing sectors of the U.S. economy. Ken Silverstein, writing for *Prison Le-*

---

97. National Institute of Corrections, "Briefing Paper: Trends in Jail Privatization."

98. Amy Cheung, "Prison Privatization and the Use of Incarceration" (Washington, D.C.: The Sentencing Project, 2004). Available online at http://www.sentencingproject.org/Admin/Documents/publications/inc_prisonprivatization.pdf.

gal News, asks, "What is the most profitable industry in America? Weapons, oil and computer technology all offer high rates of return, but there is probably no sector of the economy so abloom with money as the privately run prison industry."[99] Needless to say, this practice involves the interweaving of private business and government interests in a very complex way.

Advocates of privatization argue that it allows society to fight against crime more efficiently — i.e., at lower costs — without surrendering quality of service, social control, and/or profit. Yet according to prison activists Eve Goldberg and Linda Evans, whatever quality of service may or may not be offered, the rationale for increased imprisonment can still be connected to the interweaving of national fear, political interest, and private business, and can be summarized as follows:

> Not so long ago, communism was "the enemy" and communists were demonized as a way of justifying gargantuan military expenditures. Now, fear of crime and the demonization of criminals serve a similar ideological purpose: to justify the use of tax dollars for the repression and incarceration of a growing percentage of our population. The omnipresent media blitz about serial killers, missing children, and "random violence" feeds our fear. In reality, however, most of the "criminals" we lock up are poor people who commit nonviolent crimes out of economic need. Violence occurs in less than 14% of all reported crime, and injuries occur in just 3%. In California, the top three charges for those entering prison are: possession of a controlled substance, possession of a controlled substance for sale, and robbery. Violent crimes like murder, rape, manslaughter and kidnapping don't even make the top ten. Like fear of communism during the Cold War, fear of crime is a great selling tool for a dubious product.[100]

99. See Ken Silverstein, "America's Private Gulag," *Prison Legal News* June 1, 1997. Available online at http://www.corpwatch.org/article.php?id=867.

100. See Eve Goldberg and Linda Evans, "The Prison Industrial Complex and the Global Economy," in *Global Exchange Campaigns: United States* (Berkeley: Prison Activist Resource Center, 2004). Available online at http://www.globalexchange.org/countries/americas/unitedstates/pic.html. In the author biography, Evans is described as "a north american [sic] anti-imperialist political prisoner at FCI Dublin in California." Goldberg is said to be "a writer, film maker, and solidarity and prisoner's rights activist."

In addition to private prison management corporations, many and varied other businesses profit from prison expansion and privatization: investment houses, construction companies, and architectural firms, certainly, but also food service providers, transportation companies, and furniture manufacturers. And there is a brisk "specialty item" industry as well, providing fencing, handcuffs, drug detectors, protective vests, and other items marketed as providing "security" and "peace of mind" to prisons and to the nation.[101] Defense industry giants Westinghouse and Lockheed Martin actively lobby Washington for a share of the lucrative domestic law enforcement market. Telecommunications companies like AT&T, Sprint, and MCI have been accused of charging prisoners exorbitant rates, often six times the national average for long distance calls, by some estimates. Correctional Communications Corporation provides systematic surveillance to prisons. Investment firm Smith Barney is part owner of a prison in Florida. American Express and General Electric have invested in private prison construction in Oklahoma and Tennessee. Other "brand-name" supporters of the bureaucracy of imprisonment include Goldman Sachs & Co., Merrill Lynch, and Sodexho Marriott Services, among many others.

Currently the dominant "management-private" corrections firm is the Nashville-based Correctional Corporation of America (CCA; formerly Prison Realty Trust, Inc.).[102] CCA, the nation's largest private prison firm, operates more than 48 facilities in 11 states, Puerto Rico, the United Kingdom, and Australia. Reporting on private corrections companies in general, Goldberg and Evans contend that

> Under contract by government to run jails and prisons, and paid a fixed sum per prisoner, the profit motive mandates that these firms operate as cheaply and efficiently as possible. This means lower wages for staff, no unions, and fewer services for prisoners. Private contracts also mean less public scrutiny. Prison owners are raking in billions by

---

101. Goldberg and Evans, "The Prison Industrial Complex and the Global Economy."

102. In 1984 CCA was awarded a contract to take over a jail facility in Hamilton County, Tennessee. This marked the first time that any government in the country had turned over the complete operation of a public correctional institution to a private operator. This has led some prison observers to mark 1984 as the year of emergence and establishment of the modern private prison business. See report by Good Jobs First, "Jail Breaks: Economic Development Subsidies Given to Private Prisons," October 2001. Available online at http://www.goodjobsfirst.org/pdf/jailbreaks.pdf.

cutting corners which harm prisoners. Substandard diets, extreme overcrowding, and abuses by poorly trained personnel have all been documented and can be expected in these institutions which are unabashedly about making money. [103]

Silverstein makes a similar argument about the economic bottom line for America's private prison industry in the following summation of developments in the 1990s:

> Consider the growth of the Corrections Corporation of America, the industry leader whose stock price has climbed from $8 a share in 1992 to about $30 today and whose revenue rose by 81 per cent in 1995 alone. Investors in Wackenhut Corrections Corp. have enjoyed an average return of 18 per cent during the past five years and the company is rated by Forbes as one of the top 200 small businesses in the country. At Esmor, another big private prison contractor, revenues have soared from $4.6 million in 1990 to more than $25 million in 1995. Ten years ago there were just five privately-run prisons in the country, housing a population of 2,000. Today nearly a score of private firms run more than 100 prisons with about 62,000 beds. That's still less than five per cent of the total market but the industry is expanding fast, with the number of private prison beds expected to grow to 360,000 during the next decade.
>
> The exhilaration among leaders and observers of the private prison sector was cheerfully summed up by a headline in *USA Today:* "Everybody's doin' the jailhouse stock." An equally upbeat mood imbued a conference on private prisons held last December at the Four Seasons Resort in Dallas. The brochure for the conference, organized by the World Research Group, a New York-based investment firm, called the corporate takeover of correctional facilities the "newest trend in the area of privatizing previously government-run programs. . . . While arrests and convictions are steadily on the rise, profits are to be made — profits from crime. Get in on the ground floor of this booming industry now!"[104]

---

103. See Goldberg and Evans, "The Prison Industrial Complex and the Global Economy."

104. Silverstein, "America's Private Gulag."

According to a summary of a 1997 special report in the Washington D.C.–based *Counterpunch Newsletter,* "the clanging of the cell doors means sweet music to the growing privately owned prison industry. Thanks to tight government budgets, stricter repeat-offender sentences, the potential of a cheap labor market, and a more vigorous prosecution of the 'drug war,' the kingpin of jailing for dollars, the Correction Corporation of America, has seen its stock value soar from $8 per share in 1992 to $30 in 1996, with an 81% increase in revenue in 1995 alone."[105] It goes on to contend that for private prison companies the numbers of inmates means not only profits, but also survival. As a result, "private prisons have resorted to imposing tougher disciplinary standards (like making it harder to get time off for good behavior) and mishandling or losing parole papers and forcing inmates to stay beyond their release dates in order to maintain the requisite 90-95% occupancy rate to avoid, as Prudential Securities has said, 'low occupancy . . . a drag on profits.'"[106]

The summary goes on to argue that because prisons have fast become such a good source of continuous cheap labor, corporations are utilizing the nation's jails and prisons to maximize profits:

Where prisoners used to hammer out license tags for the state, now they saw, sew, and solder such items as car parts, clothing, furniture, and computer circuit boards for major U.S. companies. The tactic has proven so lucrative that a U.S. company operating in Mexico closed down its operations and moved them to San Quentin, while another firm dumped 150 workers in Texas and set up shop in a private prison in Lockhart, where prisoners now assemble circuit boards for such outfits as IBM and Compaq. State legislator Kevin Mannix of Oregon has issued an invitation to Nike to shift its operations from Indonesia to his state. While pay scales may be as high as $400 per month "take home" in government prisons, wages are as low as 17 cents per hour in private prisons. Pay rates at CCA prisons max out at 50 cents per hour for "highly-skilled labor."[107]

---

105. Citizens for Better Government, "The Emerging American Gulag: America's New Slave Business" (April 7, 1997). Available online at http://www.afn.org/~govern/Prisons.html. This article is based on a special report in the Washington, D.C.-based *Counterpunch Newsletter,* January 1-15, 1997.

106. Citizens for Better Government, "The Emerging American Gulag," p. 1.

107. Citizens for Better Government, "The Emerging American Gulag," p. 1. See also

It seems clear that the private prison industry, and the cheap (some say "slave") labor it provides, has become a pot of gold for other private businesses. Serious are the social consequences of public policies that encourage the maintenance of a significant work force that receives substandard wages inside institutions that prohibit worker strikes and union organizing and that provide no unemployment insurance or worker's compensation. Indeed, it would be no exaggeration to say that prison culture has effectively introduced a significant slave-like class into the American social fabric, one of whose significant functions is that of feeding profits to big business. Justice advocacy groups like Global Exchange appear correct when they summarize the cyclical connection between society's low-wage workers, crime, corporate profits, and prison labor:

> An American worker who once upon a time made $8/hour, loses his job when the company relocates to Thailand where workers are paid only $2/day. Unemployed, and alienated from a society indifferent to his needs, he becomes involved in the drug economy or some other outlawed means of survival. He is arrested, put in prison, and put to work. His new salary: 22 cents/hour. From worker, to unemployed, to criminal, to convict laborer, the cycle has come full circle. And the only victor is big business.[108]

All this raises a serious question: As a matter of public policy, should prisoners really be doing data entry for Chevron, making telephone reservations for (the now defunct) TWA, raising hogs, shoveling manure, or making circuit boards, limousines, waterbeds, and Victoria's Secret lingerie?[109] Some, no doubt, see nothing wrong with any of this and may correctly point out that even the Fourteenth Amendment to the Constitution, which abolished slavery, excludes prisoners from its protections. Others will no doubt claim that the connection between private business and prison labor is part of a rehabilitation process aimed at teaching inmates the value of hard work and responsibility. Thus private business offers a variety of employment development opportunities that, along with other life skill programs, provide

---

Robin D. G. Kelley, *Yo' Mama's Disfunktional!: Fighting the Culture Wars in Urban America* (Boston: Beacon Press, 1997), pp. 97-99.

108. See Goldberg and Evans, "The Prison Industrial Complex and the Global Economy."

109. Lotke, "New Growth Industries."

opportunities for positive changes to take place in an inmate's life. If the inmate decides to put these skills to use upon their return to society, then a better person will have been returned to the nation's communities.

Others might take issue with such arguments, contending that even if the most basic standards of employment do not legally apply to prison labor according to the Constitution, it is nonetheless unethical for a nation to create and maintain public policies that connect increased imprisonment to increased private corporate profits. A prison system that allows "jailing-for-dollars," it might be argued, encourages private industry to support lobbying and legislation efforts that guarantee an endless supply of cheap prison labor rather than encouraging the enhancing and expanding of flourishing communities.

Countering this argument however, one could point out that pressure to privatize prisons is not driven primarily by those seeking a profit, but rather by federal, state, and local governments dealing with escalating costs and overcrowded facilities, as well as by ever-increasing popular dissatisfaction with government administration of prisons. After all, as the National Institute of Corrections has pointed out, "Privatization is something seen as a practical option when a jurisdiction needs to bring facilities on-line quickly in response to a court order requiring additional capacity. Advocates claim that private operators can run facilities more efficiently and cost-effectively."[110]

In dismissing and/or disagreeing with cost comparisons, some who oppose prison privatization on public policy grounds insist that the fundamental point is simply that it is the responsibility of the government to operate corrections. On this view, as summarized by public policy analyst John DiIulio, society's correctional institutions are "a public trust to be administered on behalf of the community and in the name of civility and justice."[111] Here again, a serious concern can be raised about whether private operators of prisons might put profit ahead of the public good. NIC points out that "professional corrections associations have addressed privatization through policy statements that range from cautious (American Corrections Association) to negative (National Sheriffs' Association). The American Federation of State, County, and Municipal Employees

---

110. National Institute of Corrections, "Briefing Paper: Trends in Jail Privatization."
    111. Quoted in National Institute of Corrections, "Briefing Paper: Trends in Jail Privatization."

[AFSCME] has been opposed from the beginning, and the American Bar Association in 1989 urged a moratorium on privatization until more information was available."[112]

As I noted above, the largest private prison corporation currently is the Corrections Corporation of America, or CCA, and we would do well here to consider it in a bit more depth. CCA is currently the sixth largest corrections system in the nation, after those of Texas, California, the federal government, New York, and Florida. According to *Hoover's Online*, of the more than 48 prisons built and owned internationally by CCA as of December 2002, about 40 were located in 12 states and Washington D.C. *Hoover's* reports that at year-end 2002, CCA had supervision of 61,000 inmates at nearly 65 facilities (including some facilities not owned by CCA) in more than 20 states. CCA is paid by state, federal, and local agencies based on the number of prisoners housed in a facility. The company's current occupancy rate is almost 90 percent. The Federal Bureau of Prisons is CCA's largest customer. The Bureau of Prisons, the U.S. Marshals Services, and the Department of Homeland Security together account for almost 30 percent of the firm's business. CCA also has a subsidiary called TransCor America, which offers prisoner transport services.

Coterminous with the then-nascent "war on drugs, CCA became the first private U.S. correction company in 1983." CCA says approvingly of itself that, "We have grown to become the largest corrections company in the country." Contrary to the negative portrait painted above by people like Silverstein, and Goldberg and Evans regarding CCA's and other private prison companies' record of substandard care and concern for inmates in the service of ever-increasing corporate profit, CCA claims about itself that

> All CCA facilities must meet standards set by our customers. These standards are the same as those in government correctional facilities. In addition, CCA facilities are often more closely monitored by our customers to ensure compliance. We are committed to achieving accreditation of our facilities by American Correctional Association (ACA). Currently, 85% of all our facilities are ACA accredited, an achievement which far surpasses most public and private correction systems.

112. Quoted in National Institute of Corrections, "Briefing Paper: Trends in Jail Privatization."

At CCA we believe in trying to return a better person to our communities. At every facility you will find a variety of programs geared to the inmate population. These programs range from substance abuse to behavior modification to life skills to education and job training. While we provide the opportunity for changes to take place in an inmate's life, it is up to the individual to put those skills to use once they return to society.

Why use private corrections? Many governments are under court order to lower inmate populations in their facilities. CCA provides an immediate and efficient solution for these governments that cannot adequately house their inmates. Secondly, all governments are looking to cut costs. By working with private correction companies, such as CCA, governments are able to provide the same level of service at lower costs.[113]

Notwithstanding CCA's positive portrait of itself, one simply must face the fact that the labor of incarcerated persons in the U.S., as well as their simply being incarcerated in very large numbers, increasingly provides raw material for economic success. Industry grows richer as prisons and jails ensnare more people. Criminal justice policy is now as influenced by the Corrections Corporation of America as defense policy is by McDonnell Douglas and Lockheed Martin, which has recently begun handling information technology for some justice and corrections institutions. The Sentencing Project documents the close connection between corporate contributions and sentencing policy:

[B]oth CCA and Wackenhut are major contributors to the American Legislative Exchange Council (ALEC), a Washington, D.C. based public policy organization that supports conservative legislators. . . . One of ALEC's primary functions is the development of model legislation that advances conservative principles, such as privatization. Under their Criminal Justice Task Force, ALEC has developed and helped to successfully implement in many states "tough on crime" initiatives including "Truth in Sentencing" and "Three Strikes" laws.[114]

---

113. Corrections Corporation of America, "The CCA Story." Web page no longer available.

114. Cheung, "Prison Privatization and the Use of Incarceration."

This is in spite of the fact that "private prison companies deny that they are motivated to take proactive steps in pursuing legislation to keep their private facilities filled."[115]

Despite denials by private corporate interests, prison entrepreneurs and policymakers do often work together. Private companies routinely lobby politicians for favors that override democratic processes, thereby limiting public oversight with regard to prison philosophy, policy, and practice. A consequence of their bottom-line orientation is a widespread tendency by private prison companies to avoid the costs of (for example) drug treatment, group counseling, and literacy training.[116] Eric Lotke argues that, "The companies' bottom-line orientation drives them toward sterile, technologized solutions to prison management — fewer guards, more video cameras — rather than the labor-intensive human interactions needed to assist the troubled people in their care."[117] The evidence seems to support Lotke's contention, despite CCA spokesperson Susan Hart's denials that her company's facilities are guilty of these sorts of charges: "We want facilities to be as program intensive as possible because it gives the inmates something to do, making them easier to manage."[118]

Some analysts continue to view the prison boom of the past three decades as a social success for the nation, however regrettable the consequences for some communities of peoples. These analysts see a cause and effect relationship between a still-rising prison population and a decade-long fall in the national crime rate. David B. Muhlhausen, a policy analyst at the Heritage Foundation, has been quoted as saying, "If you put somebody in prison, you can be sure they're not going to rob you."[119] Muhlhausen argues that "quality research shows that . . . increasing incarceration decreases crime." When pondering the fact that there are still at least 12 million serious crimes committed each year in the U.S., Muhlhausen reportedly suggests that, "Maybe we're not incarcerating enough people."[120]

Cait Murphy, summarizing a study by Steve Levitt, a professor of economics at the University of Chicago, points out that it is "estimated

115. Cheung, "Prison Privatization and the Use of Incarceration," pp. 4-54.
116. Lotke, "New Growth Industries."
117. Lotke, "New Growth Industries."
118. Lotke, "New Growth Industries."
119. Shane, "Locked Up in the Land of the Free."
120. Shane, "Locked Up in the Land of the Free."

that the effect of imprisoning one additional lawbreaker for a year was to prevent two fewer violent crimes and about a dozen fewer property crimes."[121] Morgan Reynolds, director of the Criminal Justice Center at the National Center for Policy Analysis in Dallas, Texas, and professor of economics at Texas A&M University, concedes that the U.S. prison incarceration rate is growing, but that this is a good thing because it has given the nation safer streets. For Reynolds, the equation is simple: "punishment reduces crime."[122] Reynolds argues that, "Yes, prison takes a toll on the family the convict leaves behind. But crime also takes a toll on its victims and society at large. And crime rates have fallen by one third over the past decade while the prison and jail population have risen to 2 million. Most people are able to connect these dots."[123]

Reynolds does acknowledge that despite the nation's high rate of incarceration, violent crime rates remain high. Yet he, nonetheless, sees a "silver lining" of progress related to crime: "True, our violent-crime rate remains too high, concentrated on inner-city victims. But we no longer have high property-crime rates by international standards; our burglary rate, for example, is below average for industrial nations. And the improved trends have come as we have handed out more and longer prison sentences. There is a connection."[124] Nonetheless, Reynolds understands correctly that simply putting increasing numbers of offenders in jail or prison is not enough to ensure individual transformation or domestic security: "Putting criminals in jail is not enough, of course. We punish by denying the criminal freedom, but if we want him to change, he must learn to cope responsibly with life's challenges, including respecting the rights of others and earning a paycheck. We need prisons that truly correct."[125] Reynolds concedes that currently there are no model prisons in the U.S., i.e., prisons that "truly correct." On Reynolds's view, "true correction" would retain retributive punishment as the prison's *raison d'être*. He contends that, "Study after study shows that real employment before release not only improves behavior behind bars, but serves as the strongest known antidote to crime after release. Everyone prefers prevention to prison, yet

121. Murphy, "Crime and Punishment," p. 110.
122. Morgan Reynolds, "Crime and Punishment," *Newsweek*, November 13, 2000, p. 46.
123. Reynolds, "Crime and Punishment," p. 46.
124. Reynolds, "Crime and Punishment," p. 46.
125. Reynolds, "Crime and Punishment," p. 46.

apprehension, conviction, and punishment must remain the backbone of the system. It's sad and expensive but true."[126]

Despite the views of those who do believe that the benefits of large-scale imprisonment outweigh the negatives, many governors and legislators across the political spectrum are beginning to rethink whether they can afford to house more and more prisoners. Reginald A. Wilkinson, director of the Ohio Department of Rehabilitation and Corrections and president of the Association of State Prison Chiefs, has been quoted as saying, "Even some of your more right-wing people are saying, 'Let's see what we can do to get some people out of prison to save money.'"[127] Like many prison professionals, according to Scott Shane of the *Baltimore Sun*, Wilkinson has always thought too many people are being locked up.[128] Indeed, by 2000, even John DiIulio, who can hardly be mistaken for a "bleeding-heart" liberal, was writing an article for the editorial page of the *Wall Street Journal* titled "Two Million Prisoners Is Enough."

Conclusion

Each year some 644,000 persons are incarcerated for various offenses, while some 625,000 are released back onto the streets. It is widely estimated that about 50 to 75 percent of released inmates will be returned to prison within a few years. With regard to those who commit the most serious of crimes, it has been estimated that "about 40 percent of all felony probationers are rearrested for [new] felonies within three years of being placed under community supervision."[129] Increasing numbers of inmates leave prison in a condition University of Nebraska criminologist Roy Roberg characterizes as "socially crippled and profoundly alienated." John Irwin, a sociologist at the University of California–Berkley, and James Austin, executive vice president of the National Council on Crime and Delinquency, argue that when hundreds of thousands of prisoners are "crowded

126. Reynolds, "Crime and Punishment," p. 46.
127. Shane, "Locked Up in the Land of the Free."
128. Shane, "Locked Up in the Land of the Free."
129. John J. DiIulio Jr. and Joseph P. Tierney, "An Easy Ride for Felons on Probation," *New York Times*, August 29, 2000. John J. DiIulio Jr. is a senior fellow at the Manhattan Institute and professor of politics at the University of Pennsylvania. Joseph P. Tierney is vice president at Public/Private Ventures, a social and urban policy research group.

into human (or inhuman) warehouses, where they are increasingly deprived, restricted, isolated, and consequently embittered and alienated from conventional worlds, and where less and less is being done to prepare them for their eventual release," most will be "rendered incapable of returning even to a meager conventional life after prison."[130] We as a society should be deeply concerned about what happens to inmates during their imprisonment, particularly in light of the ways in which their incarceration serves the goals of the prison-industrial complex.

In Chapter Two we will turn to a discussion of some of the salient ("invisible") collateral social consequences of the current unprecedented scale of U.S. imprisonment, considering the worsening stigmatization of "people of color" (particularly Black people); the overburdening of women, children, and poor and working class communities; the erosion of necessary social unity; and the expanding and unproductive undermining of civil liberties and regard for others.

130. Austin and Irwin, *It's About Time*, pp. x, 65.

63

2. The Collateral Social Consequences of Large-Scale Imprisonment

The Growth of Imprisonment

Over the last three decades, one dimension of criminal corrections has overshadowed all others: *growth*.[1] Today the United States locks up a larger portion of its residents, both juveniles and adults, than ever before. Karen Fulbright, Director of Research for the Vera Institute of Justice, reports that federal records indicate that the combined total of state and federal prisoners in 1980 was 400,000; by the end of that year the number had increased to over 500,000, meaning that one in every 453 U.S. residents was incarcerated. By the end of 1993 one in every 189 U.S. residents was behind bars. And by 1994 the total number of inmates in state and federal prisons had grown to over one million. On any given day in 1993 an average of 93,000 youths were being held in public or private juvenile correctional facilities.[2] In less than the span of a decade — from 1994 to 2001 — the total number of U.S. inmates swelled from more than one million to over two million.

---

1. Todd Clear, "The Problem with 'Addition By Subtraction': The Prison-Crime Relationship in Low-Income Communities," in *Invisible Punishment: The Collateral Consequences of Mass Imprisonment,* ed. Marc Mauer and Meda Chesney-Lind (New York: New Press, 2002), p. 183.

2. See the editor's foreword to Karen Fulbright, ed., *The Unintended Consequences of Incarceration: Conference Papers* (New York: The Vera Institute of Justice, 1996), p. i. Fulbright draws much of her data on the growth in U.S. prison populations from Allen J. Beck and Darrell K. Gilliard, *Prisoners in 1994* (Washington, D.C.: Bureau of Justice Statistics, 1995). The information on juveniles comes from the Office of Juvenile and Delinquency Prevention. Also see Clear, "Addition by Subtraction," pp. 183-84.

Imprisonment at such an unprecedented rate brings with it a variety of unintended social consequences. Marc Mauer and Meda Chesney-Lind, researchers for the Sentencing Project, have observed that over the past thirty years mass incarceration as a social policy aimed at controlling crime has significantly

> transformed family and community dynamics, exacerbated racial divisions, and posed fundamental questions of citizenship in democratic society. Imprisonment was once primarily a matter of concern for the individual prisoner, but the scale of incarceration today is such that its impact is far broader — first, on the growing number of family members affected financially and emotionally by the imprisonment of a loved one; beyond that, by the way incarceration is now experienced by entire communities in the form of broad-scale economic hardship, increased risk of fatal disease, and marked economic and social risk for the most vulnerable children. And, ultimately, a society in which mass imprisonment has become the norm is one in which questions of justice, fairness, and access to resources are being altered in ways hitherto unknown.[3]

University of Pennsylvania sociologist Elijah Anderson has echoed some of the same concerns, arguing that the development of "prison culture and its values are contaminating entire communities, making it difficult for even the best-intentioned parents to protect their children."[4] Dina Rose, a sociologist at the John Jay College of Criminal Justice in New York City, notes that high-crime communities tend to be socially isolated and racially segregated. Her fear is that "locking up ever more people may be so damaging to neighborhood social cohesion that it destabilizes the very areas it is supposed to make safe."[5] Some analysts maintain that while debates about society's increased use of imprisonment have focused principally on its value in reducing crime rates, "these discussions have, by and large, ignored the ways in which our heavy use of incarceration affects individuals, families, and communities across prison walls."[6]

---

3. Mauer and Chesney-Lind, *Invisible Punishment,* pp. 1-2.
4. Quoted in Ellis Cose, "The Prison Paradox," *Newsweek,* November 13, 2000, p. 44.
5. Quoted in Cose, "The Prison Paradox," p. 44.
6. Fulbright, foreword to *Unintended Consequences,* p. i.

In view of today's use of large-scale imprisonment as a principal means of social control, especially in low-income communities of color that are beset with numerous other social difficulties, I want in this chapter to demonstrate that, contrary to the goal of securing increased societal stability, large-scale imprisonment helps foster a variety of "collateral consequences," which ultimately undermine societal well-being. To make this argument, I will examine some of the salient collateral social consequences of large-scale imprisonment: the intensified stigmatization of "people of color" (particularly Black people); the overburdening of women, children, and poor and working-class communities; the erosion of necessary social unity; and the counterproductive undermining of civil liberties and regard for others.

Stigmatizing "Communities of Color"

Black Males

We begin with a focus on Black males. It should be confessed from the start that Black males are not the only demographic disproportionately targeted by the U.S. criminal justice systems — Angela Davis points out that the prison-industrial complex "trains its sights on black women and other men of color, as well as on poor white people," and this is a fact that cannot be ignored.[7] I do, however, think that some initial focus on Black men, and on Black people in general, is appropriate because they represent what I view as the nerve-center of the debate over race in general, and imprisonment in particular. To put it another way, no other large community of U.S. residents shares the same burden of disproportionate confinement and overall criminal corrections supervision.

With the possible exception of the one or two percent or so of the U.S. population that is Native American, the prominence of Black "affirmative action" in the nation's carceral matrix is difficult to overstate. African American males make up less than seven percent of the U.S. population, yet they compose (perhaps conservatively) approximately 37.5

---

7. Angela Y. Davis, "Race, Gender, and Prison History: From the Convict Lease System to the Supermax Prison," in *Prison Masculinities*, ed. Don Sabo, Terry A. Kupers, and Willie London (Philadelphia: Temple University Press, 2001), p. 35.

percent (or 750,000) of the nation's jail and prison population. Taken together, African American males and females represent half the nation's inmates.[8] In 1996, ninety percent of the prison admissions for drug offenses were either African American or Latino/a.[9] Data gathered by the Department of Health and Human Services (DHHS) shows that in 1991, 1992, and 1993, approximately five times more White people had used cocaine than Black people, yet Black people (especially Black males) were imprisoned at a rate many times that of Whites.[10]

Today these disparities are particularly striking in some individual states. For example, in Maryland, where Black people make up 27 percent of the population, 90 percent of those sent to prison on drug charges are Black, a rate 28 times greater than for White people. In Virginia, where Black people represent 20 percent of the population, 82 percent of those sent to prison on drug charges are Black, a rate 21 times greater than for White people.[11]

The latest data indicates that the nation is fast approaching 600,000 Black males between the ages of 20 and 39 being imprisoned, a devastatingly high number.[12] I say "devastatingly" because this age bracket is critical to the establishment of a community's long-term "human capital." Human capital refers to the education, occupational status, and earning capacity that help establish a community's social, economic, and political stability. Such a high rate of incarceration for such a significant portion of the Black population represents a tremendous loss of human capital to the communities from which they come.

Writing for the Urban League, James Lanier reports that the loss of

8. If Joseph Ryan, writing for *Socialist Action*, is correct, by April 1999 Black people accounted for 65 percent of U.S. inmates. See Joseph Ryan, "Black Prison Population Approaches One Million," *Socialist Action*, April 1999. Available online at http://www .socialistaction.org/news/199904/prison.html.

9. Steven R. Donziger, ed., *The Real War on Crime: The National Report of the National Criminal Justice Commission* (New York: HarperPerennial, 1996), p. 103.

10. Michael A. Fletcher, "War on Drugs Sends Blacks to Prison at 13 Times Rate of Whites," in *The American Prison System*, ed. Peter G. Herman (New York: H. W. Wilson, 2001), p. 121.

11. Fletcher, "War on Drugs," pp. 121-122.

12. As of July 2003, more than 596,400 Black males between the ages 20 and 39 were incarcerated. James R. Lanier, "The Harmful Impact of the Criminal Justice System and War on Drugs on the African-American Family," *National Urban League Annual Report 2003*, p. 4.

human capital is "a circumstance underscored by the fact that more black males are in prison or jail than in higher education: for every black male who graduates from college, one hundred others are in prison or jail. This is a dramatic change from 1980, when there were about 430,700 black men enrolled in colleges and about 143,000 incarcerated."[13] Given the importance of education for a community's ability to sustain itself economically, and to advocate on behalf of its best civic and cultural interests at the local, state, and national levels, communities that have their males sentenced to prison at 100 times the rate they graduate from college can hardly be expected to be socioeconomically viable. Lanier goes on to point out that "the same disproportionate pattern is occurring with African-American females, whose rate of inmate growth has now surpassed that of males."[14] The large-scale imprisonment of Black women, who are routinely the primary caretakers of children, increases the financial and social risks for some of the most vulnerable of the nation's children as well; we will look at some of these risks later in this chapter.[15]

It is now well established that a significant amount of crime committed in low-income and working-class Black communities is predicated on a search for drug money and other drug-related activity. Using data readily obtainable from the Bureau of Justice Statistics, Lanier reports that 4,810 Black males per 100,000 U.S. residents are incarcerated, compared to 649 per 100,000 White males. The incarceration rate for Black females is also alarmingly high, at 349 per 100,000, compared to 68 per 100,000 White women. About 75 percent of these prisoners have a history of drug and/or alcohol abuse and are in desperate need of medical treatment and other social services that could help them avoid criminal activity once released from prison.

What are we to make of such statistics? As I mentioned above, I recognize that Black men are not the only group overrepresented among those imprisoned. I also do not suggest that they, or most imprisoned people for that matter, have not committed a crime of one sort or another. The problem in my judgment is not so much whether society has a right to expect accountability from its residents, particularly those en-

13. Lanier, "The Harmful Impact of the Criminal Justice System," p. 4.
14. Lanier, "The Harmful Impact of the Criminal Justice System," p. 4.
15. See, for example, Jeremy Travis and Michelle Waul, eds., *Prisoners Once Removed: The Impact of Incarceration and Reentry on Children, Families, and Communities* (Washington, D.C.: Urban Institute Press, 2003).

gaged in some type of behavior that is proscribed by law. The problem, rather, is that large-scale arrests and jailings compound the very problems they are meant to solve. When disproportionately large numbers of young Black men are doing time in overcrowded, single-sex, racist, and routinely violent fortresses of social vengeance and degradation, it is not reasonable then to expect (on balance) positive contributions from them when they return to their communities and to society at large. After some three decades of experience with the social practice of large-scale imprisonment we have not achieved a significantly less fearful or safer society.

Black Females (and Women in General)

As already hinted at above, not only has the prison-industrial complex — "based on an 'iron triangle' [among] government bureaucracy, private industry, and politicians" — resulted in a staggering number of imprisoned Black men. Black women now constitute the most rapidly expanding segment of all imprisoned populations.[16] Social scientists John Irwin and James Austin have pointed out that, "African American women have experienced the greatest increase in correctional supervision, rising by 78 percent from 1989 through 1994."[17] The proportion of women being incarcerated has risen to unprecedented heights, with Black women increasingly subjected to a rate of criminalization paralleling that of their Black male counterparts.

Angela Y. Davis argues that, similar to the situation for poor Black men, poor Black women have increasingly become targets of police surveillance and control for reasons of race and economic status, as well as for reasons of gender.[18] Davis cites the dismantling of welfare, the war on drugs, and the societal demonization of single Black mothers[19] as signifi-

16. Angela Y. Davis, "Race, Gender, and Prison History," p. 36, and Paulette Thomas, "Making Crime Pay: Triangle of Interests Creates Infrastructure to Fight Lawlessness," *Wall Street Journal*, May 12, 1994.

17. Quoted in Davis, "Race, Gender, and Prison History," p. 36. See also John Irwin and James Austin, *It's About Time: America's Imprisonment Binge,* 2d ed. (Belmont, Calif.: Wadsworth Publishing Company, 1997), p. 4.

18. Davis, "Race, Gender, and Prison History," p. 36.

19. Cf. Patricia Williams's excellent analysis of the demonization of single Black

cant contributing factors that lead large numbers of poor Black women to prison. Davis charges that, in the popular consciousness, single Black mothers "are represented as procreators of crime and poverty." With specific reference to the disparity between the rate of incarceration for poor Black women versus middle-class women, Davis argues that, "differential criminalization of drug use means that those unfortunate enough to become addicted to crack can be arrested and thrown in jail, while their middle-class counterparts, who have access to licit drugs such as Valium or Prozac, are free to indulge their drug habits."[20]

Not only Black women, but women of color in general are overrepresented in penal institutions throughout the United States. Meda Chesney-Lind, professor of criminal justice at the University of Illinois, has argued that women offenders have been largely forgotten by the harsher criminology that has emerged "to complement, explain, and occasionally critique state efforts to control and discipline unruly and dangerous men."[21] Chesney-Lind views the startling increase in the number of women sentenced to jail and prison since the early 1980s as "simply an unintended consequence of the nation's move to mass incarceration as a result of a 'war on drugs' and a host of other 'get tough' sentencing policies."[22] The dramatic increase in women's incarceration is not viewed by Chesney-Lind as a consequence of any substantial increase in women's involvement in serious crime; rather it is "a reflection of public policy decisions that have ignored any consideration of women's needs and behaviors."[23]

The story of Monica Clyburn, a Florida mother on welfare with a history of drug use, three small children, and a baby on the way provides a good illustration of what H. Jay Stevens, the chief federal public defender for the middle district of Florida, confirms as the reality for women all over the country in the name of getting tough on crime. Carl M. Cannon, writing for the *Nation Journal*, chronicled Clyburn's case as an example of the perverse way gun law "enhancements" are being applied:

---

women in *The Rooster's Egg: On the Persistence of Prejudice* (Cambridge, Mass.: Harvard University Press, 1995), pp. 1-14.

20. Davis, "Race, Gender, and Prison History," p. 36.

21. Meda Chesney-Lind, "Imprisoning Women: The Unintended Victims of Mass Incarceration," in *Invisible Punishment*, p. 79.

22. Chesney-Lind, "Imprisoning Women," p. 79.

23. Chesney-Lind, "Imprisoning Women," pp. 79-80.

In 1994, Clyburn . . . accompanied her boyfriend to a pawnshop so they could peddle a .22-caliber pistol. Her testimony, uncontroverted by the government, was that the gun was not hers and she only filled out the required federal forms because her boyfriend did not bring his identification. Months later, when agents from the Bureau of Alcohol, Tobacco, and Firearms did a routine check of records, Clyburn, who had several previous convictions on minor theft and drug charges, was arrested for being in felon possession of a firearm. She was indicted and pleaded guilty and received the mandatory minimum of 15 years in prison. She did not use the gun to commit a crime, never even redeemed the pawnshop ticket.[24]

Evidently being tough on crime includes sending people to prison even when they *get rid of* guns.

In 1980 there were a total of about 12,000 women in state and federal prisons. By 1999, this number had risen to over 90,000. In 1980, women accounted for just 3.9 percent of those in prison. By 1999, women represented 6.7 percent of prison inmates. From 1990 to 1999 the number of women in prison increased 110 percent, while the number of male prisoners increased 77 percent. The patterns are similar for jails, where women constituted 7 percent of that population by the mid-1980s, but were 11.4 percent of the total by 2001.[25]

Today the number of women incarcerated in U.S. prisons and jails is about ten times greater than the number of women incarcerated in all of Western Europe; this despite the roughly equivalent populations of the two regions.[26] According to Chesney-Lind, correctional authorities appear to have been taken by surprise when the numbers of women sentenced to prison began to increase in the 1980s. State authorities initially responded to the expansion in women prisoners by housing them in remodeled hos-

24. Carl M. Cannon, "America: All Locked Up," in *The American Prison System,* ed. Peter G. Herman (New York: H. W. Wilson, 2001), p. 72.

25. Chesney-Lind, "Imprisoning Women," pp. 80-81. See also Margaret Calahan, *Historical Corrections Statistics in the United States, 1850-1984* (Washington, D.C.: Bureau of Justice Statistics, 1986); and Allen Beck and Jennifer C. Karberg, *Prison and Jail Inmates at Midyear 2000* (Washington, D.C.: Bureau of Justice Statistics, 2001).

26. Chesney-Lind, "Imprisoning Women," p. 81. See also Amnesty International, *Not Part of My Sentence: Violations of the Human Rights of Women in Custody* (Washington, D.C.: Amnesty International, 1999).

pitals, abandoned training schools, and converted motels, and then, more recently, by opening new prisons. Whereas the United States was opening an average of two or three facilities for women per decade between 1930 and 1950, more than thirty-four facilities were built and filled in the 1980s alone. Chesney-Lind reports that, "By 1990, the nation had seventy-one female-only facilities; five years later, the number had jumped to 104 — an increase of 46.5 percent."[27] Note that between 1990 and 1999, women's criminal activity increased by 14.5 percent, yet the number of women in prison increased by 105.8 percent.[28] In addition to this, Chesney-Lind maintains that, "despite media images of hyperviolent women offenders, the proportion of women doing time in state prisons for violent offenses has been declining steadily from about half (48.9 percent in 1970) to just over a quarter (28.5 percent) in 1998."[29]

While the Bureau of Justice Statistics claims that growth in the number of violent offenders was the primary factor for male prison growth in the 1990s, the Bureau reports that the major factor for the rise in female prison populations was drug offenses. This leads Chesney-Lind and others to conclude that, "the 'war on drugs' has become a largely unannounced war on women":

> Two decades ago (1979), one in ten women in U.S. prisons was doing time for drugs. By 1998, it was one in three (33.9 percent). Finally, while the intent of "get tough" drug policies was presumably to rid society of drug dealers and so-called kingpins, many of the women swept up in the war on drugs are minor offenders. An analysis by Human Rights Watch of women incarcerated under New York's draconian Rockefeller drug laws, for example, documented that nearly half

27. Chesney-Lind, "Imprisoning Women," pp. 81-82; Nicole Hahn Rafter, *Partial Justice: Women, Prisons and Social Control* (New Brunswick, N.J.: Transition Books, 1990). See also Meda Chesney-Lind and Randall G. Shelden, *Girls, Delinquency and Juvenile Justice* (Belmont, Calif.: Wadsworth Publishing, 1998).

28. Chesney-Lind, "Imprisoning Women, p. 87; U.S. Department of Justice, *Crime in the United States: 1999 Uniform Crime Reports* (Washington, D.C.: U.S. Department of Justice, 2000); Allen Beck, *Prisoners in 1999* (Washington, D.C.: Bureau of Justice Statistics, 2000), p. 6.

29. Chesney-Lind, "Imprisoning Women," pp. 87-88; U.S. Department of Justice, *Profile of State Prison Inmates, 1986* (Washington, D.C., Bureau of Justice Statistics, 1988); Beck, *Prisoners in 1999*, p. 10.

(44 percent) had never been in prison before, and 17 percent had never been arrested before.[30]

While the "War on Drugs" certainly has been a major factor in the dramatic increase in women's incarceration rates, it has become increasingly clear that other policy changes, rather than a change in the seriousness of women's crime, have also played a role. The implementation of a number of sentencing reform initiatives, particularly at the federal level, has intensified the negative consequences of mandatory sentencing. For example, new federal sentencing guidelines intended to "reduce race, class and other unwarranted disparities in sentencing males," are now applied to women, seriously disadvantaging them in relation to men.

By refusing to consider the gender-based factors that result in women's prison sentences being considerably harsher than those of their male counterparts, federal judges place many women under a double punishment. Not only do women receive the same harsh mandatory minimums men get, but they also face the threat of termination, sometimes permanently, of their parental rights. Since so many more women are sole custodial parents, the so-called "equity clauses" in federal sentencing law lead to more extreme family hardships for women prisoners. In addition, the federal guidelines generally allow no consideration of women's histories of physical and/or sexual abuse, experiences that might appropriately mitigate women's sentencing.[31]

Women face similar disadvantages in many state prison systems. For example, ostensibly gender-blind mandatory sentencing results in a considerable disadvantage for women in plea negotiations. One of the very few ways a mandatory sentence can be altered is if a defendant can offer authorities information that could be useful in the prosecution of other drug offenders, most of whom are male. The difficulty for women here, argues Chesney-Lind, is that, "Because women tend to be working at the lowest levels of the drug hierarchy, they are often unable to negotiate plea

30. Chesney-Lind, "Imprisoning Women," p. 88; Beck, *Prisoners in 1999*, p. 10; Jamie Fellner, *Cruel and Unusual: Disproportionate Sentences for New York Drug Offenders* (New York: Human Rights Watch, 1997).

31. Chesney-Lind, "Imprisoning Women," pp. 88-89; Myrna Raeder, "Gender and Sentencing: Single Moms, Battered Women and Other Sex-based Anomalies in the Gender Free World of the Federal Sentencing Guidelines," *Pepperdine Law Review*, 20:3 (1993): 905-90; especially pp. 939-45 and 954.

reductions successfully. Added to this is the ironic fact that it is not uncommon for women arrested for drug crimes to be reluctant to testify against their boyfriends or husbands."[32] As a result of the "War on Drugs" and mandatory sentencing, women involved in drug-related crime are now sentenced to jail at a significantly increased rate. Drawing on the work of Myrna Raeder in the *Pepperdine Law Review,* Chesney-Lind summarized that

> Twenty years ago, nearly two-thirds of women convicted of federal felonies were granted probation. But after the implementation of sentencing guidelines in 1987, along with mandatory minimums, these proportions changed considerably. By 1991, only 28 percent of women were given straight probation. Further, the mean time to be served by women drug offenders increased from twenty-seven months in July 1984, to a startling sixty-seven months in June 1990.[33]

Of course, it will no doubt be argued that women who get involved in crime should have been thinking about the consequences for themselves and their children before they did so in the first place. Furthermore, it could be argued that if women insist on protecting husbands and boyfriends who commit crime, then they, in effect, also agree to accept the consequences. Here again, while I readily admit that it is appropriate to focus attention on the individual agency and responsibility of offenders themselves, it is inappropriate to do so without assigning at least as much responsibility to the various economic, social, and political factors that exert strong influences on them.[34] And even where legitimate guilt for serious breaches of social responsibility is established, the practice of large-scale imprisonment as a solution has not made us safer, nor has it effectively reduced crime. By placing offenders — both females and males — under harsher sentences for longer periods of time, we create more problems than we solve.

32. Chesney-Lind, "Imprisoning Women," p. 89.

33. Chesney-Lind, "Imprisoning Women," p. 89; Raeder, "Gender and Sentencing," pp. 31-32; 34.

34. See, for example, Juanita Díaz-Cotto, "Race, Ethnicity, and Gender in Studies of Incarceration," in *States of Confinement: Policing, Detention, and Prisons,* ed. Joy James (New York: Palgrave, 2002), p. 130.

Large-Scale Imprisonment and the Erosion of Social Unity

I have tried so far in this chapter to offer a sense of the dramatic growth of imprisonment in the United States, particularly among Black men and women. Along the way, I have also raised some questions concerning the collateral consequences of imprisonment on a large scale — specifically that of the destabilization of (especially) low-income and working-class Black communities. I will now consider in more depth the erosion of necessary social unity in local communities and in society at large.

While it may be tempting for residents of the United States to simply accept high levels of imprisonment as an unavoidable cost of living in our society, we might be less inclined to accept the current state of affairs if more were known about the collateral and unanticipated costs of excessive imprisonment. The choice to favor large-scale imprisonment is only one part of a complex matrix of policy choices that create and maintain what some social scientists call "high-risk settings." High-risk settings, for our purposes, are social locations that maximize risk to the health of families, communities, and the wider society, and which do not "just happen," but rather have identifiable causes.

While considering the collateral consequences generated by large-scale imprisonment within settings of retributive degradation, it is essential to keep in mind that high-risk settings "are a result of policies and choices that cumulatively determine whether families will have adequate incomes, whether neighborhoods will be safe or dangerous, whether schools will be capable of teaching, whether health care will be available."[35] In short, the issue is whether people in already "at risk" communities will be helped or hindered in their efforts to maintain viable and flourishing lives.

Prisoners and Children

One significant consequence of large-scale imprisonment is the often-irreparable damage that is done to women's roles as mothers and their le-

---

35. Although this quote was stated with specific reference to the effects of high-risk settings on children, it is also quite relevant when speaking of entire communities. See National Research Council, *Losing Generations: Adolescents in High Risk Settings* (Washington, D.C.: National Academy Press, 1993), pp. vii-viii.

gal status as parents when they are detained in correctional facilities. Beth Richie, a professor of criminal justice and women's studies at the University of Illinois at Chicago, conservatively estimates that 75 percent of women in prison are mothers, and that two thirds have children under the age of eighteen. Since poor women of color, particularly Black women, make up the majority of women sentenced to prison, the communities from which they come are hardest hit.

About 1.5 million children under age eighteen have a parent in prison. Of these, 125,000 have a mother in prison. Richie argues that these numbers underrepresent the true extent of the problem because they fail to account for the large numbers of other caretakers of dependent children who end up behind bars for significant periods of time. Many such women are arrested "while raising their younger siblings, nieces and nephews, or children in their extended social network."[36]

This is a problem that goes largely unrecognized in our society, due to the predominantly male image of the "criminal." Yet excessive imprisonment has taken a particularly heavy toll on the approximately 3.2 million women per year who are arrested, charged with a (usually drug-related) crime, removed from their communities, and placed in jail to await trial or some other disposition of their case. While some women of means do get released within a short time of their arrest, Richie reports that "approximately 156,000 women are held prior to trial or as sentenced prisoners, representing more than a tripling of the female inmate population since 1985."[37] While it is true that the actual number of women in jail is far smaller than their male counterparts, the rate of increase has been nearly double that for men in the period between 1980 and 1997 (573 percent for women versus 294 percent for men).[38]

---

36. Beth E. Richie, "The Social Impact of Mass Incarceration on Women," in *Invisible Punishment*, p. 139. See also Jeremy Travis and Michelle Waul, "Prisoners Once Removed: The Children and Families of Prisoners," in *Prisoners Once Removed*, pp. 1-29.

37. Richie, "The Social Impact of Mass Incarceration on Women," p. 137.

38. Richie, "The Social Impact of Mass Incarceration on Women," p. 137. See also Stephanie R. Bush-Baskette, "The War on Drugs as a War against Black Women," in *Crime Control and Women: Feminist Implications of Criminal Justice Policy*, ed. Susan Miller (Thousand Oaks, Calif.: Sage Publications, 1998); U.S. Department of Justice, *Prior Abuse Reported by Inmates and Probationers* (Washington, D.C., Bureau of Justice Statistics, 1999); U.S. Department of Justice, *Prison and Jail Inmates at Midyear 2000* (Washington, D.C.: Bureau of Justice Statistics, 2001).

It goes without saying that under conditions of confinement, serious obstacles to parenting will exist:

First, there is the obvious: sudden and unexpected forced separation of mothers and children. Then, most state and federal facilities are located long distances from the urban neighborhoods where children of incarcerated women live, making visiting logistically and economically difficult if not impossible. The lack of accessible public transportation, obscure visiting hours, and long waits present serious barriers to children's visits. In the case of jail visits, the policy trend is to limit contact with visitors, to prohibit children from entering jails altogether, or to otherwise create regulations that interfere with maintaining family bonds. With a few notable exceptions, correctional facilities do little to support mothers in their parenting role despite evidence that suggests that parenting may hold a central place in women's rehabilitation and future success.[39]

When mothering — as one of many important aspects of women's lives — is delegitimized in these ways, the direct impact on children can be devastating, essentially penalizing children for their mothers' crimes. Children of incarcerated women are destabilized "when they are passed from household to household and when their material needs go unmet as financial resources are absorbed by the costs associated with a family member's incarceration."[40]

Many children of incarcerated mothers are placed in the foster care system, where all too often poor monitoring of the quality of the child's environment is the norm rather than the exception. Additionally, there is generally not much incentive for foster parents to maintain a relationship with an incarcerated parent — mother or father. As a consequence, the feelings and emotional responses of most of these children will be predictable: "Shame, guilt, anger, and resentment are typical reactions of children to the loss of a parent through incarceration, and the lack of acknowledgement, support, and services may result in long-term consequences for them."[41] University of North Carolina–Chapel Hill criminologist John

39. Richie, "The Social Impact of Mass Incarceration on Women," pp. 139-140.
40. Richie, "The Social Impact of Mass Incarceration on Women," p. 141.
41. Richie, "The Social Impact of Mass Incarceration on Women," p. 142.

Hagan summarizes the typical road to criminality that too many children, particularly those of incarcerated mothers, will travel:

> The children of women in prison have a greater tendency to exhibit many of the problems that generally accompany parental absence including: low self-esteem, impaired achievement motivation and poor peer relations. In addition, these children contend with feelings like anxiety, shame, sadness, grief, social isolation and guilt. The children will often withdraw and regress developmentally, exhibiting behaviors of younger children, like bedwetting. . . . As the children reach adolescence, they may begin to act out in anti-social ways. Searching for attention, pre-teens and teens are at high risk for delinquency, drug addiction and gang involvement.[42]

The example of children of incarcerated parents, and of incarcerated mothers in particular, helps us to understand that current high rates of imprisonment may contribute to the indirect re/production of problematic antisocial behavior in children, by throwing inmates' families (more or less) into destitution. The children in these families have been increasingly referred to as orphans or as "children of the prison generation."[43] The current rate of incarceration is so high in some locations that the future stability of whole communities is jeopardized. With increasing numbers of parents being incarcerated, more children are reduced to destitution and abandonment or are placed with social service and foster care agencies that are already underfunded, understaffed, and far overworked.

In the state of New Jersey, dozens of teenage foster children each month are being housed in the state's array of "secure" juvenile detention

---

42. John Hagan, "The Next Generation: Children of Prisoners," in *The Unintended Consequences of Incarceration: Conference Papers,* ed. Karen Fulbright (New York: Vera Institute of Justice, 1996), p. 23; Women's Prison Association, *Breaking the Cycle of Despair: Children of Incarcerated Mothers* (New York: Women's Prison Association, 1995); Clear, "Backfire," in Fulbright, *Unintended Consequences,* pp. 12-13; Ted Conover, *New Jack: Guarding Sing Sing* (New York: Vintage Books, 2001), p. 287.

43. National Research Council, *Losing Generations;* John Hagan and Ronit Dinovitzer, *The Unintended Consequences of Sentencing: Children of the Prison Generation* (Toronto: University of Toronto Press, 1998); Michel Foucault, *Discipline and Punish: The Birth of the Prison,* trans. Alan Sheridan (New York: Vintage Books, 1995), p. 268.

centers. The overwhelming majority of these children have at least one parent under some form of correctional supervision. *New York Times* reporters Richard Lezin Jones and Leslie Kaufman explain that child welfare officials often admit to placing young people in detention centers "because there is simply a lack of more appropriate places to put them." Children are being placed in detention inappropriately "often while officials skirt state laws meant to limit how long children can be held at such places."[44] Jones and Kaufman summarize the problem, which is not unique to New Jersey, as follows:

> Some of the adolescents, ranging in age from 11 to 18, are guilty of nothing more than violating court orders prohibiting them from skipping school or running away from their homes. Others who have committed minor crimes like marijuana possession or shoplifting, and who would be released quickly if there were available foster families or group homes to take them in, remain locked up for months alongside young people awaiting trial for arson, sexual assault and murder. It is a problem that states across the nation face.
>
> Still others in New Jersey have committed crimes that their judges felt warranted punishments more compassionate than jail. In Newark, for example, one public defender recalls two girls who were charged with breaking and entering after being repeatedly found after hours in stores playing with toy dolls. They wound up held for weeks in the Essex County detention center, which was once criticized by the state for using isolation rooms and excessive restraints.
>
> The director of the Camden County Youth Center said that in recent weeks 25 of the 103 inmates were children who should have instead been in foster-care group homes, where they might get intense mental health care and regular education. At the Ocean County juvenile center, the administrator, Bob Coughlin, said that, on average, one-third of the children in his 30-person-capacity juvenile jail are simply waiting for the state child welfare agency to put them in foster care. One child has been there for 189 days.[45]

44. Richard Lezin Jones and Leslie Kaufman, "New Jersey Youths Out of Foster Homes End Up in Detention," *New York Times*, May 31, 2003; available online at http://www.nytimes.com/2003/05/31/nyregion/31CHIL/th.

45. Lezin Jones and Kaufman, "New Jersey Youths."

Here one sees the contribution being made to the indirect promotion and preservation of criminality by the very institutions charged with assisting young people in difficult, sometimes tragic, life situations. Most citizens would deem it wholly unacceptable that increasing numbers of the nation's children, many having committed either minor offenses or none at all, are subject to violence and humiliation.

In communities where substantial numbers of adults are imprisoned, the threshold of absent parents becomes so high that it is reasonable to suggest that parental incarceration itself contributes indirectly to criminality in children. Similar to numerous other observers, Marc Mauer argues that

> for children whose parents are imprisoned, feelings of shame, humiliation, and loss of social status may result. Children begin to act out in school or distrust authority figures, who represent the people who removed the parent from the home. Lowered economic circumstances in families experiencing imprisonment also leads to greater housing relocation, resulting in less cohesive neighborhoods. In far too many cases, these children come to represent the next generation of offenders.[46]

This problem is not limited to just local and state jurisdictions; federal authorities also contribute to the problem with their treatment of international children fleeing danger in their home nations. Rachel Swarns, writing for the *New York Times* and drawing on a study by Amnesty International, reports that "foreign children fleeing violence and persecution in their home countries are often improperly detained for months in bleak detention centers within the U.S. without access to lawyers or psychological services. . . ."[47] The study, which surveyed 33 detention centers around the country, reported that undocumented children who arrive in the U.S. without adult caretakers "are often strip-searched, shackled, and housed with juveniles who have been convicted of crimes."[48] Here again it is reasonable to suspect that for many of these children, who are some of

46. Mauer, *Race to Incarcerate*, p. 185.
47. Rachel L. Swarns, "Study Says Government Has Improperly Detained Foreign Children," *New York Times*, June 19, 2003.
48. Swarns, "Study Says Government Has Improperly Detained Foreign Children."

the most vulnerable and frightened of our residents, the effect of this kind of maltreatment at the hands of people who should be protecting them will be to breed criminality.

Weakening Community Cohesion

In addition to the specific impact of imprisonment on women and children, a significant collateral consequence of large-scale imprisonment is its function related to the destabilization of whole communities. And again, poor communities of color feel the impact of large-scale imprisonment the most.

The overwhelming majorities of those sentenced to prison and jail time are from low-income communities that are already beset with more than their fair share of social problems. For example, in New York City 80 percent of Rikers Island[49] inmates come from, and return to, just seven out of the literally hundreds of distinct communities in New York City.[50] Indeed, in 1992 75 percent of the New York State's entire prison population came from these same seven neighborhoods, according to a report by *New York Times* columnist Francis X. Clines. The communities are the Lower East Side of Manhattan, the South Bronx, Harlem, Brownsville, Bedford-Stuyvesant, East New York, and South Jamaica. Clines, citing data culled by inmate researchers at Green Haven Prison in Stormville, New York, also notes that 85 percent of New York state prisoners were already Black or Latino by 1992.[51]

This phenomenon is not unique to New York: between 1985 and 1992, 37 percent of all persons admitted to California state prisons were from Los Angeles County, which at the time comprised only 12 percent of the state's population. In the same period residents of Baltimore represented more than 50 percent of Maryland's prison admissions, although that city had

---

49. Rikers Island is a large correctional facility serving New York City. It is the largest penal colony in the United States, housing some 15,000 inmates on any given day. Rikers is also known as "The Rock" and "Land of Darkness."

50. The Fortune Society, a New York City nonprofit organization for ex-offenders, also publicized this statistic. Cf. Francis X. Clines, "Ex-Inmates Urge Return to Areas of Crime to Help," *New York Times*, December 23, 1992, and Lola Obudekun, *The Vera Institute Atlas of Crime and Justice in New York City* (New York: Vera Institute of Justice, 1993), p. 42.

51. Clines, "Ex-Inmates Urge Return to Areas of Crime to Help."

just 15 percent of the state population.[52] Similar patterns appear in other American cities with significant numbers of Black residents.

It may seem reasonable to assume that since one of the significant social problems affecting low-income communities is crime, getting troublemakers off the streets actually helps to increase community cohesion and flourishing. In what follows, we will consider just a few of the reasons why I believe such a presumption to be false in the context of large-scale U.S. imprisonment.

The Depenalization of Imprisonment

The prison experience has become so concentrated and routine in some low-income communities that the decidedly negative view of prison once common in many communities has waned somewhat. Thus the social sanction of prison time for criminal behavior is less a deterrent today than it once may have been: "The more often the sanction of imprisonment is employed, the less it deters," argues criminologist Todd Clear.[53] It is reasonable to suspect that part of the effectiveness of deterrence as a penal theory lies in its power to induce an avoidance of shame and to cultivate a widespread and normative sense of fear regarding the dreaded unknown that lay behind the walls of a prison or jail. But when incarceration becomes almost as commonplace in a community as going to school, terrifying, threatening, and humiliating notions of prison eventually lose their power to induce fear and intimidation with regard to "doing time." In such an environment, placing significant numbers of people in jail does not make things better; rather, "the word" routinely carried back to the streets by those in prison or jail is, "We can do this." Not only this, but many young people, especially young men and boys, view surviving prison as a rite of passage, wherein one's "rep" and "street cred" get firmly established — or not. Indeed, many young men emerge from their prison experiences with dispositions that make them greater threats to stability than they were before their extraction from the community. And these are the people who too often provide life models for the generation to come.

---

52. Hagan and Dinovitzer, *Unintended Consequences of Sentencing*, p. 9. See also James P. Lynch and William J. Sabol, "Did Getting Tough on Crime Pay?" (Washington, D.C.: The Urban Institute, 1997).

53. Clear, "Backfire," p. 10.

James Finckenauer's 1982 study of Rahway Prison's "Scared Straight" program illustrates what happens to juveniles when they are overexposed to the hard realities of prison life. The Scared Straight program was initiated in the 1970s by prisoners serving life sentences in an attempt to frighten (or "scare straight") first-time juvenile offenders into "obedience with the law in order to avert the inevitability [of a] horrifying prison experience."[54] However, an unintended result of the program was that the juveniles who participated in the program actually did worse than a comparison group not exposed to the program. Summarizing Finckenauer's results, Todd Clear explains the reasons for this unintended result:

> The kids in [Finckenauer's] study were exposed to the most hostile version of prison life imaginable, and yet far from being scared straight, they were likely to keep offending. Several explanations of this finding are possible, but the most obvious is that exposure to the brutalizing nature of prison normalizes the experience and provides images of survival to replace pre-existing images of doom. The youth now have a grounded experience of prison at its most brutal, and of tough men not only surviving the experience but thriving within it. Finally, that the youth themselves survived their prison experience diminishes the mystery of prison life. Popular American images of the prison were dominated by the "big house" myth and Edward G. Robinson tough-guy characters. Real-life experience replaces popular ideation with grounded reality.[55]

Play Tebout, a 26-year-old Black man who has been serving time since 1992 and speaking from personal experience, offers a more anecdotal assessment of Scared Straight that is worth quoting at length:

> I don't believe the "Scared Straight" program, as it exists today, is an effective crime prevention tool. The program seeks to discourage students from wanting to come to prison by highlighting the dangers of incarceration. This approach fails to take into account that many program candidates come from dangerous communities; communities

54. Clear, "Backfire," p. 10; James O. Finckenauer, *Scared Straight: The Panacea Phenomenon* (Englewood Cliffs, N.J.: Prentice Hall, 1982).
55. Clear, "Backfire," p. 10.

where they may be threatened by violence and aggression on a daily basis. Furthermore, violence and danger, in general, are romanticized by the media and entertainment industry. More specifically, prison violence is often promoted by men who have done time, as proof of their manhood, evidenced by their ability to "hold it down, Up North" (meaning that they were not taken advantage of while doing time). These men tend to glamorize the hardships they endured on lockdown as exciting, even character building, or as some sort of crucible which separates the boys from the men.

I feel the Scared Straight program only serves to further enforce these glamorizations, by showing students a white-washed, exaggerated, and often fictitious view of the jail experience. To illustrate my point, the Scared Straight tour takes students to see the cleanest living and eating areas, and the quietest programs. The staff conducting the tour is always on their best behavior, and guide the students to meet the so-called "worst" inmates.

These inmates are rarely very tough, but are actually pre-instructed by staff to put on their best performance. So they make the meanest faces, flex their muscles, and may go so far as to verbally harass the students in an attempt to intimidate them. This depiction of prison as a basically nice, clean environment filled with hardened men is far from accurate, but can give an already hardened or troubled youth the impression that all he has to do to survive the penitentiary, and qualify as "officially thugged out," is to become even harder than he already is. That's not necessarily discouraging. On the contrary, it can be quite encouraging.[56]

With only 200,000 prisoners nationwide in 1973 — the year of Nelson Rockefeller's "get tough" State of the State Address — true-life images of prison were rare compared to the present. With more than two million people now behind bars, far greater numbers of people have direct and indirect real-life knowledge of the prison experience. As Clear correctly argues, "The real-life experience of each prisoner grounds an understanding of the prison for each parent, child, and loved-one known to that prisoner. If each prisoner's personal experience reaches ten others, then the 1973 prison population reflected two million knowledgeable consumers on any

56. Play Tebout, "Unafraid of Scared Straight."

given day, while today's [1996] figures indicate ten million."[57] Following Clear's math, the experiences of today's two million plus prisoners reflects more than 20 million "knowledgeable consumers" on any given day.

We noted above that an estimated 80 percent of all Riker's Island inmates come from and return to just seven neighborhoods in New York City. Therefore, we could expect the children, mothers, brothers, sisters, cousins, friends, etc., of prisoners residing in, for example, the South Bronx or Harlem to be some of the nation's most well-informed consumers of the unintended "Scared Straight" irony. In poor communities all over the nation, where rates of imprisonment are highest, residents know that men, and increasingly women, who go to prison eventually get out and continue their lives — occasionally for the better, but often for the worse. Todd Clear's work indicates that in communities where incarceration is imposed on a large scale the average resident

> can repeat the stories of prison technique — what to do in prison in order to survive the experience. They know that the people in prison include some brutal and repulsive types as well as people like their father and brother. Instead of a dark fear of prison, they have a grounded image of what day-to-day life there entails. This is almost certainly not a pleasant image, but it is reality-based. They have an expectation of survival of the physical and emotional aspect of prison life.[58]

Clear is careful to note that the normalization of the prison experience is just one of the responses residents of poor communities will have to the incarceration of those they love, a range that is "likely to include anger at the system, personal shame, loving support, and rejection."[59]

Just as fear of physical and psychic deprivation within the prison may be lessened by knowledge and the experience that many people survive imprisonment, so too is this the case with regard to the prison's stigmatizing capacity: "If nearly everyone has a brother, father, or uncle who has gone to prison, the mortification one feels at the experience is less powerful."[60] The implications of this fact are ominous when viewed alongside the racial, ethnic, and class distribution of incarceration. For example,

---

57. Clear, "Backfire," p. 10.
58. Clear, "Backfire," p. 11.
59. Clear, "Backfire," p. 11 n. 14.
60. Clear, "Backfire," p. 11.

as imprisonment becomes a more routine experience in the neighbor-hoods in which large numbers of low-income African Americans live, shame and fear of prison life decline significantly. This, of course, does not mean that prison life ceases to be an experience of brutality and/or humili-ation. However, increasing numbers of people know that they can survive the prison experience, and even be looked up to by many in the commu-nity for having survived society's attempt to "break them." For many in such communities, the forbidding nature of the institution is lessened.

This phenomenon may also be related to the increasing numbers of lower-level nonviolent offenders who are being locked up.[61] In general, the far too frequent practice of imprisonment as a negative reinforcement re-sponse to crime inevitably loses some of its sting — like most any overused negative reinforcement strategy: "The more prison is used, the more real are the images people have of prison. As these images are normalized, [the prison's] mythological potency is diminished and so is the prison's power to deter criminal behavior."[62]

Fed up with fear of crime, the assumed incorrigibility of criminal of-fenders, and a sense that most criminal sanctions are "not so bad," society has turned to making prison life a harsher experience; but we appear to be fighting a losing battle. I contend that the threat of doing prison time does not work as a sufficient deterrent when prison life no longer needs to be imagined, where there is no longer any mystery: "No matter how brutal — and today's prison's can be undeniably cruel places — the widespread use of prison will continue to create growing numbers of informed consumers who know people who have survived and count them among friends and family."[63] Hence, for too many communities across the nation one collat-eral consequence of excessive imprisonment is a paradoxical and ironic "depenalization" of punishment.

The Revolving Door

Not only does the excessive use of imprisonment undermine the prison's value as a significant deterrent to would-be offenders; it also undermines

---

61. Mauer, *Race to Incarcerate*, pp. 182-83.
62. Clear, "Backfire," p. 11.
63. Clear, "Backfire," p. 12.

neighborhood cohesion by producing and maintaining a constant exit and reentry of community residents. Of course high crime rates undermine community cohesion and stability as well, but to remedy this problem with large-scale imprisonment exacerbates the problem. This is so because the constant back-and-forth flow of exit and reentry of adults puts families at serious economic risk, thereby intensifying the problem of crime for whole neighborhoods. When so many adults continually get locked up for significant periods of time and then are returned to community — many after being imprisoned far from home — difficult family relocations may result, "which in turn creates transitory populations and less integrated neighborhoods."[64]

This negative effect of large-scale incarceration is particularly acute for low-income African American children, for whom the family experience of imprisonment is now almost commonplace. Mauer and Chesney-Lind report that one out of every fourteen African American children has a parent in prison on any given day. As a result of various difficulties related to prison visitor policies and visiting schedules, "more than half of children with a parent in prison have never even visited their parent since his or her incarceration," according to Mauer and Chesney-Lind. This presents a particularly tough situation for women, who are often the custodial parents. Imprisoned mothers unfortunate enough to have no available relative or friend to care for their children will see their children placed in foster care. In addition to this, these women face having their custodial rights severed as a result of 1997 federal legislation mandating that parental rights can be terminated for individuals whose children have been in the care of the state for fifteen months. At fifteen months, it becomes increasingly likely that the children of an imprisoned custodial parent in the care of the state will be placed for adoption.[65]

"Locked Down" Consciousness

The dramatic expansion of imprisonment has become so intense in some communities that it has become part of the lives of many residents in unconscious ways. In Geoffrey Canada's book *Reaching for Manhood*, as well

---

64. Clear, "Backfire," p. 13.
65. Mauer and Chesney-Lind, *Invisible Punishment*, 4.

as in Jonathan Kozol's book *Amazing Grace,* one finds good examples of the impact of large-scale imprisonment on the conscience and language of low-income communities. "Locked-down consciousness" refers to the linguistic and other communicative symbols that represent the socially truncated customs and common practices of the prison culture. This locked-down consciousness becomes embedded in the collective ethos of a community, and severely limits the possibilities for human flourishing in such a community. Locked-down consciousness as a cultural dynamic has been well demonstrated in the autobiography of Harlem Children's Zone president Geoffrey Canada. Canada recalls the following conversation he and some buddies had with two older men, Ronald and Sam, who were former South Bronx gang members and prison inmates:

> "Listen, when you go to jail, don't take no shit from nobody," Ronald began. I was immediately stunned. Ronald didn't say if you go to jail, he said when. It was clear to me that he expected me to go to jail one day. I wondered why we all had to go.
>
> "That right," Sam chimed in. "Don't take no cigarettes, no candy bars, no nothing. If you ain't got no money, fuck it. Do without. Be a man."
>
> "And when they try to make a move on you," Ronald continued, "Fuck them up. I mean fuck them up good. Not with your hands. Pick up something, a tray, a stool, anything you can get your hands on. Don't say anything. Just bust them upside their fucking head. Try to tear their fucking head off. Yell and scream and shit like a madman. Let everyone know you ain't afraid to kill a motherfucker."[66]

Ronald and Sam's words represent a salient example of locked-down consciousness, which routinely gets transported from the prison back to the streets. Back on the street, former inmates like Ronald and Sam often enjoy "instant respect" from the younger men and boys — and increasingly from young females as well.

A locked-down consciousness results in the reduced ability of many

---

66. Quoted in Don Sabo, Terry A. Kupers, and Willie London, "Gender and the Politics of Punishment," in *Prison Masculinities,* ed. Sabo et al. (Philadelphia: Temple University Press, 2001), p. 7; also see pp. 12-13. See also, Geoffrey Canada, *Reaching for Manhood: Transforming the Lives of Boys in America* (Boston: Beacon Press, 1998).

residents to imagine a greater world of possibility and potential beyond the limitations placed on community flourishing by the routine and normalizing effects of large-scale imprisonment. Another example of locked-down consciousness can be seen in an interview conducted by Kozol in the South Bronx. A twelve-year-old Black boy named Jeremiah informs the researcher that, "since 1960 white people started moving away from black and Spanish people in New York." Intrigued with the specificity of the date, Kozol asks, "Where do you think white people went?" A second (unnamed) boy answers, "I think — to the country." Jeremiah then returns to the conversation to explain, "It isn't where people live. It's *how* they live. . . . There are different economies in different places." When asked to elaborate on his comments, Jeremiah makes reference to Riverdale, a mostly White, mostly middle-class neighborhood in the northwest Bronx: "Life in Riverdale is opened up. Where we live, it's locked down."[67] It is not unreasonable to suspect that former inmates like Ronald and Sam would have had an impact on the perceptions of a child like Jeremiah. Jeremiah's words indicate a feeling now prevalent among many residents in poor communities where the high rates of crime, intense police surveillance, and the large-scale imprisonment of residents are all too common.

The negative social impact of being "locked down" in prison is so comprehensive a reality in some communities that it now transverses the prison walls and soaks the consciousness of entire neighborhoods from which inmates come and return. It is no longer unusual in many communities to hear children describe being grounded by a parent or being kept after school as being "locked-down." It is similarly not unusual to overhear fighting youth on the streets with a locked-down consciousness speak of not wanting to be another person's "punk" or "bitch" or "pussy" — words which convey the same negative anti-female identity recognitions prevalent among contemporary prison populations. A locked-down consciousness is often represented in the "body language" of young men walking down a city street conveying in their gait an unmistakable message to all would-be threats: "Don't even think about fucking with me!" Indeed, the locked-down consciousness is one that is far more concerned with the garnishing and maintaining of *respect* in the service of a will-to-survive with "props" (i.e., the "honor" due one) than with the will to contribute to the evolution of community and societal flourishing.

67. Jonathan Kozol, *Amazing Grace: The Lives of Children and the Conscience of a Nation* (New York: Crown, 1995), p. 32.

Imprisonment and Social Capital

Large-scale imprisonment as a social practice constitutes a serious threat to the development of the positive "social capital" necessary for communities to flourish. In agreement with Harvard public policy professor Robert Putnam, I suggest that positive "social capital" refers to the thick networks of social relations in a community and the norms of reciprocity, trust, and honesty that arise from them.[68] The practice of expansive imprisonment creates a large, embittered, and frustrated population of ex-offenders, too many of whom return to their communities changed for the worse. Statistics demonstrating the high rate of recidivism illustrate that high crime rates in many inner-city and poor neighborhoods are virtually guaranteed. Further, intensifying the social impact of bitterness and frustration on the parts of many ex-offenders as a result of their imprisonment, "little support is expressed for the communities and families affected by the dynamic," reports Ernest Drucker, writing in 2003 for the Urban League on the State of Black America.[69] Drucker contends that, "Each prisoner's family must carry its own burdens and find ways to compensate for the loss. When this phenomenon occurs on a large scale and for an extended period of time, it may significantly damage the mental and physical health of individuals, families and entire communities — and create and intensify the very social conditions that enable crime to flourish."[70] All of this undermines the positive social capital that is necessary for shaping wider civic virtue. Civic virtue involves the active participation of all citizens in the positive evolution of society toward the promotion and preservation of community with justice.

Undoubtedly many observers will contend that the primary responsibility for undermining positive social capital lies squarely with offenders. After all, one might argue, a good number of offenders were already not contributing significantly to the support of a family, community, or nation even before being imprisoned. And it is true that many prisoners were

68. Robert Putnam, *Bowling Alone: The Collapse and Revival of American Community* (New York: Touchstone, 2000), pp. 19, 134-47.

69. Ernest M. Drucker, "The Impact of Mass Incarceration on Public Health in Black Communities," in *The National Urban League Annual Report: The State of Black America 2003*, p. 2.

70. Drucker, "The Impact of Mass Incarceration on Public Health in Black Communities," pp. 2-3.

causing family and friends a great deal of difficulty prior to being sent to prison. But many were trying. In a survey of offenders, criminologists John Irwin and James Austin found that "about 40 percent [of offenders] indicated that they had been employed most of the time in the period before arrest."[71] Many of those sent to prison are married and have children, and nearly all have mothers, fathers, brothers, sisters, uncles, aunts, or cousins. I am not contending that there should be no consequences for crime, but I believe Irwin and Austin are correct in their contention that

> Perhaps the highest cost of our careless extension of the use of imprisonment is the damage to thousands of people, most of whom have no prior prison record and who are convicted of petty crimes, and the future consequences of this damage to the society. These persons are being packed into dangerous, crowded prisons with minimal access to job training, education, or other services that will prepare them for life after prison. Some marginally involved petty criminals are converted into hard-core "outlaws" — mean, violence-prone convicts who dominate crowded prison wards.
>
> Making matters worse, a growing number of prisoners are being subjected to extremely long sentences. These long-termers are not only stacking up in prisons and filling all available space, but their long terms, much of which they serve in maximum-security prisons that impose deprivation on them, result in more loss of social and vocational skills, more estrangement, and more alienation.
>
> It must be kept in mind that virtually all of these profoundly damaged individuals will be released from prison and will try to pick up life on the outside. For the most part, their chances of pursuing a merely viable, much less satisfying conventional life after prison are small. The contemporary prison experience has converted them into social misfits and cripples, and there is a growing likelihood that they will return to crime, violence, and other forms of disapproved deviance.[72]

In an argument similar to that of Irwin and Austin, Joan Moore, a criminologist at the University of Wisconsin–Milwaukee, has pointed out

71. Irwin and Austin, *It's About Time*, p. 167.

72. Irwin and Austin, *It's About Time*, pp. 167-68. See also Joan Petersilia and Susan Turner, *Prison Versus Probation in California: Implications for Crime and Offender Recidivism* (Santa Monica, Calif.: Rand Corporation, 1986).

what has become an obvious collateral social consequence of large-scale imprisonment under hostile and humiliating conditions: the negative aspects of imprisonment on such a large scale being exported onto the streets of the nation. Hence, re/producing criminality, the theme of Chapter One, is itself one of the collateral consequences of large-scale imprisonment. As suggested in Chapter One, the prison functions as what could be called a school of crime "mis/education." This mis/education contributes to the circularity and intensification of crime, from the streets to the prison and back to the streets again. Moore contends that, "Prisons and jails are ideal institutions for strengthening peer-group relationships that have later repercussions on the streets."[73] Indeed, if a majority of drug dealers in the neighborhood, gang member and nonmember alike, are swept into jail at or around the same time, the strengthening and expansion of negative criminal social capital will be a predictable result.

That neighborhood ties outside prison get reinforced in prison has led criminologist Richard Curtis to suggest that New York City's Rikers Island correctional facility has been turned "into a [neighborhood] block party!"[74] Moore argues that the export of prison criminality is not the only negative aspect of street networks that include high numbers of ex-offenders. She maintains that, "Researchers and practitioners speculate that the increased violence in street networks may be affected by the export of violent interpersonal styles. There is some evidence that ex-inmates hang around with younger men, who are impressed with these 'veteranos.'"[75]

Another export from the prison is the relative imperviousness large interconnected groups of ex-inmates have to being sanctioned — formally or informally. Moore explains that, "Their members become inured to criminal justice sanctions, and their friends don't stigmatize them if they do wind up in prison. The prison subculture is intensely hostile to established authority, and these attitudes, too, are exported to the streets."[76]

Indeed, not only are socially destructive attitudes and associated an-

73. Joan Moore, "Bearing the Burden: How Incarceration Weakens Inner-City Communities," in Fulbright, *Unintended Consequences,* p. 74.

74. Quoted in Moore, "Bearing the Burden," p. 74. See also Richard Curtis et al., "Street-Level Drug Markets: Network Structure and HIV Risk," *Social Networks* 17 (1995): 229-49.

75. Moore, "Bearing the Burden," p. 74.

76. Moore, "Bearing the Burden," p. 74.

tisocial behaviors exported from prisons and jails back onto the streets of the nation, so too has imprisonment on such a large scale raised the rates of infectious disease in the general population. Half a million people are released from the nation's prisons and jails each year, and many of them spread illnesses they caught while incarcerated. Social scientist Donald F. Sabo contends that, "The prison system is in many ways becoming a Petri dish for the spread of HIV/AIDS, tuberculosis, and hepatitis."[77] This unfortunate reality is now widely acknowledged among prison analysts and public health professionals. Since the vast majority of the nation's prisoners, and hence a majority of those being released, are young, the public health threat to society in terms of the spread of infectious diseases is considerable to say the least.

Civil Liberties and "Other Regard"

Of course it is difficult to identify and measure accurately the full range and depth of the collateral social consequences tied to the practice of large-scale imprisonment. Nonetheless, I would like to suggest that a nation that relies on retributive and degrading imprisonment as a principal means of crime control may well be committing felony assault on the kinds of human and social capital that are necessary to facilitate prisoner participation in the building of better communities in society at large. Consider the right to vote: currently, a felony conviction often means the loss of the right to vote, sometimes for life. Soon the nation can expect there to be some four million citizens who have lost their right to vote due to a felony conviction. Half of the current 3.9 million residents who have lost voting rights are African American. For African Americans, this consequence, predominantly as a result of drug convictions, has meant "political disempowerment writ large," according to Ernest Drucker, professor of epidemiology and population medicine at Albert Einstein College of Medicine.

The rate of disenfranchisement is so high for individual Black people that entire communities have, in effect, been disenfranchised. Drucker re-

77. Quoted in Peter Monaghan, "Madness in Maximum Security: When Scholars Get a Look Inside America's Secretive Prisons, They See Chaos," *Chronicle of Higher Education,* June 18, 2004, A14-15.

ports that "thirty to forty percent of black males age 18 to 30 are disenfranchised. Given that the usual voting rate of this age group, regardless of race, is about 25 percent, it may be that in those areas with high incarceration rates, the number of young black men barred from voting may be greater than those who are legally eligible."[78] Intensifying the issues of civil liberties and justice related to the right to vote, ex-felons, especially drug felons, are now ineligible for public housing, for Temporary Aid to Needy Families (TANF) assistance, for governmental aid to pursue education, and for a host of other governmental and state resources and benefits that might provoke better citizenship once a prisoner is discharged from prison.[79] To give just one example, this retributive and status-reducing spirit of punishment could be discerned in 1995 when Democratic President Bill Clinton together with the Republican-controlled Congress decided to terminate inmate eligibility for federal Pell Grant awards for higher education for anyone who had been convicted of a drug-related felony.

A serious social consequence of all this is that a significant fraction of ex-offenders will find the obstacles to obtaining basic shelter, education, and employment (all of which enhance the establishment of stable family, communal, and societal relationships) insurmountable. As a consequence, many ex-felons will end up homeless on the streets of the nation, and many of them will eventually land back in jail. Moore, drawing on substantial anecdotal data regarding what Irwin and Austin see as society's "dereliction," has reported that, "After they exhaust family resources, many ex-offenders wind up on the streets, homeless. Merging the findings of 12 studies of the homeless, [Peter] Rossi (1989) found that an average of 21.3 percent had served prison sentences. Many die on the streets."[80]

The drug war has been particularly influential on political decision-making, with profound consequences for civil liberties. Not only have leg-

---

78. Drucker, "The Impact of Mass Incarceration on Public Health in Black Communities," p. 3. See also Mauer and Chesney-Lind, *Invisible Punishment*, pp. 4-5; and Mauer, "Mass Imprisonment and the Disappearing Voters," in Mauer and Chesney-Lind, *Invisible Punishment*, pp. 50-58.

79. Lanier, "The Harmful Impact of the Criminal Justice System and War on Drugs on the African-American Family," p. 2. Also see Gwen Rubinstein and Debbie Mukamal, "Welfare and Housing — Denial of Benefits to Drug Offenders," in Mauer and Chesney-Lind, *Invisible Punishment*, pp. 37-49.

80. Moore, "Bearing the Burden," p. 75; Irwin and Austin, *It's About Time*, p. 138; Peter Rossi, *Down and Out in America* (Chicago: University of Chicago Press, 1989).

islators adopted ever more punitive sentencing measures against anyone convicted of a drug offense, but we are now also faced with "the bizarre situation whereby a convicted armed robber or rapist can apply for higher education or welfare benefits, but a drug offender cannot."[81] This will hardly help reduce the collateral damage done to ex-offenders' children, families, and communities. In another example of the direct assault on civil liberties faced by prisoners, Mauer and Chesney-Lind have reported that, "through the guise of asset forfeiture legislation, the presumption of innocence has been ignored as local and federal law enforcement agencies are empowered to seize the property of suspected drug dealers and deposit it in police coffers, even if the suspect is not convicted."[82] This, of course, constitutes a serious affront to the principles of civil liberty on which the nation allegedly stands.

It is distressing that a mere decade after the civil rights victories of the 1950s and 1960s succeeded in dismantling the legal structures of segregation and discrimination, the nation's attitudes and policies on crime and imprisonment began to prominently reintroduce serious questions concerning racial, ethnic, class, and gender fairness. The degree of negative consequences associated with the contemporary prison-industrial complex may now equal (or exceed) the levels of human trauma and social alienation known during the civil rights reform era.

Not only does the phenomenon of large-scale imprisonment for extended periods of time in ever harsher forms result in numerous, perhaps unintended, social consequences for people of color living in lower-status communities, it negatively affects the conscience and social cohesion of the entire nation. The social practice of large-scale imprisonment inflicts a massive wound on any public compassion we might share with other humans. As Mark Lewis Taylor, a professor of theology and culture at Princeton Seminary, has correctly observed, the more than two million people in U.S. prisons (including a burgeoning death row), along with the often routine brutality associated with imprisonment, is a threat because it destroys the whole fabric of fellow-feeling, or "other regard": "It disrupts and divides the unity we want to feel and build, with our neighbors and with all humanity."[83]

81. Mauer and Chesney-Lind, *Invisible Punishment*, p. 6.
82. Mauer and Chesney-Lind, *Invisible Punishment*, p. 6.
83. Mark C. Taylor, *The Executed God: The Way of the Cross in Lockdown America* (Minneapolis: Fortress, 2001), pp. 42; 25-41.

There may well be many citizens who are not at all concerned about the promotion and preservation of "fellow-feelings," but even they should care about the social implications of the way society punishes. Taking a pragmatic interest in maintaining a society that punishes better than it now does helps produce a better (i.e., safer, more just, and flourishing) society for even a self-interested person to inhabit. The present practice of imprisonment poisons the entire social order, afflicting even those who refuse to value a prisoner's life as highly as their own. Of course, it would be a higher and better principle, in my estimation, to see others as being as valuable as oneself, but there is also a baser pragmatic interest that society might have to appeal to in an imperfect world. One would be a safer egoist if punishment were more humanely applied.

Reliance on large-scale imprisonment and the retributive degradation of prisoners undermines the pursuit of sufficient levels of collective social capital to improve the living conditions of individuals, families, communities, and society at large. And this makes it difficult, if not impossible, to avoid the kinds of collateral social consequences I have attended to in this chapter. Continuing to imprison such large numbers of people under sentence of vengeful social retribution and status humiliation can hardly avoid lessening the tangible substances of good will, other regard, empathy, and appropriate social intercourse among the very people who call for, and want to practice, these for the sake of the common good.[84]

Summary

By continuing to imprison millions of people under intolerably cruel and dangerous conditions, the United States has effectively put its own racial, ethnic, and class-based apartheid into place. As authorities continue to stigmatize, scapegoat, and disproportionately "disappear" Black, Latino/a, Native American, poor, mentally ill, drug addicted, homeless, miseducated, and other prisoners from the nation's democratic hopes, they unravel some of the important gains of the Civil Rights era. Using a term as contentious as "apartheid" to describe our national obsession with imprisonment may seem rash and unfair to some, but a look at the collective

---

84. See Robert Putnam's good discussion of the social necessity of positive forms of social capital if human community is to flourish, in *Bowling Alone*, p. 19; 16-28.

portrait of prisoners in the U.S. is quite telling: the overwhelming majority of prisoners come from poor or working-class communities, and over two-thirds are so-called racial and ethnic minorities. This has a ripple effect as racial, ethnic, and class tensions are exacerbated throughout the whole society. For example, distrust of the police in Black and Latino/a communities is now more common than ever. Joan Moore maintains that

> In many African-American and Latino communities there is strong suspicion that the sudden burgeoning of the drug market and the resulting wave of incarcerations are no accident. They are seen by many as a deliberate plan on the part of the white establishment to weaken communities that might offer a political threat (Edsall and Edsall, 1991). Right or wrong, this view contends that the drug epidemic was designed to remove men from the community to prison and thereby depress the birth rate and the political potential of the population, and also to corrupt the lives of those remaining in the community. This alienation reinforces the social and political isolation of inner-city communities. As Glasgow (1995) remarks, "policies that destroy the connectedness of people with each other and the community drive people away from socialization with community institutions, and they destroy the vitality of the future."[85]

In addition to this, there are other indicators related to the excessive use of imprisonment that insure social apartheid: seventy-five percent of prisoners have a history of drug or alcohol abuse; we are fast approaching a point where one in five suffer from mental illness; a majority of inmates are functionally illiterate; and over half of the nation's female inmates suffer from a history of sexual and/or physical abuse.[86] Imprisoning such persons at such excessive rates indicates strong societal willingness to isolate our most vulnerable residents without much thought of our collective national collusion in their problems. Here society's most entrenched social problems go largely unaddressed as we make the lives of most undesirable human beings among us more matters of crime control than matters of healing care and difficult love. Cultivation of a vindictive disregard for those judged to be the criminal other entitles us to feel good about hating

---

85. Moore, "Bearing the Burden," p. 80.
86. Mauer and Chesney-Lind, *Invisible Punishment*, p. 2.

offenders, whom we can only see as victimizers unworthy of our affection. Such affection is extraordinarily and understandably difficult to muster.

As we debate the collateral social consequences of large-scale imprisonment for poor and working-class communities and for the nation as a whole, a central quandary articulated by criminologist Todd Clear should be kept in mind: "A profound penological paradox of the twentieth century is this: Between 1973 and 1995, prison populations quintupled in size and incarceration rates quadrupled, yet crime rates have remained high."[87] In 2002 the nation's prison population grew 2.6 percent despite a small decline in serious crime. This represents the largest increase since 1999, according to the Justice Department. At the start of 2003 there were more than 2,166,260 U.S. residents being held in local jails, state and federal prisons, and juvenile detention facilities.[88]

Refusing to truly work at the transformation of the ever-increasing number of prisoners and ex-prisoners, who are "more or less psychologically and socially crippled and excluded from conventional society," means that offenders will continue to pose a nuisance and serious threat to others.

By refusing to develop a justice system that not only truly corrects but also deals effectively with the nation's substantial levels of anxiety and fear related to crime, we foster a nation of retribution, degradation, and substantial imprisonment. This severely undermines some of society's most cherished humanitarian values: individual, communal, and societal peace with justice. Our national vindictiveness as evidenced by our excessive thirst to imprison greater numbers of people will further divide our nation into the predominantly (but not exclusively) White affluent classes on one side, and a poor, mostly non-White underclass on the other. Far too many of the latter will become convicts and ex-convicts.[89] This is the social apartheid, now in full bloom, which must be arrested.

87. Clear, "Backfire," p. 3.
88. Fox Butterfield, "Study Finds 2.6% Increase in U.S. Prison Population," *New York Times*, July 28, 2003.
89. Irwin and Austin, *It's About Time*, p. 170.

3. Prisons and Social Alienation

So far in this book I have argued that criminality is re/produced and maintained by the punitive practice of retributive degradation and that this practice is now practiced on a grand scale due to the growth in imprisonment that is the result of a web of interlocking relationships known as the prison-industrial complex. I have also examined the collateral social consequences of this dramatic rise in the rate of incarceration: the intensified stigmatization of "people of color" (particularly Black people); the over-burdening of women, children, and poor and working-class communities; the erosion of necessary social unity; and the undermining of civil liberties and regard for others.

In this chapter I will now situate the contemporary problem of imprisonment within the context of a deeper problem of the human condition: that of alienation. In particular, I want to deal with representative social alienations that are made greater or exacerbated by the nation's reliance on large-scale imprisonment as a means toward what passes for safety and happiness, and our widespread tolerance for the unfortunate collateral consequences that are fed well by our "race to incarcerate."

Alienation Defined

By employing the term "alienation," I mean to focus attention on a basic and tragic human tendency: namely, to turn away from our mutual affections for one another, to participate in neglectful indifference toward — and even the most virulent oppression of — persons and groups other than the ones to which we believe ourselves to belong.[1] Alienation is an extremely complex topic, and it has been analyzed philosophically, theologically, socially, politically, and economically throughout human history. The more limited purpose of this chapter is to show that contemporary large-scale imprisonment practice, and its collateral social consequences, reinforce the socially corrosive factors of (scientific) atomism, (vulgar) individualism, and especially racism, all of which are salient forms that alienation takes (sometimes, as I shall show, with critical contributions from religion).

In what follows, I want to consider briefly the matters of atomism and individualism before focusing in depth on the development and phenomenon of racism as a principal factor in the alienating productions and representations of the "Black criminal." Alienating racial conceptions and relationships have resulted in the disproportionate imprisonment of Americans of African descent, and they also play a significant role in the collateral social consequences experienced by Black communities due to the scale of Black imprisonment. It is my contention that atomism and individualism both intensify and are intensified by racism, the effect of which is the disproportionate level of misery experienced by Black people vis-à-vis the American prison system.

---

1. This brief and general working definition of "alienation" (or "estrangement") draws from the significant philosophical and theological works of Hegel, Marx, and Paul Tillich. See G. W. F. Hegel's discussion of "Self-alienated Spirit Culture" in *Phenomenology of the Spirit* (Oxford: Oxford University Press, 1977), pp. 294-328; Terry Pinkard's commentary on Hegel's understanding that the coming-to-be of the human community's awareness of its meaning in terms of dialectical history occurs only within the context of "the community's linguistic and cultural practices and the socially instituted structures of mutual recognition that provide the grounds for determining who one is . . . ," in *Hegel's Phenomenology: The Sociality of Reason* (Cambridge: Cambridge University Press, 1994), pp. 249-52; Bertell Ollman's discussion of Marx's theory of alienation, which essentially names as a "mistake," or "defect," "any state of human existence which is 'away from' or 'less than' unalienation," in *Alienation: Marx's Conception of Man in Capitalist Society* (Cambridge: Cambridge University Press, 1976), pp. 131-35; and finally Paul Tillich's discussion of human estrangement and the three-fold concept of sin — "unbelief," "hubris," and "concupiscence," in *Systematic Theology*, vol. 2, *Existence and the Christ* (Chicago: University of Chicago Press, 1975), pp. 44-59.

Alienating Dimensions of Criminal Punishment

The Atomized Individual, Community, and Society

Throughout the twentieth century, thought and discussion about crime policy were dominated by a focus on individuals. Earlier in the century, the predominating idea was that offenders, as distinct and separate individuals, required reform or rehabilitation. From the early 1970s on, the general belief has been that offenders, as distinct and separate individuals, require control. A notable exception to this emphasis on criminals as individuals took place during a brief period of debate in the 1970s concerning the "reintegrative" view of criminal corrections, which focused not only on the needs of individual offenders, but also on those of the communities to which they would return.[2]

While it is obviously true that crime policy approaches that focus primarily on reform differ in several important respects from those that focus primarily on control, both approaches have shared a common, and unfortunate, analytic foundation, according to criminologist Todd Clear: that "crime and its control are best understood in regard to the thoughts and emotions of specific individuals who commit crimes."[3] Clear argues that both reform and control views of punishment in their traditional formulations may be termed "atomistic" "because offenders are seen as individual actors who behave largely in isolation from their environments."[4] An atomistic view is one in which phenomena are generally seen as being made up of numerous unrelated elements. To hold to an atomistic view, whether with regard to crime policy or to any other field, is to imply that the universe is made up of tiny, simple, indivisible particles.

Tying atomistic theory to a general understanding of criminal justice, Clear contends that, "Rehabilitation models have always treated the offender as the unit of analysis, to be diagnosed or classified for correctional intervention based on his or her individual characteristics. Similarly, the criminal control model describes the offender's life as though it were a

2. Todd Clear, "Backfire," in *The Unintended Consequences of Incarceration: Conference Papers*, ed. Karen Fulbright (New York: Vera Institute of Justice, January 1996), p. 2.

3. Clear, "Backfire," p. 2.

4. Clear, "Backfire," p. 2.

self-contained system, bounded by age on onset, duration, rates of behaviors, and dates of desistence."[5] Clear goes on to explain that, "Both the rehabilitation and control models consider the effects of various individual characteristics, but both focus on understanding individual offenders as the key to knowing about crime at large. . . . The tendency to view crime as a phenomenon defined by wayward individuals and their desires is not only ingrained in penology, it is reinforced in public consciousness by the popular media's focus on individual criminal events as news stories."[6]

In addition to treating offenders as individual units of analysis and offenders' lives as self-contained systems, the dominant viewpoint of criminal corrections is atomistic in another important aspect. The imprisonment of specific offenders "is considered to be a self-contained process — affecting that offender and almost nobody else," according to Clear. He contends that under this "self-contained" view of the incarceration process,

> The walls of the prison stand symbolically as a black box into which citizens disappear for a time and later emerge — changed or not. The number of black boxes in existence and the frequency of experiences within them are therefore important only for the individuals who go through the process. This perspective ignores the potential impact of incarceration upon families, communities, economics, and politics.[7]

Yet there is a critical, and ironic, exception to this general observation: "From the atomistic point of view, deterrence means that when the state punishes person X, other persons are unaffected by that punishment in every way except in calculations of the desirability of engaging in crime."[8]

The atomistic (or scientifically[9] individualized) model of criminal

---

5. Clear, "Backfire," p. 2. Here Clear is drawing on Alfred Blumstein, Jacqueline Cohen, Jeffrey A. Roth, and Christy Visher, eds., *Criminal Careers and "Career Criminals"* (Washington, D.C.: National Academy Press, 1986).

6. Clear, "Backfire," p. 2, nn. 2, 3.

7. Clear, "Backfire," p. 3.

8. Clear, "Backfire," p. 3, n. 4.

9. What makes this "atomistic" view "scientific" is the close attention social researchers pay to "scientific method" in the study of criminal behavior: i.e., the disciplined, systematic, and "objective" gathering, comparing, and classifying of data in the service of developing generalizations, theories, or laws that explain the phenomena of criminality. The

corrections led, in the 1970s, to speculations about the nature and impact of individual criminal careers. The initial development of the individual criminal career paradigm was developed in 1975 by the researchers Shlomo Shinnar and Revel Shinnar.[10] Shinnar and Shinnar's work was broadly coterminous with the dramatic rise of excessive imprisonment, which, as I have already outlined, started its upward trend in 1973.

Another central difficulty with atomistic views of punishment, regardless of whether their primary goal is rehabilitation or control, lies in their failure to adequately consider and acknowledge the collateral "ripple effects" of punishment on communities and society at large. An atomistic view of punishment is socially corrosive insofar as it fails to understand that no human process, practice, or institution can ever function in a self-contained way. Indeed, even the atomistic model of punishment is reflexive in the sense that the knowledge it generates gets injected back into, and therefore shapes, interpretations of the reality it describes. When we act as if we can disconnect the ways we punish from the social consequences that issue from them, we cannot deal effectively with the corresponding social corrosion that may result. Social practices are reflexive; they have ways of bending back upon themselves. When offenders are incarcerated on a large scale under conditions of social vengeance and status humiliation, there will certainly be a degree to which the alienating effects of such practices will bend back upon communities and society at large. Imprisonment as a large-scale social practice has attached to it a constitutive circularity — as noted in Chapter Two, the negative social capital that is produced and maintained in the prison routinely gets exported to the streets, and vice versa. What goes on behind the prison walls affects, and is affected by, what goes on in the streets of the nation at large.

While it is true enough that offenders, like all human beings, are discrete subjects with agency and thus should demonstrate a good measure of personal responsibility, they do not choose crime in a social vacuum. The

---

relationship between "scientific atomism" and individualism, discussed below, is that scientific atomism is a social scientific tool or technique inspired by, and expressive of, the individualism of the wider social-political-cultural U.S. ethos.

10. Shlomo Shinnar and Revel Shinnar, "The Effects of the Criminal Justice System on the Control of Crime: A Quantitative Approach," *Law and Society Review* 9 (1975): 581-612. For a good full-scale review of the individualistic model of penology see Barbara Hudson, *Justice Through Punishment: A Critique of the "Justice" Model of Corrections* (New York: St. Martin's Press, 1987).

economic and political context in which crime occurs must be given a certain amount of weight; I contend it should receive at minimum as much weight as individual responsibility. While it may well be the case that many of those classified as criminal are antisocial, pathological, mentally ill, drug addicted, and so forth, such persons are also products of the economic, social, and political reality in which they live. In failing to acknowledge that offenders always act within thick networks of social interconnectedness, we fail to understand that the idea of reflexivity is absolutely essential for the process of social analysis.[11]

(Vulgar) Individualism

The United States is a nation that prizes individualism. Unfortunately, it is not unusual for expressions of U.S. individualism to be of a simplistic, often vulgar kind, which resists comportment to the inextricable bondedness of humanity and nature. From the stoic and self-reliant cowboy and the self-made millionaire on one end of the spectrum to the notorious outlaw on the other, American society places an excessive emphasis on the notion that great and terrible actions are primarily the product of *individual* effort and responsibility.[12] Even in American popular religion, Jesus Christ is seen as a kind of individualistic hero, committing salvific deeds on behalf of humankind. It is perhaps no surprise, then, that mainstream criminal justice processes often give little attention to the overlapping social, economic, and political interests inextricably tied to them.

In spite of the mightiest social efforts of the twentieth century to encourage more associational civil and political arrangements, gross individualism remains deeply embedded in U.S. custom and common practice. So often even our best efforts at creating associational groups have resulted in a species of alienation, namely, separatism as an end in itself. Self-imposed group sectarianism as a social aim may be produced and reinforced on the bases of various combinations of, for example, class, ethnicity, gender, race, national origin, or sexual orientation. Robert Putnam has characterized

11. See Pierre Bourdieu and Loïc J. D. Wacquant, *An Invitation to Reflexive Sociology* (Chicago: University of Chicago Press, 1992), pp. 36-38; 62-260.

12. See, for example, Richard Slotkin, *Gunfighter Nation: The Myth of the Frontier in Twentieth-Century America* (Norman, Okla.: University of Oklahoma Press, 1998).

this kind of "bonding social capital" as inward-looking, with a tendency to reinforce exclusive identities and homogeneous groups.[13] While this kind of self-imposed group separation and solidarity is, in fact, a necessary requirement for groups acting to cast off the virulent oppression of other groups, it should never be considered an end in itself. As my Black slave ancestors knew all too well, a measure of "stealing away" for the sake of group survival and flourishing can be absolutely necessary. Stealing away (often "to Jesus"), along with "hush harbors" and all other manner of secret and separate gatherings, signified social survival and/or freedom from the social and physical death of slavery. However, such separation should not be considered an ultimate goal, but rather as a step along the way to embracing our common humanity.

Throughout America's history, religion has played a major role in undergirding many of the nation's institutions and social practices. Alexis de Tocqueville (1805-1859) spoke of American church religion, in particular, as a political institution that powerfully served the maintenance of a democratic republic among Americans.[14] Although the founders of the republic aimed to never directly mix religion and government, de Tocqueville observed that for Americans religion was, nonetheless, "the first of their political institutions; for if it does not give them the taste for freedom, it singularly facilitates their use of it."[15] In 1902, observing the critical influence of religion in American society, Henry Bargy noted, "American religion has always had as its aim the well-being of the (human) race. It is the poetry of public-mindedness".[16] Indeed, the historical influence of religion on the civil and political institutions of U.S. society has always been prominent.

In this milieu, certain streams of Christianity have been more influential than others. Specifically, there are certain Christian, particularly

---

13. Robert D. Putnam, *Bowling Alone: The Collapse and Revival of American Community* (New York: Simon & Schuster, 2000), p. 22. Putnam correctly observes that many social capital networks bond and bridge simultaneously. Bridging social capital (which Putnam endorses) is outward looking, encompassing people across diverse social cleavages. Bonding and bridging forms of social capital are not strict either-or categories where neat divisions are always discernable. The dimensions cover a spectrum of "more or less."

14. Alexis de Tocqueville, *Democracy in America*, ed. and trans. Harvey C. Mansfield and Delba Winthorp (Chicago: University of Chicago Press, 2000), p. 275.

15. Tocqueville, *Democracy in America*, p. 280.

16. Henry Bargy, *La Religion dans la Societé aux Etats-Unis* (Paris: Librairie Armand Colin, 1902), p. 31. The original French reads: "La religion américaine eut toujours pour but le bien-être de la race. Elle est la poésie du civisme."

Protestant Christian, understandings of the sin of pride, human responsibility, and free will that have contributed to unhelpful individualistic views of punishment that we are considering here. Versions of Christianity focusing on individual righteousness within strictly defined (holy) communities tend to separate "us" from "them," "saint" from "sinner," "righteous" from "unrighteous," "damned" from "blessed," and so forth. The problem with these bipolar categories is that they fail to account for the radical interconnectedness of all creation, including the mutuality of human interconnectedness.

In Chapter One I presented Thomas Aquinas's description of the function of punishment in the kingdom of heaven in his *Summa Theologiae*. Whatever his other reasons for lifting up the horrific divine vengeance meted out upon the damned as a means of intensifying the delight of the righteous, it seems clear that Aquinas failed to see the negative impact such a situation could have on the development of human interconnectedness. Even if one were to grant for the sake of argument that the damned deserve God's vengeful and status-reducing judgment, would it not be more appropriate, and more consonant with Christian teaching, to say that this ought to be an occasion for Christian sorrow and lament rather than delight? Aquinas failed to ask himself the same critical questions contemporary Christians must consider today, that is, how have "righteous" Christians contributed to the necessity for divine revenge and humiliation for the damned? Put another way, how have righteous Christians contributed to the damnation of the damned? Why is the righteous gaze upon the damned a necessary component of Christian delight? Why do we not mourn for the suffering of the damned or view their suffering as a dimension of our own suffering as an interconnected humanity? If it is true that the damned were created by eternal love, what, then, for Christians, are the implications for our treatment of those whom society imprisons?

From Aquinas's point of view the damned serve a necessary function as "transgressing carcasses" (Isa. 66:24), the sight of which urge the holy to a more profound praise of God: "Nothing should be denied the blessed that belongs to the perfection of their beatitude. Now everything is known the more for being compared with its contrary, because when contraries are placed beside one another they become more conspicuous."[17] To the

---

17. Thomas Aquinas, *Summa Theologiae*, III, Supplementum, Q. 94, Art. 1 (New York: Benziger Brothers, 1948).

extent that Christians affirm the contemporary criminal justice system's routine meting out of vengeance and status-humiliation on its prisoners, it continues in the legacy of Aquinas's strict saint/damned dualism, which in its effects is one of the uglier streams of Christianity. In a society where offenders are often viewed as "trash," "scum," "filth," "pieces of shit," and so forth, we too easily draw a dichotomy between "us" and "them" in which our supposed beatitude is contrasted with their supposed wickedness.

Many Christians today continue to affirm imprisonment practices informed by such views as this, in which prisoners are exclusively guilty and therefore worthy of societal revenge and status-humiliation. And so just as God is seen as punishing transgressors, contemporary society imprisons those who transgress against the metaphysical authorities and principles of civil religion: the state, liberty, happiness, and fraternity.[18] Those who breach these authorities and principles are popularly believed to deserve social retribution and degradation. Here too exists the radical separation of "us" from "them," thus intensifying a socially corrosive state of human alienation from one another.

To be sure, some criminal transgressions are so horribly beyond the pale of human imagination that long-term separation is required to insure the public safety and welfare. We must indeed recognize that there are persons who are imprisoned because they have committed the worst sorts of violence on other persons: rape, homicide, child abuse, armed robbery, battery, etc. Even within thick social networks of goodness and reciprocity, there will be those seriously troubled individuals who commit horrific crimes, and these must take responsibility, and be held responsible, for

18. I am using the term "civil religion" here in the sense employed by Robert Bellah in his *The Religious Situation:* "what I mean by civil religion is a set of religious beliefs, symbols, and rituals growing out of the American historical experience interpreted in the dimension of transcendence." Quoted in Vine Deloria, Jr., *For This Land: Writings on Religion in America* (New York: Routledge, 1999), p. 166. Also see Chapter 8, Book 4 of Jean-Jacques Rousseau's *The Social Contract* (New York: Penguin, 1968). Rousseau outlines the foundational dogmas of civil religion as the existence of God, the afterlife to come, the rewarding of virtue and punishment of vice, and the rejection of religious intolerance. Even if one does not wish to endorse an argument for the direct influence of Rousseau's writings on the founders of the republic, similar ideas regarding "civil religion" as part of the cultural understanding of the late eighteenth century had a profound affect on the founding fathers and on modern leaders of the American Republic. See for example Robert Bellah's discussion in his essay "Civil Religion in America," in *Beyond Belief: Essays on Religion in a Post-Traditionalist World* (Berkeley: University of California Press, 1970), pp. 173-176.

their decisions and actions. But the *way* we punish even the most blood-thirsty child-murdering rapist has serious social implications for families, communities, and society at large.

Hatred and a desire for vengeance are understandable emotions, particularly in response to horrific violent crimes. Yet the overwhelming majority of offenders have not committed crimes of such a degree, and so the vengeance and status-humiliation to which these lesser offenders are subjected serves only to make the whole society worse off. This is true from the guards on the frontlines, who are likely to take habits of vengeance, status-humiliation, and intolerance home with them, all the way out to society in general, which will find itself less able to enhance and extend liberty, justice, and fraternity. To the extent that those who administer the prison are being routinely habituated in vices detrimental to human dignity, they too suffer. What writer and broadcaster David Cayley has correctly noted with regard to Canadian prisons applies in the United States as well:

> The suffering of prison staff is not normally included when the costs of imprisonment are reckoned up. Locking people up gets trouble out of the way, at least temporarily; but the trouble doesn't actually disappear by being put out of sight and out of mind; it's just put in a new place, where someone else has to deal with it. This is what is asked of Canada's various correctional services and their front line, the prison guards. They bear the scars of imprisonment as surely as their prisoners.[19]

The alienation produced by criminal acts is often made worse by the ways in which society punishes its prisoners. By meting out ever-harsher prison terms, under motivation of vengeance and status humiliation, the circularity of alienating relations continues unabated. Thus it can be said that the contemporary prison contributes to the undermining of the best of human possibilities for the future of community and society. The paradox and irony of this situation is that prison authorities and the wider society at large fail to see that our own tendency to normalize vengeance and degradation reinforces the very human conditions that help produce the individuals we tend to view as individually responsible for their crimes. In

19. David Cayley, *The Expanding Prison: The Crisis in Crime and Punishment and the Search for Alternatives* (Cleveland: Pilgrim Press, 1998), pp. 113-14.

a way, the process of meting out retributive degradation victimizes society beyond what prisoners have done. This is due to the fact that by practicing retributive degradation we tend toward a social direction more spiritually and behaviorally in sync with the very people we deem criminal. Indeed, we can expect a certain percentage of society members who favor and/or practice retributive degradation themselves to become negatively affected by the practice because they cannot see that what we do habitually is often what we become. And on a larger scale, we as a society fail to see the connection between what individuals become when they routinely practice revenge and status-humiliation on others and what the whole society is threatened with becoming.

In contemporary prisons and jails, practices that contribute to an intensification of human pain and misery also contribute to the corrosion of human community outside the prison. If it is true that a society is to be judged by the kinds of peoples it produces, then surely a society that habituates itself in the scientific method of atomism, and in vulgar individualism reinforced by certain versions of the Christian narrative, and then applies these to the excessive imprisonment of its residents under conditions of retributive degradation, will produce individuals less willing to take on the risks of participation in a common democratic hope necessary to produce a society of mutual well-being.

While perhaps unsatisfying in its brevity, the foregoing sprint through a description of two basic forms of alienation gives us some understanding of the contemporary social landscape against which the coming discussion of racial alienation and the conception of the "Black criminal" find intelligibility.

Anti-Black White Racism and Alienation

A particularly salient and vicious form of alienation infecting U.S. imprisonment practice is racism, especially anti-Black White racism. A vast institution, the American criminal justice system reinforces systemic racism on a macro level, and hence reinforces social alienation. Routine and ordered perpetuation of racial subordination and inequality are significant dimensions of the U.S. prison system's functioning.

The racial ethos of the prison gets created and re/created on the micro level by the routine discriminatory actions of individuals under various sorts of pressures, such as excessive anxiety, fear, hate, vindictiveness, cynicism, profit motive, and the desire to control and manage "surplus populations." Drawing on the work of Philomena Essed, sociologist Joe Feagin argues that "individual acts of discrimination regularly activate whites' group power. Discriminatory practices based on racial prejudices express the collective interests of whites and regularly activate and sustain the underlying racial hierarchy."[20] The continued construction of hierarchical racial images, attitudes, and identities, which have been inextricably connected to the creation, development, and maintenance of White privilege, economic wealth, and sociopolitical power over nearly four (American) centuries, contribute significantly to the alienating racist relationships infecting penal practice in the United States. The alienation caused by racism is experienced in the day-to-day complexity of our common interactive lives. Feagin argues persuasively that

> People do not experience "race" in the abstract but in concrete recurring relationships with one another. Individuals, whether they are the perpetrators of discrimination or the recipients of discrimination, are caught in a complex web of *alienating racist relations*. These socially imbedded racist relations distort what could be engaging and egalitarian relationships into alienated relationships. The system of racism categorizes and divides human beings from each other and thus severely impedes the development of common consciousness and solidarity. It fractures human nature by separating those defined and elevated as the "superior race" against those defined and subordinated as the "inferior race." As a result, life under a system of racism involves an ongoing struggle between racially defined human communities — one seeking to preserve its unjustly derived status and privileges and the other seeking to overthrow its oppression.[21]

Although alienating racist relations were an indisputable and major dimension of the nation's most savage institution, slavery, Alexis de Tocqueville made the provocative suggestion that the White "prejudice"

20. Joe R. Feagin, *Racist America: Roots, Current Realities, and Future Reparations* (New York: Routledge, 2001), pp. 19-20; Philomena Essed, *Understanding Everyday Racism* (Newbury Park, Calif.: Sage Books, 1991), p. 20.

21. Feagin, *Racist America*, pp. 19-20.

that sought to repel Black people in the United States seemed to grow after Black people ceased to be slaves.[22] That race as a moral problem, and Blacks, in particular, as a "problem people," have been deeply and powerfully engraved in the mores of the United States has been well summarized by the Swedish economist and political philosopher Gunnar Myrdal:

> There is a "Negro problem" in the United States and most Americans are aware of it, although it assumes varying forms and intensity in different regions of the country and among diverse groups of the American people. Americans have to react to it, politically as citizens and, where there are Negroes present in the community, privately as neighbors.
>
> To the great majority of white Americans the Negro problem has distinctly negative connotations. It suggests something difficult to settle and equally difficult to leave alone. It is embarrassing. It makes for moral uneasiness. The very presence of the Negro in America; his [sic] fate in this country through slavery, Civil War and Reconstruction; his recent career and his present status; his accommodation; his protest and his aspiration; in fact his entire biological, historical and social existence as a participant American represent to the ordinary white man in the North as well as in the South an anomaly in the very structure of American society. To many, this takes on the proportion of a menace — biological, economic, social, cultural, and, at times, political. This anxiety may be mingled with a feeling of individual and collective guilt. A few see the problem as a challenge to statesmanship. To all it is a trouble.[23]

In 1900 the Black genius W. E. B. Du Bois declared, "The problem of the 20th century will be the problem of the color line: the relationship of the white races of Europe and America to the darker races of Asia, Africa, Latin America, and the Islands of the sea."[24] Three years later, Du Bois

22. Tocqueville, *Democracy in America*, p. 330. This is a curious observation for today's reader since *Democracy in America* was published in 1835 (Volume I) and 1840 (Volume II), well before abolition. I assume, then, that Tocqueville is referring to runaway slaves and/or to those set free for one reason or another.

23. Gunnar Myrdal, *An American Dilemma*, Vol. 1: *The Negro in White America* (New York: McGraw-Hill, 1964), p. lxix.

24. William Edward Burghardt Du Bois, "To the Nations of the World," in *W. E. B. Du Bois: A Reader*, ed. David Levering Lewis (New York: Henry Holt, 1995), p. 639. Primary

asked the question many White Americans wanted to know about Black people: "How does it feel to be a problem?"[25]

According to historian George Fredrickson, racism is said to be present whenever the antipathy or hostility of one ethnic group or people toward another "is expressed and acted upon with a single mindedness and brutality that go far beyond the group-centered prejudice and snobbery that seem to constitute an almost universal human failing."[26] Racism is more than simple-minded ethnocentric dislike and distrust of the "other." The word "racism" came into popular (that is, common) usage in the 1930s, "when a new word was required to describe the theories on which the Nazis based their persecutions of the Jews."[27] However, the phenomenon of "racism" existed well before the coinage of the word that is used to describe it today.

A critical dimension of racism is the systemic (or structural) character of group belief in a particular race's inherent biological, social, cultural, and/or political inferiority. As Allan A. Boesak has correctly pointed out,

> Racism is not merely attitudinal, it is structural. It is not merely a vague feeling of racial superiority, it is a system of domination, complete with the structures of domination — social, political, and economic . . . racism excludes groups on the basis of race or color . . . for the purpose of subjugating or of maintaining subjugation.[28]

Similarly, pointing toward the crucial systemic character of American racism in particular, Charles Lawrence, writing for the *Stanford Law Review*, has correctly pointed out that

> Racism in America is much more complex than either the conscious conspiracy of a power elite or simple delusion of a few ignorant bigots.

---

source: the *Report of the Pan-African Conference, held July 23-25, 1900 at Westminster Town Hall, Westminster S.W.* (London, 1900), pp. 10-12.

25. Du Bois, *The Souls of Black Folk* (New York: Alfred A. Knopf, 1903; Everyman's Library Edition, 1993), p. 7.

26. George M. Fredrickson, *Racism: A Short History* (Princeton, N.J.: Princeton University Press, 2002), p. 1.

27. Fredrickson, *Racism*, p. 5.

28. Allan A. Boesak, *If This Is Treason, I Am Guilty* (Grand Rapids, Mich.: William B. Eerdmans, 1987), p. 3.

It is part of our common historical experience and therefore, a part of our culture. It arises from the assumptions we have learned to make about the world, ourselves and others as well as from the patterns of our most fundamental social activities.[29]

Racism, in summary, can be defined as race prejudice plus systemic power: that is, race prejudice of one or more cultural groups of people(s) against another cultural group(s), plus the power to oppress and exploit other group(s) in a comprehensive, significant fashion. Racism is always a systemic category in my view; an individual may possess race prejudice, but racism is not an individual phenomenon.[30] Thus I do not believe, for example, that Black people *in the United States* can be classified as racist since they, as a group, do not possess the requisite collective systemic power to negatively and comprehensively affect another cultural group's "being-in-the-world." Black people, however, are quite capable of race prejudice, which I view as a more individual and/or socially localized state of mind and being which, similar to racism, can become virulent and produce deadly practical results. It should also be said that racist peoples need not have superior numbers but could be a relative minority in possession of overwhelming political, economic, and police/military powers, which they employ against a majority. Of course, the former White South African apartheid regime is but one historical example of this, although probably the most well-known.

The Development of Anti-Black Racism

One of the two principal forms of modern racism is the color-coded, White-over-Black variety, which is mainly a product of the modern period. The other principal form of racism can be seen in the racial anti-Semitism of the twentieth century. Contemporary anti-Semitism has medieval antecedents (especially among Christians) and could be seen "in the popular tendency to see Jews as agents of the Devil and, thus, for all practical pur-

29. Charles Lawrence, "The Id, The Ego and Equal Protection: Reckoning with Unconscious Racism," *Stanford Law Review* 39 (1987): 317; 330.

30. For a good and brief summary of racism as group phenomenon see C. Eric Lincoln, *Coming Through the Fire: Surviving Race and Place in America* (Durham, N.C.: Duke University Press, 1996), pp. 145-47.

poses, beyond redemption and outside the circle of potential Christian fellowship. . . ."[31] We will now turn to focus on anti-Black White racism.

According to Fredrickson, European perceptions of peoples of darker hues were ambivalent during the medieval period. As a matter of fact, according to Fredrickson, in some cases "there was a definite tendency towards Negrophilia in parts of northern and western Europe in the late Middle Ages, and the common presumption that dark pigmentation inspired instant revulsion on the part of light-skinned Europeans is, if not completely false, at least highly misleading."[32] Regarding the medieval European ambivalence toward dark-skinned peoples, Fredrickson goes on to argue that

> Before the middle of the fifteenth century, Europeans had little or no direct contact with sub-Saharan Africans. Artistic and literary representations of these distant and exotic peoples ranged from the monstrous and horrifying to the saintly and heroic. On the one hand, devils were sometimes pictured as having dark skins and what may appear to be African features, and the executioners of martyrs were often portrayed as black men. The symbolic association of blackness with evil and death and whiteness with goodness and purity unquestionably had some effect in predisposing light-skinned people against those with darker pigmentation. But the significance of this cultural proclivity can be exaggerated. If black *always* had unfavorable connotations, why did many orders of priests and nuns wear black instead of white or some other color?[33]

Despite the fact that representations of Black Africans were ambivalent in the twelfth through fourteenth centuries, Fredrickson does finally (and correctly) contend that Negrophilia was never well established among Europeans, nor did the Negrophilia that was present arrest the development of anti-Black racism.

31. Fredrickson, *Racism*, pp. 26; 18-26.

32. Fredrickson, *Racism*, p. 26.

33. Fredrickson, *Racism*, pp. 26; 26-28. See also Winthrop D. Jordan, *White over Black: American Attitudes Toward the Negro, 1550-1812* (Baltimore: Penguin Books, 1969), pp. 4-11; Jean Devisse, *The Image of the Black in Western Art*, Vol. 2, *From the Early Christian Era to the "Age of Discovery,"* pt. 1, "From the Demonic Threat to the Incarnation of Sainthood" (Cambridge, Mass.: Harvard University Press, 1979), passim.

The representation of the African as Christian saint or hero was admittedly a relatively superficial cultural phenomenon. It provided no warrant for expecting that Europeans would be greatly influenced by it when they came into sustained contact with Africans under conditions that encouraged other attitudes. It does, however, weaken the argument that Europeans were strongly prejudiced against blacks before the beginning of the slave trade and that color-coded racism preceded enslavement. The one place where one can perhaps find an anticipation of antiblack racism in the late Middle Ages is in fourteenth and early-fifteenth century Iberia. Here the association of blackness with slavery was apparently already being made. According to historian James H. Sweet, it was during the period when Christians and Muslims coexisted in Iberia that the former learned from the latter to identify blackness with servitude.[34]

The concept of "race" as a scientific and moral category is a modern one, with antecedents in a certain stream of ancient Near Eastern religion and ancient Greek culture. An early modern and commonplace rationale for European and Anglo American exploitation, genocide, and enslavement of non-White peoples drew significantly on an ancient religious myth based on the biblical narrative of Noah and his sons (Genesis 9–10). This ancient story relates an episode in which the intoxicated patriarch Noah is seen naked by his youngest son Ham (the father of Canaan) as he lay uncovered in his tent. Ham goes back outside the tent and tells his two brothers, Shem and Japheth, of their father's uncovered state. Shem and Japheth, walking into the tent backward and with faces turned away, respectfully cover their drunken father without gazing upon his nakedness. The unfortunate consequence of this perceived act of disrespect for Ham was that his son Canaan was cursed by Noah and informed that he was to become the slave of his brethren. Drawing on work done by historian Winthrop Jordan, sociologist Joe Feagin has pointed out regarding the myth of Ham that

A later version of this religious myth views Ham as African and as suffering the divine punishment of his descendants being made [slaves]

34. Fredrickson, *Racism,* p. 29; James H. Sweet, "The Iberian Roots of American Racist Thought," *William and Mary Quarterly* 54 (1997): 143-66.

to other peoples, the descendants of Ham's brothers. However, in the [biblical text] there is nothing about Ham's African characteristics. It was later, in the Talmudic and Midrashic (Jewish) religious tradition, that Ham (or Canaan) was said to have "darkened the faces of mankind" and thus was asserted to be father to African peoples.[35]

The mythical story of Ham was picked up in pre-Enlightenment Christian communities by the 1500s, and became relatively common by the seventeenth century, first more as an *explanation* of color and then later as a *justification* for colonial European subjugation and enslavement of African peoples in the Americas.[36]

By the eighteenth century, "the Age of Enlightenment," religious and aesthetic conceptions of race converged in the production of a "scientific" dogma of White supremacy which would contribute heavily to a more disciplined and systematic rationale for penal notions of Black incorrigibility. The foundations of the modern development of "race" as a significant biological, civic, and political phenomenon did not rely solely on a religious foundation, but also involved what philosopher of religion Cornel West, drawing partly from the work of George Mosse, characterized as "the recovery of classical antiquity in the modern West." The content of this recovery was a "normative gaze" or "ideal of beauty, proportion, and human form, and standards of moderation, self-control, and harmony" drawn primarily from classical Greek aesthetics.[37] West argues that, "the role of classical aesthetic and cultural norms in the emergence of white supremacy as an object of modern discourse cannot be underestimated."[38]

Greek aesthetic and cultural norms were intentionally projected and

35. Feagin, *Racist America*, p. 74. See also Jordan, *White Over Black*, pp. 18-19.

36. Feagin, *Racist America*, p. 74, and Jordan, *White Over Black*, pp. 18-20. It should be noted that historians Bernard Lewis and William McKee Evans have produced considerable evidence supporting the view that the Muslim world preceded the Christian in representing sub-Saharan Africans as descendants of Ham, who were "condemned to perpetual bondage" because of their ancestor's ill-treatment of Noah. See Fredrickson, *Racism*, pp. 29; 43-47; Bernard Lewis, *Race and Slavery in the Middle East* (Oxford: Oxford University Press, 1990), pp. 44-45; 55; William McKee Evans, "From the Land of Canaan to the Land of Guinea," *American Historical Review* 85 (1980): 15-43.

37. Cornel West, *Prophesy Deliverance!: An Afro-American Revolutionary Christianity* (Philadelphia: Westminster Press, 1982), pp. 53-54. See also George L. Mosse, *Toward the Final Solution: A History of European Racism* (New York: Howard Fertig, 1997).

38. West, *Prophesy Deliverance*, p. 54.

promoted by numerous influential Enlightenment philosophers and artists. West argues that the most famous of these was J. J. Winckelmann (1717-1768), author of the widely read book, *History of Ancient Art*, which characterizes ancient Greece as a world of beautiful bodies: "[Winckelmann] laid down rules — in art and aesthetics — that should govern the size of eyes and eyebrows, of collarbones, hands, feet and especially noses."[39] Not only was the epitome of physical beauty thought to reside in the Greek bodily form, so too was virtue or moral excellence. Winckelmann, without ever setting foot in Greece and seeing almost no original Greek art along the way to being murdered in midlife, argued that "the expression in the figures of the Greeks reveal a great and composed soul in the midst of passions."[40]

In a vein similar to that of Winckelmann, Johann Friedrich Blumenbach (1752-1840), one of the founders of modern anthropology, praised the symmetrical face of Europeans as the most beautiful human face because it was the closest approximation of the "divine" found in the anatomical proportions found in Greek art, specifically in Greek sculpture.[41] In his essay entitled, "Varieties of the Human Species," Georges Léopold Cuvier (1769-1832), takes Winckelmann's and Blumenbach's sentiments to their anticipated conclusion: "The race from which we are descended has been called Caucasian . . . the handsomest on earth."[42]

There have been numerous noteworthy premodern racist viewpoints derived from the ancients and aimed directly and indirectly at non-Whites, particularly at Black peoples. Drawing on the work of Winthrop Jordan and Thomas Gossett, West has noted, for example, that

39. West, *Prophesy Deliverance*, p. 54. Note that Paracelsus (1493-1541), perhaps meaning "higher than high," is the pseudonym of Philippus Aureolus Theophrastus Bombastus (Baumastus) von Hohenheim, reformer of pharmacology and medicine, chemist, and philosopher. Giordano Bruno (1548-1600) was an Italian philosopher trained as a Dominican who was eventually burned at the stake in Rome as a heretic. Lucilio Vanini (1585-1619) was an Italian philosopher who gave himself the name Julius Caesar. He was condemned and burned alive at the stake at Toulouse, France, for atheism and witchcraft, and for claiming that humans evolved from apes.

40. Quoted in West, *Prophesy Deliverance*, p. 54. Quote also cited in George L. Mosse, *Toward the Final Solution*, p. 10.

41. West, *Prophesy Deliverance*, p. 57.

42. Georges Léopold Cuvier, "Varieties of the Human Species," in *Race and the Enlightenment*, ed. Emmanuel Chukwudi Eze (Cambridge, Mass.: Blackwell, 1997), pp. 104-108.

[I]n 1520 Paracelsus held that black and primitive peoples had a separate origin from Europeans. In 1591, Giordano Bruno made a similar claim, but had in mind principally Jews and Ethiopians. And Lucilio Vanini posited that Ethiopians had apes for ancestors and had once walked on all fours. Since theories of the separate origin of races were in disagreement with the Roman Catholic Church, Bruno and Vanini underwent similar punishment: both were burned at the stake. Of course, biblically based accounts of racial inferiority flourished, but the authority of the church prohibited the proliferation of nonreligious, that is, protomodern, accounts of racial inferiority.[43]

West goes on to argue (and this is a critically important point) that, "*What is distinctive about the role of classical aesthetic and cultural norms at the advent of modernity is that they provided an acceptable authority for the idea of white supremacy, an acceptable authority that was closely linked with the major authority on truth and knowledge in the modern world, namely, the institution of science.*"[44]

While it is true that the "scientific" structuring of racial difference became systematized during the Enlightenment, the Enlightenment was never a monolithic movement. Indeed, the philosopher Allen Wood is correct that "its underlying principles have always been subject to change, reinterpretation, and continuing dispute." Nonetheless, some of the most rudimentary affirmations of the Enlightenment are still debated in American civil and political discourse today: "the expansion of liberty in human thought and action, equality in the social, political and economic spheres, and tolerance regarding religious and cultural diversity."[45] Yet the "twin" sciences of anthropology and physical geography as developed by the eighteenth-century European founders of the Enlightenment often belied the lofty goals of mutual respect and self-esteem. Indeed, respect for the individual rights and equal worth of *all* human beings as coworkers in the evolution of broad and interactive cosmopolitan human communities and

---

43. West, *Prophesy Deliverance*, p. 54; Jordan, *White Over Black*, pp. 217-218; Thomas Gossett, *Race: The History of an Idea in America* (Oxford: Oxford University Press, 1997), pp. 32-34.

44. West, *Prophesy Deliverance*, p. 54.

45. Allen W. Wood, *Kant's Ethical Thought* (New Haven: Yale University Press, 1999), p. 1.

cultures was frequently undermined along a racial fault line by some of the West's most prominent thinkers.

Philosopher Emmanuel Chukwudi Eze has argued for example that Immanuel Kant's notions of racial difference "sought to establish an inherent human rational capacity responsible for historical progress from the 'primitive' to the 'civilized,' partly by classifying mankind [sic] into various races on the basis of skin color."[46] Eze reminds us that in 1756 Kant was the first to introduce geography into the curriculum of study at the University of Königsberg. Later, in the winter of 1772-3, Kant began teaching anthropology at Königsberg. According to Eze, "it was the first such program of study in any German university."[47] Eze points out that, "Quite often, teachers and students of the history of modern science and the history of modern philosophy pay little or no attention to the enormous amount of research and writing undertaken and accomplished by the philosophical luminaries of the eighteenth century, the Age of Reason. For example, in nearly all standard programs of study of Immanuel Kant, rarely is it noted that Kant devoted the largest period of his career to research in, and teaching of, anthropology and geography."[48] Kant offered more courses in his career in anthropology and geography (72) than in subjects he is more noted for: logic (54), metaphysics (28), moral philosophy (20), and theoretical physics (20). Eze goes on to argue that since "questions of race and of the biological, geographical, and cultural distribution of humans on earth occupied a central place in both Kant's science of geography and anthropology, it can hardly be said that his interest in the 'race problem' was marginal to other aspects of his career."[49]

46. Immanuel Kant, "A Review of J. G. von Herder's Ideas on the Philosophy of the History of Mankind," in *Race and the Enlightenment,* ed. Emmanuel Chukwudi Eze (Cambridge, Mass.: Blackwell, 1997), p. 65. For a good very brief summary of the eighteenth-century invention of the inheritability of race, and the related understanding of the relationship between genetics and social status, see Dorothy E. Roberts, "The Genetic Tie," in *Critical White Studies: Looking Behind the Mirror,* ed. Richard Delgado and Jean Stefancic (Philadelphia: Temple University Press, 1997), pp. 186-89.

47. Eze, *Race and the Enlightenment,* p. 2.

48. Eze, *Race and the Enlightenment,* p. 2.

49. Eze, *Race and the Enlightenment,* p. 2. It should be noted that even some contemporary social and political conservatives acknowledge Kant's racism (as well as that of other major Enlightenment philosophers). For example, while arguing that racism "did not make up the main part of their philosophy," Dinesh D'Souza admits that, "We see racism . . . in the greatest thinkers of the Enlightenment. Hume, Voltaire, Montesquieu, Kant, and Hegel were

It is apparent to me that the powerful currents of contemporary racism in the United States have modern roots in the uglier streams of the Enlightenment. The Enlightenment development of racial differentiation set some of the core foundations for notions of the natural inferiority of peoples of darker hues. In particular, European notions of the innate intellectual, social, and political inferiority of peoples of African decent was assumed by the founders of the American Republic and, consequently, have always had considerable impact on notions of Black incorrigibility in penal theory.

In a vein in sync with that of Kant, basic beliefs and tenants concerning *homo sapiens* in the system of nature were developed in Carl Linnaeus' *The System of Nature* (1735). In this work, Linnaeus articulated and advanced a notion that was pervasive in the eighteenth century, namely (as well summarized by Eze) that

> an underlying hierarchical order in nature was established by God, or by providence itself, and that it is the duty of humans to discover this order and to classify everything that exists from human to fauna and flora accordingly. This worldview led many writers . . . to the assumption that their classification of humans into races and their theories about this classification were guaranteed by an inviolable "order of nature."[50]

In the introduction to *The System of Nature*, entitled "The God-given Order of Nature," Linnaeus sets a standard for human classification which I believe still infects the popular conscious and unconscious view of humanity in general, and contributes to penal philosophy in particular:

Mammalia

Order I. Primates

Foreteeth cutting: upper 4; parallel teats 2, pectoral

HOMO
Sapiens. Diurnal; varying by education and situation

---

among the many who entertained racist views. . . ." See D'Souza, "Ignoble Savages," in *Critical White Studies: Looking Behind the Mirror,* ed. Richard Delgado and Jean Stefancic (Philadelphia: Temple University Press, 1997), p. 62.

50. Eze, *Race and the Enlightenment,* p. 10.

1 Four-footed, mute, hairy. *Wild man.*
2 Copper-coloured, choleric, erect. *American.*
   Hair black, straight, thick; *nostrils* wide; *face* harsh; *beard* scanty; obstinate, content, free. *Paints* himself with fine red lines. Regulated by customs.
3 Fair, sanguine, brawny. *European.*
   Hair yellow, brown, flowing; *eyes* blue; gently, acute, inventive. *Covered* with close vestments. *Governed* by laws.
4 Sooty, melancholy, rigid.
   Hair black; *eyes* dark; *fevere,* haughty, covetous. *Covered* with loose garments. *Governed* by opinions.
5 Black, phlegmatic, relaxed.
   Hair black, frizzled; *skin* silky; *nose* flat; *lips* tumid; crafty, indolent, negligent. *Anoints* himself with grease. *Governed* by caprice.[51]

Following in the ("rational") European logic of Linnaeus nearly a century later, Georg Wilhelm Friedrich Hegel, in his "Lectures on the Philosophy of World History" (1822-1828), argued that

The characteristic feature of the Negroes is that their consciousness has not yet reached an awareness of any substantial objectivity — for example, of God or the law — in which the will of man could participate and in which he could become aware of his own being. The African, in his undifferentiated and concentrated unity, has not yet succeeded in making this distinction between himself as an individual and his essential universality, so that he knows nothing of an absolute being which is other and higher than his own self. Thus, man as we find him in Africa has not progressed beyond his immediate existence ... he is dominated by passion, and is nothing more than a savage. All our observations of African man show him as living in a state of savagery and barbarism, and he remains in this state to the present day. The Negro is an example of animal man in all his savagery and lawlessness, and if we wish to understand him at all, we must put aside all our European attitudes. We must not think of a spiritual God or of moral laws; to comprehend him correctly, we must abstract from all rever-

51. Eze, *Race and the Enlightenment,* p. 13.

ence and morality, and from everything we call feeling. All this is foreign to man in his immediate existence, and nothing consonant with humanity is to be found in his character. For this very reason, we cannot properly feel ourselves into his nature, no more than that of a dog, or of a Greek as he kneels down before the statue of Zeus.[52]

The posthumous edition of Kant's published lectures, *Physical Geography*, in Volumes 2 and 8 of his *Gesammelte Schriften* (Berlin: Reimer, 1900-66), also convey much of the same logic concerning racial hierarchy or what he called the "Innate characteristics of the human being considered throughout the world": "Humanity is at its greatest perfection in the race of whites. The yellow Indians do have a meager talent. The Negroes are far below them and at the lowest point are a part of the American peoples."[53] Kant goes on to argue that

The inhabitant of the temperate parts of the world, above all the central part, has a more beautiful body, works harder, is more jocular, more controlled in his passions, more intelligent than any other race of people in the world. That is why at all points in time these peoples have educated the others and controlled them with weapons.[54]

The superior peoples of temperate climates to whom Kant refers are the Greeks, Romans, ancient Nordics, and Europeans after Columbus's "discoveries." The "others" in need of education and control are Africans, Negroes, Indians, and other lower-status peoples.

Philosopher Tsenay Serequeberhan has pointed out that the eighteenth-century philosopher David Hume (1711-1776) was another pivotal precursor of thought whose opinions were considered of cardinal importance on matters of racial difference. Hume asserted that "I am apt to suspect that the negroes, and in general all the other species of men (for there are four or five different kinds) to be naturally inferior to whites. There never was a civilized nation of any other complexion than white."[55] Sereque-

52. George Wilhelm Friedrich Hegel, "Geographical Basis of World History," in *Race and the Enlightenment*, ed. Eze, pp. 127-128.

53. Immanuel Kant, *Physical Geography*, in *Race and the Enlightenment*, ed. Eze, p. 63.

54. Kant, *Physical Geography*, in *Race and the Enlightenment*, ed. Eze, p. 64.

55. Tsenay Serequeberhan, *The Hermeneutics of African Philosophy: Horizon and Discourse* (New York: Routledge, 1994), p. 61.

berhan goes on to point out that, in agreement with Hume, Kant asserted that, "so fundamental is the difference between the two races of men, and it appears to be as great in regard to mental capacities as in color."[56]

Two of the most prestigious and popular sources of eighteenth-century support for the widespread and alienating belief that racial differences were fixed in nature were the *Encyclopédie* and the *Encyclopaedia Britannica*. For example, one cannot overestimate the influence of the entry "Nègre" in what Eze has called one of the monuments of the Enlightenment, the *Encyclopédie ou Dictionnaire raisonné des sciences, des arts, et des métiers*, co-edited by Denis Diderot and Jean le Rond d'Alembert, and published from 1751 to 1772. The entry was written by M. le Romain.

Nègre

Man who inhabits different parts of the earth, from the Tropic of Cancer to the Tropic of Capricorn. Africa has no other inhabitants but the blacks. Not only the color, but also the facial traits distinguish them from other men: large and flat noses, thick lips, and wool instead of hair. They appear to constitute a new species of mankind. If one moves further away from the Equator toward the Antarctic, the black skin becomes lighter, but the ugliness remains: one finds there this same wicked people that inhabits the African Meridian. If one goes east, the features soften and become more regular, but the skin color remains black as inside Africa. After these [eastern peoples], one encounters a greatly tanned people, distinguishable from others by their narrow and obliquely positioned long eyes. If we pass through this vast part of the world which appears to be separate from Europe, from Africa and Asia, one finds — if several travelers are to be believed — a different human variety. There is absolutely no white person: the land is peopled by red nations tanned in a thousand ways. . . . Many physicians have researched the causes of the blackness of the negro. The major opinions that the physicians hold on this matter can be reduced to two: one attributes the cause to bile, the other to some fluid contained in the veins of the mucous membrane.[57]

56. Serequeberhan, *Hermeneutics of African Philosophy*, p. 61. The comments attributed to Hume and Kant by Serequeberhan are as quoted by Richard H. Popkin in his essay "Hume's Racism," *The Philosophical Forum* 9:2-3 (Winter-Spring 1977-1978); for Hume's remarks, see p. 213; for Kant's, see p. 218.

57. Eze, *Race and the Enlightenment*, p. 91.

In a similar vein, consider the following extract from the first American edition of the *Encyclopaedia Britannica* in 1798:

> **Negro**
>
> Negro, *Homo pelli nigra,* a name given to a variety of the human species, who are entirely black, and are found in the torrid zone, especially in that part of Africa which lies within the tropics. In the complexion of negroes we meet with various shades; but they likewise differ far from other men in all the features of their face. Round cheeks, high cheek-bones, a forehead somewhat elevated, a short, broad, flat nose, thick lips, small ears, ugliness, and irregularity of shape, characterize their external appearance. The negro women have the loins greatly depressed, and very large buttocks, which give the back the shape of a saddle. Vices the most notorious seem to be the portion of this unhappy race: idleness, treachery, revenge, cruelty, impudence, stealing, lying, profanity, debauchery, nastiness and intemperance, are said to have extinguished the principles of natural law, and to have silenced the reproofs of conscience. They are strangers to every sentiment of compassion, and are an awful example of the corruption of man when left to himself.[58]

Considering even this all too brief outline of the development of alienating racial theorizing during the Enlightenment, it is perhaps not unreasonable to suggest that today's criminal justice discourse and practice functions as an ongoing representation of the highly influential Enlightenment construction of "race" as a biological and aesthetic human category with profound social, political, and economic significance.

Anti-Black Racism and Imprisonment

The general and popular refusal to acknowledge that the criminal justice system is in some significant ways a living monument to Enlightenment racist discourse and practice contributes to the nation's significant levels of interpersonal and intergroup alienation. Philosopher Angela Y. Davis argues that, "Because the racist-informed discourse on criminality goes

58. Eze, *Race and the Enlightenment,* pp. 93-94.

largely unchallenged Black male bodies are treated as dispensable by communities in the 'free world' that have all but forsaken those who are marked as criminal."[59] As Davis correctly observes, many hundreds of thousands of Black men are currently trapped in a proliferating web of state and privately run prisons. Jerome G. Miller, president of the National Center on Institutions and Alternatives, argues that Black men today are the primary targets of a criminal justice system mission to "search and destroy."[60] Ken Roth, executive director of Human Rights Watch, argues that "[t]hese racial disparities are a national scandal." This scandal, according to Roth, threatens democratic notions of fairness: "Black and white drug offenders get radically different treatment in the American justice system. This is not only profoundly unfair to blacks, it also corrodes the American ideal of equal justice for all."[61]

Roth's observation echoes those of Steven Donziger: "There are so many more African-Americans than whites in our prisons that the difference cannot be explained by higher crime among African-Americans — racial discrimination is also at work, and it penalizes African-Americans at almost every juncture in the criminal justice system."[62] Donziger goes on to argue that whether the disparity in Black rates of imprisonment is caused by higher crime among that population or discrimination or both, "this country is on the verge of a social catastrophe because of the sheer number of African-Americans behind bars — numbers that continue to rise with breathtaking speed and frightening implications."[63] The reason that this constitutes a social catastrophe is that "our criminal justice policies are preventing many African-Americans from claiming their stake in the American dream, thereby contributing to the destruction of our national ideal of racial harmony."[64]

59. Angela Y. Davis, "Race, Gender, and Prison History: From the Convict Lease System to the Supermax Prison," in *Prison Masculinities*, ed. Don Sabo, Terry A. Kupers, and Willie London (Philadelphia: Temple University Press, 2001), p. 35.

60. See Jerome Miller, *Search and Destroy: African-American Males in the Criminal Justice System* (Cambridge: Cambridge University Press, 1996).

61. Quoted in Michael A. Fletcher, "War on Drugs Sends Blacks to Prison at 13 Times Rate of Whites," *Washington Post*, June 8, 2000.

62. Steven R. Donziger, ed., *The Real War on Crime: The National Report of the National Criminal Justice Commission* (New York: HarperPerennial, 1996), p. 99.

63. Donziger, *The Real War on Crime*, p. 99.

64. Donziger, *The Real War on Crime*, p. 99.

Angela Davis has argued that the current rise in the numbers of imprisoned Black men and women in particular, and "people of color" in general, is because of "the peculiarly racialized and gendered history of punishment in the United States, that has, in part, facilitated the structural and ideological transformation of the penal system into a Prison Industrial Complex that imprisons, dehumanizes, and exploits ever-increasing numbers of people, the vast majority of whom are poor and black."[65] On Davis's view,

> It is not a coincidence that rehabilitation, the historical goal of the prison, has receded theoretically and practically as U.S. prisons have come to house spiraling numbers of black men. The current notion that the "criminals" with whom prisons are overcrowded are largely beyond the pale of rehabilitation — that is, that "nothing works" — is very much connected with the fact that, in the contemporary era, the combined terms "black" and "male" have become virtually synonymous with "criminal" in the popular imagination.[66]

Indeed, narratives of rehabilitation, whether constructed under philosophical, religious, or medical frameworks, have historically been informed by certain racial assumptions. So too has the category of recidivism figured prominently in measurements of success of rehabilitation. Law enforcement officials have accepted no uniform definition of recidivism. Criminologists Richard Hawkins and Geoffrey Alpert argue that official measurements of recidivism are conservative and point out that, "One reviewer of various recidivism definitions notes thirteen different indicators of 'failure,' ranging from a recorded police contact to being returned to prison."[67]

The current understanding of imprisonment as the inevitable destiny of significant numbers of Black men has a long history in U.S. penology. Hence it really should be no surprise that today's prisons, populated far disproportionately by Black men often viewed as incorrigible, are being increasingly divested of educational, recreational, therapeutic, and other

65. Davis, "Race, Gender, and Prison History," p. 36.
66. Davis, "Race, Gender, and Prison History," p. 36.
67. Richard Hawkins and Geoffrey P. Alpert, *American Prison Systems: Punishment and Justice* (Englewood Cliffs, N.J.: Prentice Hall, 1989), pp. 198-99.

programs historically associated with rehabilitation projects. No longer, for the most part, is the early architectural and theoretical plan of the modern prison (both centered on the moral reformation of the individual) in evidence.

While Davis and many others imply that the nation ought to champion a return to rehabilitation as a goal of the prison, I have already suggested above that even that goal as generally practiced tends to reinforce an atomistic social view of individuals and social processes. Excessively individualistic or not, the goal of criminal rehabilitation has historically never really been intended for Black men and others who were not included in the Enlightenment-age assumption that reason formed the core of every human being.[68] Indeed, modernity's vision of inevitable progress, even for criminals, has always contained a strong racial bias and caveat, regardless of whether the purpose of punishment was viewed primarily as reformation or retributive control. The philosopher David T. Goldberg has noted that the "defining of humanity in relation to rationality clearly prefaces modernity's emphasis on rational capacity as a crucial differentia of racial groups."[69] And this perceived difference has always colored — pun intended — the way society punishes.

Manhood and Black Incorrigibility

In the context of modernity's racialized assumptions about and constructions of rational humanity, the penitentiary was largely conceived of as an institution for the reformation of White men. (This notwithstanding the contention by some scholars that "the term 'penitentiary' originated from a plan in England to incarcerate 'penitent' prostitutes."[70]) Underlying the goal of reformation for White male offenders was the critical Enlighten-

---

68. See, for example, Paul Gilroy, *The Black Atlantic: Modernity and Double Consciousness* (Cambridge, Mass.: Harvard University Press, 1993), pp. 1-40 (especially 8-11); 49.

69. Quoted in Angela Y. Davis, "Race, Gender, and Prison History," p. 37. See also, David T. Goldberg, *Racist Culture: Philosophy and the Politics of Meaning* (Cambridge: Cambridge University Press, 1993), p. 23. Of course (in the words of Davis), "modernity's construction of rational humanity was not only racialized; it was gendered as well"; see Davis, "Race, Gender, and Prison History," p. 37.

70. Davis, "Race, Gender, and Prison History," p. 37. See also Hawkins and Alpert, *American Prison Systems*, p. 30.

ment conception of manhood, which was tied to the expressive language of freedom in the minds of the American founders. Mark Kann, a professor of political science at the University of Southern California, has argued that Benjamin Franklin's proclamation that his grandfather's essay on liberty was written with "manly freedom," and Thomas Paine's explication that *Common Sense* is what prepared the way for "manly principles of independence," laid some of the significant foundation for perceptions of race, crime, and punishment. Kann goes on to point out that John Adams, too, "praised his ancestors for their 'manly assertion of . . . rights' against tyranny, while Thomas Jefferson applauded his American brethren for demonstrating 'manly spirit' by declaring independence."[71] While the founders' use of gendered language to urge true men into battle was typical of the ancient fusion of manhood to militarism, connecting concepts of manhood to the restoration of wrongdoers to a state of freedom was new, according to Kann: "[the founders'] use of manhood to promote self-discipline in the exercise of liberty, to deter and punish criminal activity, and to rehabilitate some convicts and restore their liberty was innovative."[72]

In the aftermath of leading a successful revolution against the British in the name of liberty, the founders of the republic soon encountered what they took to be men's tendency toward licentious behavior. They came to view fairly commonplace male vices like swearing, gambling, drinking, promiscuity, and greed as threats to the new republic because such vices fostered conflict and criminality.[73] Viewing vice as ultimately leading to criminality that would subvert the foundations of society, the founders "urged men to consult religious doctrine, examine enlightened self-interest, commit to republican virtue, and follow their moral sensibilities to promote self-restraint in the exercise of liberty, social harmony, and

71. Mark E. Kann, "Penitence for the Privileged: Manhood, Race, and Penitentiaries in Early America," in *Prison Masculinities,* ed. Sabo et al., p. 21. Also see Benjamin Franklin, "The Autobiography," in *The Autobiography and Other Writings,* ed. L. Jesse Lemisch (New York: New American Library, 1961), p. 18; Thomas Paine, "Common Sense," in *The Complete Writings of Thomas Paine,* vol. 1, ed. Philip S. Foner (New York: Citadel Press, 1945), p. 40; John Adams, "Dissertation of the Canon and Feudal Law" (1765), in *The Political Writings of John Adams,* ed. George W. Carey (Washington, D.C.: Gateway, 2001), p. 16; Thomas Jefferson, "Declaration of Independence" (1776), in *The Portable Thomas Jefferson,* ed. Merrill D. Peterson (New York: Viking, 1975), pp. 236, 240.

72. Kann, "Penitence for the Privileged," p. 21.

73. Kann, "Penitence for the Privileged," p. 21.

law-abiding behavior. They also invoked the dominant norms of manhood to prompt men to moderate their conduct."[74]

In general, the founders viewed "manhood" as a mixture of individual freedom and family responsibility. This combination was seen as a crucial source of social order and stable, responsible citizenship. This view of manhood was relied upon to deter White men from falling into criminal conduct, as well as to punish and reform those who did engage in criminal activity.[75] Kann summarized the founders' appeal to manhood to deter and reform wrongdoing as follows:

> Prison reformers in the early republic threatened to deprive lawbreakers of their manly freedom and dignity by incarcerating them and isolating them from their families in newly conceived penitentiaries. Men who were actually convicted of crimes and imprisoned were encouraged to use their isolation as an opportunity to repent and reform in order to regain their manhood and liberty.[76]

From the foundations of the republic, the Enlightenment optimism of the founders with regard to deterring crime and reforming criminals had racial limits. Reflecting modernity's overarching regulation of "men of color," as well as women of all racial backgrounds, the founders saw in Black men reason's antithesis; that is, they saw creatures who were governed by nature, instinct, and the senses.[77] Davis correctly observes that with modernity came "the putative universality of reason [which] masked strong racial and gendered assumptions about the bodies in which universal reason resided."[78]

Most White leaders of the republic considered Black males inherently unmanly because they lacked individual independence and control of their families. The requirement of individual independence was that a mature male be "an autonomous thinker and actor," capable of disciplining his passions and impulses. Such a male routinely consulted reason, and relied on virtue to guide his actions.[79] Moreover, Kann argues that from

74. Kann, "Penitence for the Privileged," p. 21.
75. Kann, "Penitence for the Privileged," p. 21.
76. Kann, "Penitence for the Privileged," p. 21.
77. Davis, "Race, Gender, and Prison History," p. 37.
78. Davis, "Race, Gender, and Prison History," p. 37.
79. Kann, "Penitence for the Privileged," p. 23.

the point of view of White men of the eighteenth century, "A mature male was self-supporting, determined the nature and pace of his labor, and kept free of other men's patronage and government relief. He could afford to resist adverse pressures and exercise his own will to defend his liberty, property, and community. He was an independent agent of his personal and public destiny."[80]

Not only did White male notions of their own independence stand in opposition to subordination to other men in general, it stood in opposition to slavery in particular. Drawing on Judith Shklar's work on conceptions of citizenship in early America and Gary Nash's work on race, class, and politics, Kann contends that "a white male's sense of dignity, reputation, and public standing was a function of distinguishing himself 'from slaves and occasionally from women.' He measured his worth by his distance from dependency. The main marker of that distance was suffrage, which functioned as 'a certificate of full membership in society.' A man without the vote saw himself and was seen by others as slavish, effeminate, or childish."[81] With regard to the issue of family governance as a dimension of manliness, responsibilities included a patriarch's "provisioning and protecting his loved ones, continuing his family line, and caring for his posterity."[82] A patriarch's deep and abiding commitment to family provided an enduring foundation for societal stability and the social good. Here mature manhood was viewed as a critical joining of traditional patriarchal authority in the family to republican benevolence. As Kann points out, "Many founders saw patriarchal family status as a basis for citizenship." Indeed, independent manhood, family patriarchy, and social stability were nearly synonymous in early America.[83] It was thought by White male leaders of the early Republic that "males who exercised the self-discipline associated with independence, assumed the responsibilities of family life, and exhibited the long-term caring conducive to citizenship, would voluntarily limit licentiousness and obey legitimate laws."[84]

80. Kann, "Penitence for the Privileged," pp. 23-24.

81. Kann, "Penitence for the Privileged," p. 24. Also see Judith Shklar, *American Citizenship: The Quest for Inclusion* (Cambridge, Mass.: Harvard University Press, 1991), pp. 2, 15, 17; Gary Nash, *Race, Class, and Politics: Essays on American Colonial and Revolutionary Society* (Urbana: University of Illinois Press, 1986), p. 248.

82. Kann, "Penitence for the Privileged," p. 24.

83. Kann, "Penitence for the Privileged," p. 24.

84. Kann, "Penitence for the Privileged," p. 24.

As already suggested above, with the assumption that even some White men would eventually run afoul of the law, authorities relied on state coercion to deter criminal activity and punish criminals. But traditional state coercion was infused with an Enlightenment ethic of benevolent reform for White men only. Reformer optimism about penal rehabilitation did not extend to Black convicts who were, by nature, devoid of manly freedom, which was predicated on being self-guided and regulated by mature reason. Moreover, because Black men lacked individual independence and control of their families, many White leaders considered them inherently unmanly. Kann explains that

> This putative absence of manhood precluded public officials from deterring and punishing black men's crimes by threatening to confiscate their manhood. It also eliminated any incentive for rehabilitation, because black convicts had no manly freedom to redeem. Black convicts were often considered incorrigibles. For them, the new penitentiaries were not innovative houses of penitence but old-style prisons for punishment.[85]

Complicating the problem for Black men in early America was the reality that, juxtaposed to White men, they were not attributed a clear gender identity. They were "outcasts from humanity" who "lacked the manly ability to discipline their passions and the manly freedom to govern, provision, and protect their families."[86] Officials in the revolutionary period sometimes shamed disorderly White men by associating them with Black men. For example, public degradation of a White offender sometimes included being handcuffed to a Black man for a period of time or even being whipped by a Black man before being exiled from the community. This juxtaposition was viewed as humiliating because it rendered a White man of status as "impotent" and kindred to Black males who were viewed by White America as lower-order creatures not unlike cattle.[87]

Given the lower-order, creaturely status of Black people in general, it is not surprising that the founders found it difficult to imagine the races

85. Kann, "Penitence for the Privileged," p. 22.
86. Kann, "Penitence for the Privileged," p. 29.
87. Kann, "Penitence for the Privileged," p. 29. Cf. Ann Fairfax Withington, *Toward a More Perfect Union: Virtue and the Formation of American Republics* (Oxford: Oxford University Press, 1991), pp. xiii-xiv, 16-17, 55, 134, 184, 208, 212, 215, 217, 224, 229, 242.

living together in freedom and equality. The "great American forefather" Thomas Jefferson, in his essays entitled "Manners" and "Laws," which appeared in his only published work, *Notes on the State of Virginia* (1787), offers a telling example. While showing an "acute awareness of the cancerous effect of the institution of slavery on the moral fiber of his nation," Jefferson nonetheless, "prays for wisdom to find a way to end slavery in a manner that would not bring about a reversal of 'the wheel of fortune, an exchange of situation' between white and black."[88] Emmanuel Chukwudi Eze has noted that a disproportionately large part of Jefferson's second essay, "Laws," "is devoted to arguments in support of what Jefferson believed to be the innate or 'natural' inferiority of the Negro (and superiority of the white) in the areas of physical beauty, and mental and intellectual capacity. The Negroes, according to Jefferson, are biologically conditioned for manual labor because they are 'tolerant of heat.'"[89]

Jefferson's well-known assertions about inherent racial differences were adopted by followers such as Tunis Wortman, who argued that interracial mingling and marriage were tantamount to a "universal prostitution" that would produce "a motley and degenerate race of mulattos." Other White leaders ranted against "the infamy of such a mongrel coalition," condemned "the disgraceful and unnatural" evil of interracial unions, and proclaimed that a "free nation of black and white people [will] produce a body politic as monstrous and unnatural as a mongrel half white man and half Negro."[90] Hopelessly impassioned, oversexed, immutably lustful, and incorrigible, the uncontrollable desires of Black men threatened to pollute and debase the White race. On Jefferson's view, Black male lust and coarseness was caused by their inferiority in "body and mind" as well as "imagina-

88. Eze, *Race and the Enlightenment*, p. 95.
89. Eze, *Race and the Enlightenment*, p. 95.
90. Kann, "Penitence for the Privileged," p. 29. Cf. John Witherspoon, "The Dominion of Providence over the Passions of Men" (1776), in *Political Sermons of the Founding Era, 1730-1805*, 2nd ed., ed. Ellis Sandoz (Indianapolis, Ind.: Liberty Press, 1991), p. 537; Robert Gross, *The Minutemen and Their World* (New York: Hill and Wang, 1976), pp. 94, 96; James Dana, "The African Slave Trade" (1791), in *Political Sermons*, ed. Sandoz, pp. 508-9; Anonymous, "Rudiments of Law and Government Deduced from the Law of Nature" (1783), in *American Political Writings*, vol. 1, ed. Charles S. Hyneman and Donald S. Lutz (Indianapolis, Ind.: Liberty Press, 1983), p. 584; David Rice, "Slavery Inconsistent with Justice and Good Policy" (1792), in *American Political Writing*, vol. 2, ed. Hyneman and Lutz, p. 874; John Taylor, *Arator: Being a Series of Agricultural Essays, Practical and Political in Sixty-Four Numbers*, ed. M. E. Bradford (1804; repr. Indianapolis: Liberty Press, 1977), p. 178.

tion," where Blacks were "dull, tasteless, and anomalous." Jefferson thought of Black males as promiscuous and mindless: "Never yet could I find that a black had uttered a thought above the level of plain narration; never see even an elementary trait of painting or sculpture."[91]

Kann points out an observation made by Frank Shuffelton and others that, "Jefferson was quite blind to the diversity of African cultures and the creativity of the black artisans in his own household. This blindness allowed Jefferson and other founders to conceive of Black males as less than men."[92] There was a particular fear among the founders, and White people in general, that the prodigal lust and incorrigibility of Black males ultimately issued in the rape of White women. This assumption had a critical effect on even religiously derived penology. As early as 1682, while Pennsylvania Quakers were for a short time revoking the death penalty for White rapists, they retained hanging for Black men convicted of rape. Apparently even the Quakers, who normally viewed no one as beyond the pale of potential reform, believed that Black males were beyond the possibility of rehabilitation.[93]

Slave status meant that Black males could do little to start families, keep them together, prevent their wives' victimization, or protect children. Many male slaves lived in small, isolated households and had little or no contact with potential brides. Moreover, slave traders often forced those male slaves who were married to separate from wives and children, and slaveholder wills required the distribution of slave families' members among various heirs. Meanwhile, owners and overseers might force slave husbands "to prostitute their wives and mothers and daughters to gratify the brutal lust of a master."[94]

---

91. Kann, "Penitence for the Privileged," p. 29. See also Thomas Jefferson, *Notes on the State of Virginia,* in *The Portable Thomas Jefferson,* pp. 94-95; 187-89; 192-93; Frank Shuffelton, "Thomas Jefferson: Race, Culture, and the Failure of the Anthropological Method," in *A Mixed Race: Ethnicity in Early America,* ed. Frank Shuffelton (Oxford: Oxford University Press, 1993), pp. 198-200; and Samuel Walker, *Popular Justice: A History of American Criminal Justice* (Oxford: Oxford University Press, 1980), pp. 268-70.

92. Kann, "Penitence for the Privileged," p. 29.

93. Kann, "Penitence for the Privileged," p. 30; David Rice, "Slavery Inconsistent with Justice and Good Policy" (1792), Hyneman and Lutz, *American Political Writing,* vol. 2, p. 861; Daniel Williams, "The Gratification of That Corrupt and Lawless Passion: Types and Themes in Early New England Rape Narratives," in *A Mixed Race,* ed. Shuffelton, pp. 198-200; Walker, *Popular Justice,* pp. 33-34.

94. Kann, "Penitence for the Privileged," p. 30.

In early America Black men were thought to have little regard "for their posterity," as family paternal fondness was always being compromised by the brutality of slavery. Perceived as devoid of full human status, manly independence, family mastery, and endowed by nature with hypersexuality, Black men were viewed as such a serious threat to society that they were beyond rehabilitative redemption. Thus for the indefinite future, the disorderly among them would need to be controlled by physical coercion. The founders hoped to control incorrigible Black males with traditional capital and corporal punishments. Black males who somehow avoided execution or being tortured into cooperation were likely sold away from their families. Finally, by the modern prison age (the late eighteenth–early nineteenth centuries), many Black males would be sent to prisons.

As is the case today, the founding authorities of the republic were more likely to prosecute, convict, and execute (by hanging) Blacks for their crimes.[95] When Black offenders did not receive the death penalty, they were almost assured jail time. By the late 1790s, Black people constituted one-third of the prison population at Philadelphia's Walnut Street Jail — the earliest modern prison in the U.S. For Black convicts, however, as Kann correctly points out, "the penitentiary was not a substitute for traditional state coercion or an innovative institution for rehabilitation. Instead, it was one more option for detaining, disciplining, and controlling a select population of men whose putative passions and licentious behavior were believed to be incurable."[96]

As a consequence of this widespread White representation of the incurability of "a select population of men," retribution and control, not rehabilitation, were viewed as the proper functions of punishment for Black men. By contrast, White convicts were stripped of manhood in a calculated effort to motivate them to reform, with the promise of renewed manly freedom and dignity. William Bradford (1755-1795), appointed by George Washington as the United States' second attorney general in 1774, explained that, ideally, "the offender becomes humbled and reformed, society, instead of losing, gains a citizen."[97] Black men could not be citizens

95. Kann, "Penitence for the Privileged," p. 30.

96. Kann, "Penitence for the Privileged," p. 30. See also Louis P. Masur, *Rites of Execution: Capital Punishment and the Transformation of American Culture, 1776-1865* (Oxford: Oxford University Press, 1989), p. 39, and John Taylor, *Arator*, p. 188.

97. Quoted in Kann, "Penitence for the Privileged," p. 31. See also William Bradford,

because White leaders doubted that "these 'creatures' could learn manly self-restraint, honor family responsibility, or show respect for the law."[98] Black males needed to be controlled by the law because, by nature, they could not be redeemed.

The early republic's perceptions of the manly potential of White men in contrast to Black men (as well as in contrast to libertines, lower-class laborers, immigrants, itinerants, orphans, regular soldiers, backwoodsmen, and Indians) legitimized what was essentially a two-tiered criminal justice system. State coercion would be applied to White male criminals in the service of benevolent rehabilitation and restoration to manhood and liberty. Kann argues that it was assumed by the founders that "the certainty of punishment, not its severity, best deterred criminal behavior." In the cases of White offenders, "American elites used this principle to justify replacing traditional punishment such as hanging, branding, and whipping with ostensibly lesser penalties such as incarceration." For Blacks, on the other hand, the new penitentiaries "functioned as coercive custodial institutions for warehousing disproportionate numbers of blacks and other males whose ostensible unmanly conduct excluded them from liberty and justified severity and subordination to control them."[99]

Capital, Labor, and Black Prisoners

Another important social function of the effective control of Black bodies had to do with the critical role Black servitude played in the economic development of the new republic. Slaves, who held little or no social status as individuals, were defined by their value in the marketplace, their laboring potential, and the punishment they received for perceived criminal conduct. As I alluded to earlier, a consequence of this was the dominant White culture's refusal to unambiguously recognize human gender differentiation among Black people. Hence, as Angela Davis has pointed out, women's task quotas in the plantation fields were essentially the same as men's. Their tasks were "established in connection with their

---

An Enquiry How Far the Punishment of Death is Necessary in Pennsylvania, in *Reform of Criminal Law in Pennsylvania: Selected Inquiries, 1787-1819* (New York: Arno Press, 1972), p. 7.

98. Kann, "Penitence for the Privileged," p. 31.

99. Kann, "Penitence for the Privileged," p. 31.

size and weight rather than with their gender. Women were also targets of the whip and the lash, the primary weapons of punishment during slavery."[100]

Although Black people, particularly males, were already disproportionately represented in penitentiaries of the antebellum south, the rate of Black integration into southern penal systems increased after the Civil War. Eventually the penal system became a system of penal servitude. With the slavery-like control of Black labor becoming integrated into the penal system after the Civil War, Whites were able to continue their control of the "Black beast" and to retain control of the lucrative raw material that Black bodies represented. The creation and expansion of a southern convict leasing system from 1866 to 1928 insured that Black bodies, which were thought to require constant oversight under the discipline of the whip, would remain both under control and profitable. It was essential to many Southern White leaders after the war that the former slave status of Black people as "radically dishonored beings" be maintained.[101]

White society's widespread fear and horror of newly freed slaves, particularly in postwar Southern culture, intensified traditional Enlightenment notions of color symbolism, which identified whiteness with beauty, goodness, and purity, and blackness with ugliness, evil, baseness, and wickedness. Indeed many White people wished to encourage the perception that, even post-slavery, Black people were still to be considered trespassers on the human race. Religious symbolism vigorously reinforced the potent myth that Black Americans were descended from Ham, which confirmed "the concept of degeneration from pristine whiteness."[102] The formerly docile slave had sometimes been considered to be as loyal and as faithful as a good dog. Now, under legal emancipation, former male slaves in particular became horrible beasts and monsters who

---

100. Angela Y. Davis, "Race, Gender, and Prison History," p. 39.

101. Matthew J. Mancini, *One Dies, Get Another: Convict Leasing in the American South, 1866-1928* (Columbia, S.C.: University of South Carolina Press, 1996), p. 21. Mancini's understanding of Black slaves as "radically dishonored beings" is borrowed from Orlando Paterson's "preliminary definition of slavery on the level of personal relations: *slavery is the violent domination of natally alienated and generally dishonored persons.*" See Orlando Patterson, *Slavery and Social Death: A Comparative Study* (Cambridge, Mass.: Harvard University Press, 1992), p. 13.

102. Orlando Patterson, *Rituals of Blood: Consequences of Slavery in the Two American Centuries* (Washington, D.C.: Civitas, 1998), p. 211.

were not only devoid of manhood, but now, to the horror of Whites, were without the necessary forced status control of their vile and unredeemable existence. Status control was viewed as crucial for a population of subhumans who, now free of the legal constraints of slavery, would "naturally" act out of laziness, irresponsibility, cunning, rebelliousness, untrustworthiness, and sexual promiscuousness.[103] In an attempt to reinforce White manhood after the Civil War, a significant aim of the post-Reconstruction era included a redoubled focus on what was thought to be the most acceptable association of republican qualities: "freedom = manhood = white status."[104] Historian Matthew Mancini, borrowing partly from the work of Charles L. Flynn, offers a good summary of the post-Reconstruction efforts by Southern Whites to keep Blacks in their pre-emancipation social position:

> Before emancipation slaves might not have been a part of "society," but Reconstruction endowed the freedmen with the status of citizenship. Post-Reconstruction legislatures expressed their bewilderment and rage at this status by in effect criminalizing Negro behavior. Some illegal behavior patterns identified as specifically "black" were removed from misdemeanor status and reclassified as felonies. Charles L. Flynn Jr. has recently [1982] described with relentless thoroughness how Southern "society" was defined as an arena for white people, and blacks as "a racially defined laboring caste": "The equation of whiteness with membership in society was inseparable from the implicit equation of black labor with agricultural labor as a whole and of whiteness with capital. . . . White equaled property, equaled capital, equaled society. Black equaled poverty, equaled labor, equaled something somehow alien."[105]

---

103. Eugene D. Genovese, *Red and Black: Marxian Explorations of Southern and Afro-American History* (Knoxville, Tenn.: University of Tennessee Press, 1984), pp. 77-78. Also see David Brion Davis, *The Problem of Slavery in Western Culture* (Ithaca, N.Y.: Oxford University Press, 1966), pp. 59-60; and George Fredrickson "White Images of Black Slaves (Is What We See in Others Sometimes a Reflection of What We Find in Ourselves?)," in *Critical White Studies,* ed. Delgado and Stefancic, p. 39.

104. Patterson, *Rituals of Blood*, p. 212.

105. Mancini, *One Dies, Get Another,* p. 21; Charles L. Flynn, Jr., *White Land, Black Labor: Caste and Class in Late Nineteenth-Century Georgia* (Baton Rouge: Louisiana State University Press, 1982), pp. 8, 27.

Angela Davis sees some similarities between the convict leasing practices of the past and the contemporary burgeoning prison system. She argues that today's emergent prison-industrial complex, fueled increasingly by privatization trends, "recalls the early efforts to create a profitable punishment industry based on the new supply of 'free' black male laborers in the aftermath of the Civil War."[106] Emancipated Black men, and significant numbers of Black women, provided a virtually endless supply of raw material for the Southern punishment industry, which provided much-needed cheap labor for the economies of Southern states recovering from the devastation of the Civil War. In the contemporary era, Black men, and increasing numbers of women, constitute a continuing supply of raw material for the present-day prison-industrial complex.[107]

As I mentioned in the previous chapter, today's prison-industrial complex involves a number of the largest investment houses on Wall Street. Indeed, Steven Donziger reminds us, for example that

> Goldman Sachs and Co. and Smith Barney Shearson Inc. compete to underwrite jail and prison construction with private, tax-exempt bonds that do not require voter approval. Titans of the defense industry such as Westinghouse Electric and Alliant Techsystems, Inc., have created special divisions to retool their products for law enforcement. Publicly traded prison companies such as the Correction Corporation of America and Wackenhut Corporation, as well as correctional officer unions, also exercise a powerful influence over criminal justice policy. Private companies are growing rapidly as the correctional population expands, and they are aggressively "exporting" their formula for private jails and prisons to other countries.[108]

Drawing on the work of Norwegian criminologist Nils Christie, Donziger also offers important insight into the use of prisoners as raw material for the contemporary prison industry:

> Companies that service the criminal justice system need sufficient quantities of raw materials to guarantee long-term growth. An econo-

---

106. Davis, "Race, Gender, and Prison History," p. 40.
107. Davis, "Race, Gender, and Prison History," p. 41.
108. Donziger, *The Real War on Crime*, pp. 87-89.

mist looking at almost any industry might make the same simple state-ment. In the criminal justice field, Christie suggests a frightening sce-nario: that the raw material is prisoners, and industry will do what is necessary to guarantee a steady supply. For the supply of prisoners to grow, criminal justice policies must ensure a sufficient number of in-carcerated Americans regardless of whether crime is rising or the in-carceration is necessary.[109]

Indeed, Donziger's words are important ones to consider for the sake of just and flourishing communities and society at large. And together with a consideration of just what it is that feeds the sense of necessity "for the supply of prisoners to grow," we must keep alive the question of how and why Black bodies end up facing the social brunt of this frightening state of affairs, and what we, as a nation, will do about it in the name of the com-mon good.

Summary

From what we have just seen, it should be clear how the social alienations of atomism, (vulgar) individualism, and racism are linked to the contem-porary practice of U.S. imprisonment. All three of these phenomena are deep social alienations that are exacerbated via the collateral social conse-quences of excessive imprisonment, which we discussed in Chapter Two. As this chapter has suggested, a scientific, atomistic view of imprisonment, (vulgar) individualism, and the aesthetic-scientific construction of racist dehumanization contribute heavily to a society in which people with ma-jority power and status refuse to see that their own well-being is inextricably tied to the transformation and restoration of prisoners.

Although we have thus far been proceeding on the assumption that difficulties associated with today's prison-industrial complex, and the col-lateral social consequences associated with it, are not uniquely Christian concerns, we will nonetheless now turn in Chapter Four to a specifically Christian response to the contemporary problem of imprisonment in the United States. In critical engagement with what I view as Stanley Hauerwas's Christian social ethics of punishment in particular, and his

109. Donziger, *The Real War on Crime,* p. 87.

overarching dispositionist theological ethics in general, I will begin to envision a Christian social ethics of "good punishment." Hopefully a Christian re-envisioning of the nation's contemporary large-scale imprisoning of its residents will contribute to society's hope of enhancing and expanding justice and well-being for all its residents. It is hoped that not only will such a contribution aid us against the terror of those who truly offend, but also against the bureaucratic, political, and economic tyranny institutionalized in the form of the prison-industrial complex.

A final note: the foregoing examination of some alienating deep issues at work behind contemporary imprisonment was not undertaken simply to deepen our understanding of the socially corrosive aspects of imprisonment. At critical issue in the next chapter is the beginning of a discussion of how any good ethics (in this instance a Christian one) focusing on U.S. imprisonment will actively address problematics related to the social functions and collateral consequences of imprisonment. In the next three chapters, I begin to work toward a "politics of ontological intimacy" (as an "ethics of response"), which is expressive of a Christian social ethics of "good punishment." I offer the following as a response (always in a state of becoming) to the socially alienating and corrosive problematic of U.S. imprisonment. In other words, I intend to address a serious affront to *human* hope in the service of love.

4. Mining Stanley Hauerwas: Foundations for a Christian Social Ethics of Good Punishment

Howard Zehr, a pioneering theorist and practitioner of contemporary restorative justice, has suggested that while the Western legal system's approach to justice has some important strengths, "there is also a growing acknowledgement of this system's limits and failures. Victims, offenders, and community members often feel that justice does not adequately meet their needs. Justice professionals — judges, lawyers, prosecutors, probation and parole officers, prison staff — often express a sense of frustration as well. Many feel that the process of justice deepens societal wounds and conflicts rather than contributing to healing and peace."[1]

To the degree that retributive theories of justice aim at insuring a proportional relationship between acts classified as "criminal" and the response of authorities, they are not necessarily the polar opposite of more transformative practices of criminal justice. Transformative practices of justice aim to incapacitate wrongdoers and restore or transform them in a manner beneficial to themselves, their communities, and society. The crucial difference, though, between retributive and restorative forms of justice is that the former contends that the infliction of pain and/or suffering is what primarily vindicates wrongs, while restorative justice addresses the need for vindication in more positive ways.[2]

As I move toward the construction of a Christian social ethics of good punishment, a critical question to keep in mind throughout is,

---

1. Howard Zehr, *The Little Book of Restorative Justice* (Intercourse, Pa.: Good Books, 2002), p. 3.
2. Zehr, *Little Book of Restorative Justice*, pp. 58-59.

"What kind of people do we wish to be?" In the service of thinking about this question, a question concerning the core dispositional distinctiveness of who we are as human beings, I turn to the important work being done by the theological ethicist Stanley Hauerwas. In this chapter I will piece together[3] Hauerwas's understanding of "Christian punishment" as a resource worth considering in anticipation of inviting better Christian participation in resisting the social misery tied to the large-scale practice of retributive and degrading imprisonment. It is hoped that a consideration of Hauerwas's understanding of punishment (regardless of the degree to which one ultimately agrees or disagrees with him) will issue in better approaches to criminal justice than that of large-scale imprisonment.

Why Stanley Hauerwas?

No doubt many readers will scratch their heads, wondering, "Why Stanley Hauerwas?" "Who is he anyway?" Let me try to offer a rationale for this choice. Stanley Hauerwas is arguably one of the exemplary Christian theologians of our time. Currently the Gilbert T. Rowe Professor of Theological Ethics at Duke University Divinity School, he is the author of more than twenty books. He was the Gifford Lecturer for the year 2001 and *Time* magazine's choice for best theologian of that year.[4] More infamously, he has also been dubbed the "filthy-mouth theologian" for his well documented and fairly frequent use of expletives in his public dialogues and debates with others. Due to his family's tough Texas bricklayer roots and his somewhat brash persona, he has also been cited as the pacifist you would want most to have on your side in a barfight. He advocates for a recovery of the moral skills (or virtues) that enable a proper understanding of social reality and practice from the perspective of the Christian narrative of Israel as Jesus Christ presents it. Viewing the theologian's task as that of call-

---

3. Stanley Hauerwas's scholarly production has predominantly been in the form of the essay. So while my articulation of his ethic of punishment will pay close attention to his essay entitled "Punishing Christians" (in Stanley Hauerwas, *Performing the Faith: Bonhoeffer and the Practice of Nonviolence* [Grand Rapids, Mich.: Brazos Press, 2004]) it is necessary that I draw on a number of his essays elsewhere, as well as a number of secondary sources, in my articulation of his position.

4. Michael J. Quirk, "Stanley Hauerwas: An Interview," *Cross Currents,* http://www.crosscurrents.org/Hauerwasspring2002.htm.

ing into question distortions in the grammar of the Christian faith, and theology itself as occasional discourse in response to particular historical difficulties, Hauerwas's work aims at developing a recovery of the virtues that are based in the alternative narrative of Christian life before its compromise with Christendom.

It is true that there are numerous Christian theologians and ethicists who contribute to public debates on a variety of "hot-button" social issues, including the debate over the legitimate social function of punishment in church and society. Hauerwas's own provocative essay "Punishing Christians" was recently published in his 2004 book *Performing the Faith: Bonhoeffer and the Practice of Nonviolence*. Other recent works by Christian scholars concerned with various aspects of punishment praxis in the United States include Lee Griffith's *The Fall of the Prison: Biblical Perspectives on Prison Abolition* (1999), Christopher Marshall's *Beyond Retribution: A New Testament Vision for Justice, Crime, and Punishment* (2001), T. Richard Snyder's *The Protestant Ethic and the Spirit of Punishment* (2001), Mark Taylor's *The Executed God: The Way of the Cross in Lockdown America* (2001), and *The Spiritual Roots of Restorative Justice* (2001), edited by Michael Hadley. This list is by no means exhaustive, but it is a representative sample.

One of the main reasons why I make particular appeal to Hauerwas rather than to others who are also doing important work around issues of punishment and imprisonment is that, generally speaking, few other Christian scholars have secured a public and church-wide hearing on issues concerning peace and justice quite on the level that he has. Arguably, no other academic Christian theologian today draws as much critical engagement, fire, verbal fisticuffs, scorn, and adoration from conservatives, liberals, and moderates concerning their view of human sociopolitical arrangements. Very few Christian scholars today have Stanley Hauerwas's "juice" across disciplines and in the public arena, and so his thoughts are eminently worth considering.[5] The philosopher Michael J. Quirk contends that,

> While [Hauerwas's] favored form of writing is the short essay rather than the standard-issue scholarly book, his work is scholarly, in the

5. Jeffrey Stout, professor of religion at Princeton University and current president of the American Academy of Religion, has gone so far as to refer to Hauerwas as "the most prolific and influential theologian in the English-speaking world." See Jeffrey Stout and Robert MacSwain, eds., *Grammar and Grace: Reformulations of Aquinas and Wittgenstein* (London: SCM, 2004), p. 5.

best sense of the word: well-acquainted with the relevant theological literature, and enriched by his proficiency in understanding other genres of writing, such as philosophy, social criticism, and the novel. The craftsmanlike character of his piecework prose (which he attributes, in part, to his earlier apprenticeship as a bricklayer) dares his readership to take him seriously, because he is serious. But to accept that challenge would be to lead one to place in question certain intellectual — and moral — habits that one might find too comforting to give up.[6]

Finally, I must confess (as I have already mentioned in the introduction) that a part of my particular appeal to Hauerwas rather than to others who are also doing important work around issues of imprisonment and punishment has to do with the Anabaptist pacifist sensibilities that he, even as a (somewhat Catholic) Methodist, shares with my own Mennonite faith.

The Problem of "Liberalism"

Hauerwas was trained in religious ethics at Yale University in the tradition of the (Reinhold and H. Richard) Niebuhrs, but he now allies himself (primarily) with the thought of the Mennonite theologian John Howard Yoder and the neo-Aristotelian political philosopher Alasdair MacIntyre. Yoder, in particular, represents for Hauerwas an alternative to, rather than a continuation of, the Niebuhrian tradition. Drawing from Yoder, on Hauerwas's view the first responsibility of Christians is to be themselves; that is, accountable to a body of sacred literature (the Bible) and to the church.[7] In agreement with MacIntyre, Hauerwas describes the dominant moral ethos in contemporary American society as "liberalism." According to Hauerwas, American liberalism, at its base, holds that the best or only moral community we can have is based on guaranteeing the principle of the freedom of each individual citizen to do as he or she pleases, so long as he or

6. Michael J. Quirk, "Stanley Hauerwas: An Interview," *CrossCurrents,* http://www.crosscurrents.org/Hauerwasspring2002.htm.

7. Stanley M. Hauerwas, "Reconciling the Practice of Reason: Casuistry in a Christian Context," in *Christian Existence Today: Essays on Church, World and Living In Between* (Grand Rapids, Mich.: Baker Books, 1988), p. 67.

she does not violate the legitimate equal freedom of others. Liberalism celebrates toleration, pluralism, and respect for personal autonomy.

Hauerwas takes very serious exception to the liberal[8] claim that personal freedom and individual consent can be "truthful" bases from which to arrange our moral and political lives. Since "truthful" social arrangements represent the only social condition through which necessary virtues can be adequately developed in the service of right human desiring, liberalism (as a non-tradition on Hauerwas's view) cannot pass the litmus test for what is truthful: "Liberalism presupposes that society can be organized without any narrative that is commonly held to be true. As a result it tempts us to believe that freedom and rationality are independent of narrative — i.e., we are free to the extent that we have no story."[9] Indeed, it is essential in Hauerwas's view that church and society understand that "truthful" social arrangements emerge out of lived "narratives," "traditions," or "stories."

Hauerwas views the church (i.e., the Body of Christ) as devoted not to the principles of liberalism, but rather to a particular God and a particular way of life that follows Jesus. The members of the church know themselves not in the first instance as autonomous and free individuals, but rather as bound to God, to their tradition (or "narrative"), and to one another. The fundamental category for ensuring human agency is not freedom but narrative.[10] Being rooted in "a story formed community," the particular story being that of Jesus' kingdom,[11] church members know

8. Of course, Hauerwas's more or less essentialist version of "liberalism" will not do justice to the fact that the term "liberalism" has a dizzying array of sociopolitical, theological, ethical, and economic definitions, depending on who is employing the term. To be fair, Hauerwas does in fact recognize that "liberalism" has various expressions, but what is essentially common in all versions of liberalism is that they lack the storied-memory necessary to develop virtue for "truthful" living. This should be kept in mind as I proceed to recite Hauerwas's well-known fight against all things liberal on behalf of virtue, character, and pacifism. See and cf. Max Stackhouse's claim that "Hauerwas' definition of 'liberal' is at once too narrow and too broad" in "Liberalism Dispatched vs. Liberalism Engaged," *Christian Century*, October 18, 1995: 962-67.

9. Stanley Hauerwas, *A Community of Character* (Notre Dame, Ind.: University of Notre Dame Press, 1981), p. 12. For an excellent brief overview of this aspect of Hauerwas's thinking see William Werpehowski, *American Protestant Ethics and the Legacy of H. Richard Niebuhr* (Washington, D.C.: Georgetown University Press, 2002), pp. 80-85.

10. Stanley Hauerwas, *The Peaceable Kingdom: A Primer in Christian Ethics* (Notre Dame, Ind.: University of Notre Dame Press, 1983), p. 43.

11. Hauerwas, *Community of Character*, pp. 9-35; 36-52.

themselves as they are known by a merciful and faithful God. Living within a distinctively Christian narrative, Christians come to embody the virtues of trust, patience, hope, gratitude, hospitality, and forgiveness, seeking not to *control* history but to *witness* to God's rule within history as established by Jesus Christ. In attempting to control society, Christians have mistakenly accepted liberalism as a social strategy appropriate to the Christian story. Hence, on Hauerwas's view, Christians have lost the moral skills or virtues that enable a proper description of reality as the Christian narrative of Israel, as Jesus presents it.

The contractual ethos of liberalism, with its supreme valuation of individual freedom, destroys Christian virtue, on Hauerwas's view. For example, under liberal social arrangements family is viewed as a "contractual" agreement between individuals rather than as a community of commitment and responsibility even to persons we do not choose to be with. Hauerwas prefers to view the Christian moral life in terms of the virtues that enable Christians to describe and live it truthfully. A preeminent Christian virtue is "peaceableness," which highlights Jesus' political act of refusing recourse to violence. Hauerwas believes that nonviolence is a normative mode of Christian being-in-the-world. The nonviolent disposition of peaceable Christians is a witness to God's reign in history. The preeminent Christian *telos* in history from Hauerwas's point of view is holiness, the content of which is faithful obedience to the nonviolent politics of Jesus. A critical aspect of Hauerwas's account of holiness is that its realization is communal and deeply embedded within, and inseparable from, a common set of practices. Such practices include peaceableness, hospitality, patience, and courage, which sustain a people "who refuse to have their lives determined by the fear and denial of death."[12] Christians know that not only have they been raised with Christ, but they have also died with Christ. Since Christ subdued death on a cross, Christians should favor political arrangements that demonstrate fearlessness in the face of death. This way of living is a gift that Christians offer their non-Christian sisters and brothers as a better alternative to all politics based on a denial of death. The Christian community offers society a countercultural testimony of hope in a world devoid of the version

---

12. Stanley Hauerwas, "September 11, 2001: A Pacifist Response," in *Dissent from the Homeland: Essays After September 11*, ed. Stanley Hauerwas and Frank Lentricchia (Durham, N.C.: Duke University Press, 2003), p. 188.

of transforming hope demonstrated during the celebration of Passover in A.D. 33.[13]

Contrary to the liberal tradition stretching from Immanuel Kant to John Rawls, Hauerwas argues that moral communities cannot be arranged according to abstract principles. He understands that good people will be built differently by different groups and traditions. Mark Oppenheimer has correctly noted that for Hauerwas "tradition" refers to memories that persist over generations because parents and communities dare to indoctrinate their children. (Related to this point Oppenheimer notes just why it is that Hauerwas does not like liberal arts pedagogy in education: "Teachers who pretend to have no opinions train students who have no opinions.")[14] Hauerwas consistently argues that Christian "happiness" is a life formed rightly by the right virtues. All the virtues come together in "peaceableness." Peaceableness is an active display of the supreme Christian goal on earth, namely, *holiness* — "not because it is effective, but because it is simply true." And what is "true" for Hauerwas is that "God does not rule creation through coercion, but through a cross."[15]

Given Hauerwas's insistence that narrative-dependent virtue should always inform the social practices of church and society, it is no surprise that he insists on an understanding of Christian ethics that does not begin in the first instance with the question, "What ought we to do?" Rather, Hauerwas suggests that ethical inquiry must begin with the foundational question, "What ought we to be?" Put another way, the question is not, "What shall I do if presented with this or that dilemma?" but, "What kind of person shall I be?" As a consequence, Hauerwas has emerged as a strong opponent of "quandary ethics" and as a zealous champion of Christian virtue. He refuses to perform what he sees as the legalistic task of formulating moral principles and then subsuming cases under them, for such a methodology effectively eliminates character from ethical consideration. Any obligations and duties that characterize Christian responsibility ought to be character-dependent and appropriate to a particular narrative's time and place. An individual never "simply bumps up against decisions devoid of any human context."[16] Indeed, for Hauerwas *all* liberal social arrange-

13. Hauerwas, "September 11," pp. 181-83, 188.

14. Mark Oppenheimer, "For God Not Country: The Un-American Theology of Stanley Hauerwas," *Linguafranca: The Review of Academic Life* 11:6 (September 2001).

15. Hauerwas, *The Peaceable Kingdom*, p. 104; cf. p. 151.

16. Hauerwas, *The Peaceable Kingdom*, p. 130.

ments lack human context; that is, they lack the memory-tradition necessary for the development of virtues which undergird truthful human existence.

Constructing Hauerwas's "Christian Ethics of Punishment"

As I now turn to the task of articulating Hauerwas's Christian ethics of punishment, I keep in mind two broad areas in which Hauerwas is instructive for Christian thinking about social practices in general: (1) his insistence that the datum of Christian ethics lies in a distinctive embodiment of story-informed character, and (2) his insistence that this is good news for the whole of society.

Drawing on the work of John Howard Yoder, Hauerwas argues that those committed to Christian nonviolence cannot avoid providing an account of punishment. Nor can they avoid providing alternative practices. He understands that there are many who would suggest that pacifist responses to violence do not deserve serious consideration. This is not because nonpacifists think that criminal violence or war are good things; rather it is because "they sense that pacifism simply cannot give an account of how our daily lives depend on violent forms of behavior."[17] Nonpacifists might ask how it is possible to live in a cohesive society if residents have no understanding of crime and/or are unwilling to punish those who engage in crime.

Hauerwas first began to explore the issue of crime and punishment in an essay entitled, "McInerny Did It: or, Should a Pacifist Read Murder Mysteries?"[18] In this essay Hauerwas confesses to being "something of a 'moralist,'" which explains his avid interest in the moral significance of murder mysteries, murders, and murderers. Understanding the morality of punishment to be basic to a human understanding of civilization, Hauerwas quotes G. K. Chesterton's summary of the function of punishment in the mystery narrative:

17. Hauerwas, "Punishing Christians," p. 186.

18. This essay was first published in John O'Callaghan and Thomas Hibbs, eds., *Recovering Nature: Essays in Natural Philosophy, Ethics, and Metaphysics in Honor of Ralph McInerny* (Notre Dame, Ind.: University of Notre Dame Press, 1999), pp. 163-75. The essay appears most recently in Stanley Hauerwas, *A Better Hope: Resources for a Church Confronting Capitalism, Democracy, and Postmodernity* (Grand Rapids, Mich.: Brazos Press, 2000), pp. 201-10.

The romance of police activity keeps in some sense before the mind the fact that civilization itself is the most sensational of departures and the most romantic of rebellions. By dealing with the unsleeping sentinels who guard the outposts of society, it tends to remind us that we live in an armed camp, making war with a chaotic world, and the criminals, the children of chaos, are nothing but traitors within our gates. The romance of the police force is thus the whole romance of man [sic]. It is based on the fact that morality is the most dark and daring of conspiracies. It reminds us that the whole of noiseless and unnoticeable police management by which we are ruled and protected is only a successful knight-errantry.[19]

Drawing as well on P. D. James, Hauerwas observes that one function of the crime novel is to reassure us "that we live in a morally comprehensible universe and accordingly we have an obligation to try to put things right."[20] To put things right is to do justice; justice is served when evil is bounded by a greater good. Hauerwas appreciates James's notion that temporal justice — that is, the state of affairs at the conclusion of the modern detective story — is fallible justice precisely because it is human:

> You don't get divine justice, you can't achieve that. It is very reassuring to have a form of fiction which says that every form of human life is sacred, and if it is taken away, then the law, society, will address itself to finding out who did it. The attitude is not, "well, one more chap's got murdered — hard luck." Infinite pains and money are spent trying to find out who did it because we still have the belief that the individual human life is sacred; we all have a right to live out our lives to the last moment.[21]

Hauerwas views James's understanding of the moral presuppositions of murder mysteries as the correct ones. The insights of murder mysteries

19. Quoted in Stanley Hauerwas, "McInerny Did It: or, Should a Pacifist Read Murder Mysteries?," in *A Better Hope,* 204. The primary source is G. K. Chesterton, "A Defense of Detective Stories," in *The Art of the Mystery Story,* ed. Howard Haycraft (New York: Carroll and Graf, 1992), pp. 5-6.

20. Stanley Hauerwas, "McInerny Did It," p. 207.

21. Quoted in Hauerwas, "McInerny Did It," pp. 207-8. See also P. D. James, "The Baroness in the Crime Lab: Interview by Martin Wroe," *Books and Culture* 4, no. 2 (March/April 1998): 15.

regarding human understandings of crime (especially murder) and punishment make it "particularly important for those of us who think about as well as teach ethics to be students as well as readers of novels about crime."[22] This is a significant point to make, on Hauerwas's view, because

> one of the temptations for those of us who "do ethics" is to assume that ethics is about the more subtle aspects of our lives. As a result we forget that few things are more important for the sustaining of our lives than the conviction that murder is wrong . . . to lose our hold on to that fundamental conviction would mean to lose our hold on the very possibility of living humane, to say nothing of godly, lives. To the extent that the reading of murder mysteries reminds us that we were not created to kill one another we are made better.[23]

An important objection that Hauerwas believes might be raised in light of his advocacy for the reasonableness of a pacifist Christian's reading of murder mysteries is as follows: "If I believe murderers should be caught and punished, have I not in effect accepted the fundamental practice that justifies the restrained use of violence by public authorities?" Hauerwas correctly points out that this was just the kind of argument made by Paul Ramsey, "who insisted that just war not only provided a casuistry for thinking about war but was also a theory of statecraft."[24]

As a pacifist Hauerwas wants to be committed to thinking through the necessary conditions that would allow a Christian committed to nonviolence to consider performing police or prison functions. In his willingness to consider the possibility that a Christian committed to nonviolence could, without contradiction, perform police functions, Hauerwas rejects the presumption that police functions must be understood as controlled violence: "Rather, I assume most of what police officers do is nonviolent response to violence. After all, police officers are called peace officers. Indeed I think one of the most interesting challenges before pacifists and just-warriors is to think together about what would be required to have a society in which the police would not be required as part of their task to

22. Hauerwas, "McInerny Did It," p. 208.
23. Hauerwas, "McInerny Did It," p. 208.
24. Hauerwas, "McInerny Did It," p. 280 n. 18. See Paul Ramsey, *Speak Up for Just War or Pacifism* (University Park, Pa.: Pennsylvania State University Press, 1988), with an epilogue by Stanley Hauerwas.

use lethal weapons."[25] I would extend what Hauerwas has helpfully said here to the administration of prisons, assuming that the use of some form of (involuntary) incapacitation will always be necessary for a relatively small number of offenders. Indeed, it would serve society better if prison officials saw their primary roles as keepers of peace rather than as enforcers of control and order.

Sin, Forgiveness, and Reconciliation

A fundamental theological aspect of Hauerwas's ethics of punishment is his insistence that "'sin and forgiveness' names the realities that make the Christian commitment to peace intelligible."[26] Ontologically, argues Hauerwas, crime is a subset of sin. Since the Christian narrative of Jesus ultimately highlights forgiveness over sin, forgiveness must be viewed as a more determinative reality than punishment. God does not punish us for our sin, according to Hauerwas. On his view, sin is self-inflicted punishment that is healed through "reconciliation with God, ourselves, and our wronged neighbor." Moreover, suggests Hauerwas, reconciliation is a Christian reality that produces the space allowing "the narration of our lives, individually and collectively, through which our sins can be acknowledged without deception."[27] The "realism" depicted in the crime novel is the necessary realism required by the human acknowledgment of sin. The acknowledgment of sin is made possible through reconciliation.

On Hauerwas's view the reality of Christian sin, forgiveness, and reconciliation constitutes the heart of the Christian commitment to nonviolence. Such nonviolence in the face of crime is an act of Christian obedience, and is not intended to comport to popular societal notions of temporal effectiveness:

> Christians are not committed to nonviolence because we believe nonviolence is an effective strategy to free the world of war. Rather, we are nonviolent because we know we live in a world at war yet believe that the forgiveness wrought on the cross of Christ makes it possible for us to live

25. Hauerwas, "McInerny Did It," p. 280 n. 19.
26. Hauerwas, "McInerny Did It," p. 209.
27. Hauerwas, "McInerny Did It," p. 209.

nonviolently in a world at war. In like manner we know we do not live in a world free of murder. Indeed, like advocates of just war, we know how important it is to distinguish between murder and other ways life is taken. Yet we also know that God's forgiveness is not only for those who are the victims of murder but for murderers. Indeed we know part of the process such forgiveness names is the discovery of those who have unjustly killed. For without discovery, they have no way to be made part of the process of judgment, penance, and reconciliation.[28]

With this in mind, Hauerwas argues that it is important that Christians understand that judgment, penance, and reconciliation require that murderers not simply be condemned to absolute aloneness. When a person kills or otherwise harms another human being, they are enveloped in a substantial level of secrecy, even if others know of their relational breach. This secrecy makes a human life incapable of being shared. The autonomous, private, and individualistic aspects of liberal democracy exacerbate this problem. Hence Hauerwas favors an end to secrecy. When a criminal is "discovered" there is a kind of redemption; "the murderer is known not just by us but by themselves." Such discovery, such knowing, on Hauerwas's view, begins the process that redemption names. "The name Christians have been taught to call that process is peace."[29]

Hauerwas contends that Christian peaceableness involves understanding that the people of the Christian God cannot make our children safe; "we cannot make them safe if it means we must use violence to ensure their safety." Hauerwas claims that Christians "have been given better work to do in a world at war. We have been made part of a company of people who would not have our lives or our children's lives protected through further killing or other acts of violence. It is a dangerous way to live, but then the alternative . . . is that lives lived safely are not worth living."[30]

The Social Function of Punishment

Hauerwas makes a point of drawing on Yoder's observation that neither Jesus nor Paul ever rose up against capital punishment. Following Yoder's

28. Hauerwas, "McInerny Did It," p. 209.
29. Hauerwas, "McInerny Did It," p. 209.
30. Hauerwas, "McInerny Did It," p. 210.

lead, Hauerwas argues that this was so because the noncoercive gospel cannot eliminate such practices from secular society. The gospel, being noncoercive, cannot "rule the world" in that way. Nor, however, is the gospel's silence on the issue to be interpreted as approval of the way things stand.[31] While the political gospel of Jesus does not seek to rule the world, on Hauerwas's view, the gospel does, nonetheless, impact the world. The gospel is for the world insofar as "the new level of love and forgiveness made possible by the Holy Spirit is good news for the 'real world' because such love will work as salt and light for those who are not Christians."[32] With regard to the claim that the gospel is good news for Christians and non-Christians alike, Yoder himself suggests that

> This should be true everywhere; even more evidently should this be the case in the Anglo-Saxon world, where a large number of citizens claim some kind of Christian sanction for society's values. If Christ is not only prophet and priest but also king, the border between church and the world cannot be impermeable to moral truth. Something of the cross-bearing, forgiving love, and dignity which Jesus' life, death, and resurrection revealed to be the normative way to be human, must be the norm for all humans, whether they know it or not. We cannot *expect* of anyone, not even of believers, that that norm be lived out perfectly. Yet, it is the calling of the followers of Jesus to testify that there is no other norm. The one strategy which will not serve that calling, which could not be done in the first century, is to claim to possess, and to impose on society, a body of civil rules independent of the faith of the persons called to respect them. The alternative is to work with the acceptance of the others' unbelief which is what I call "condoning" the lesser moral level of the civil order.[33]

Hauerwas thinks that Yoder's understanding of the permeable boundaries between the world and church does not really offer Christians a view of how they ought to "think about punishment in general and/or, in

31. Hauerwas, "Punishing Christians," p. 186. See also H. Wayne House and John Howard Yoder, *The Death Penalty Debate: Two Opposing Views of Capital Punishment* (Dallas: Word Publishing, 1991), p. 141.

32. Hauerwas, "Punishing Christians," p. 187.

33. Quoted in Hauerwas, "Punishing Christians," p. 187. See also House and Yoder, *Death Penalty Debate*, p. 141.

particular, capital punishment." Indeed, after years of listening to the debate over capital punishment, and by extension, the function of punishment in general, Yoder conceded that the debate had taught him that there is no one right place to begin in terms of a Christian response to crime:

> There is no "scratch" where we must start. The argument is in full swing, with claims of different kinds flowing past each other often without meeting. People who think their view is nothing but "biblical" make unavowed assumptions about facts which the social sciences would need to test. Other people who think their view is purely "scientific" or humanistic make unavowed philosophical or religious assumptions about what is "true" or "good." It would therefore be a mistake to begin this work of Christian witness, as one might begin a textbook, with the attempt to go back to a nonpartisan beginning and neutral definition of terms. I must rather accept the fact that the debate is already under way, and must myself enter it in the form it has already taken, in midstream.[34]

Hauerwas understands Yoder's claim that there is no one right place to begin when considering legitimate responses to crime as basically accurate. He nonetheless proceeds to chastise what he sees as society's common temptation to start by restating the various theories of punishment — e.g., rehabilitation, defense against the criminal (deterrence), retribution, etc. — and then to assess the actual practice of punishment against the various theories.[35] Hauerwas contends that the problem with the standard theories is not so much that they are "wrong" per se, but that, "In particular the theories give the impression that how Christians punish is but an instance of a more general practice of punishment shared by all societies."[36] This is a presumption that Hauerwas aims to challenge, "by calling attention to the way Christians have punished and should punish."[37] Hauerwas argues that by beginning with theories, society is often given a false sense that we know what we are talking about when we talk about punishment. On Hauerwas's view, it is not clear what work theories of punishment are meant to do.

34. House and Yoder, *Death Penalty Debate*, pp. 107-8.
35. A good example of this approach can be seen in Avery Cardinal Dulles, "Catholicism and Capital Punishment," *First Things*, April 2001, pp. 30-35.
36. Hauerwas, "Punishing Christians," p. 188.
37. Hauerwas, "Punishing Christians," p. 188.

Hauerwas points out that in the particular case of capital punishment, beginning with general theories of punishment is often employed by death penalty opponents in an attempt to demonstrate that the practice fails to be justified on grounds of this or that alternative theory. For example, capital punishment is indefensible if we believe that rehabilitation or the protection of society against murder is the primary function of punishment: "You certainly cannot rehabilitate someone you have killed nor does it seem that the use of capital punishment protects society by deterring others from killing. It is often pointed out, for example, that murderers are seldom repeat offenders, unless they are professional killers, so capital punishment does little to deter. Professionals after all will not be deterred exactly because they are professionals."[38] In a clever move Hauerwas suggests that capital punishment could well deter behavior considered criminal if only society would apply the practice with the right sorts of crimes, i.e., crimes more likely to be deterred if capital punishment were a consequence: "If we killed people for stock fraud, for example, there is every reason to believe that capital punishment would deter. Erect a gallows or a guillotine on Wall Street, televise the execution of those guilty of stock fraud, and I think there is every reason to believe that stock fraud would be a much less common crime."[39] Hauerwas contends that the fact that most people in today's society would recoil against killing people for theft "indicates that questions of punishment involve more than what the various abstract theories of punishment suggest in and of themselves."

Drawing on work done by Duncan Forrester for the Penal Policy Group, which attempted to understand how Scotland's penal system worked and should work by assessing the various theories of punishment, Hauerwas argues that theories of punishment, taken separately or together, fail to explain what actually happens in a penal system. Hauerwas cites Forrester's summary findings regarding Scotland's penal system "that theories often disguise, mystify, and subtly justify what is really happening."[40]

According to Hauerwas it was only when Forrester's research group began to go more deeply into the experience of being and surviving as a

---

38. Hauerwas, "Punishing Christians," p. 188.

39. Hauerwas, "Punishing Christians," p. 188.

40. Quoted in Hauerwas, "Punishing Christians," p. 188. See also Duncan Forrester, "Priorities for Social Theology Today," in *Vision and Prophecy: The Tasks of Social Theology Today,* ed. Michael Northcott (Edinburgh: Centre for Theology and Public Issues, 1991), p. 30.

prisoner did theological themes begin to emerge to illumine the practice of punishment. Forrester's work provides for Hauerwas some of the critical theological themes necessary for a proper Christian understanding of punishment: hope, guilt, forgiveness, and discipline. Forrester suggests that it is precisely within the context of a prisoner's lived story that Christians discover aspects of the proper function of punishment:

> We discover the necessity of hope. We noted that although offense involves guilt, this is not today recognized as something with which the penal system can or should engage. And, most important of all, we noted that in the Christian tradition offense, crime and sin are met with forgiveness which wipes away the guilt and the memory, while our society remains highly punitive and former prisoners rarely experience real forgiveness and reconciliation at the hands of their neighbors and colleagues. We concluded that any Christian account of punishment must see it as a discipline directed to the good of society and of the offender. Most of those working in the system or in academic criminology found the notion of forgiveness a fresh and exciting and challenging idea. In Christian theology it is of course rooted deeply in the understanding of God, and theologians would wish to affirm that it is a universal truth that God is a God who forgives.[41]

While Hauerwas is "sure" that Forrester and his colleagues are on the right track in terms of helping Christians to think about punishment, he thinks it wrong to suggest that the Christian practice of forgiveness "wipes out memory." "On the contrary," argues Hauerwas, "forgiveness makes memory possible." Hauerwas is opposed to all forms of "no-fault" reconciliation or "forgetting" in the name of easy reconciliation. This is because crimes, be they crimes against humanity or street-level crime, can never be safely fixed in the historical past. The memories fostered by crime live eternally in the present, often crying out for revenge.[42] Related to this point, Hauerwas concurs with an important sentiment expressed by Michael Ignatieff, himself drawing on James Joyce and related to bloody conflict in Ireland: the memories of past wrongs, and hence a thirst for vengeance, are

41. Quoted in Hauerwas, "Punishing Christians," p. 189. Primary source, Duncan Forrester, "Priorities for Social Theology Today," p. 30.

42. Cf. Michael Ignatieff, *The Warrior's Honor: Ethnic War and the Modern Conscience* (New York: Henry Holt, 1997), p. 186.

never safely dead and buried; they always roam through the sleep of the living in search of retribution.[43]

In apparent agreement with Ignatieff, Hauerwas suggests that the modern moral sensibility to forget past wrongs is not only unrealistic but, even more important, morally superficial. The social consequence of a strategy of "forgiving and forgetting" is the formation of superficial people. "No-fault reconciliation" disregards the fact that even "[g]ood people, morally substantive people, rightly want revenge."[44] In order to drive home the point that revenge is an understandable human desire in the face of the criminal abuse of other persons, Hauerwas quotes Ignatieff on the matter:

43. See Hauerwas's essay "Why Time Cannot and Should Not Heal the Wounds of History, But Time Has Been and Can Be Redeemed," in *A Better Hope*, pp. 144-45. See also, Ignatieff, *Warrior's Honor*, p. 186.

44. Hauerwas, "Why Time Cannot and Should Not Heal the Wounds of History," p. 145; see also pp. 143-44; 149-53. Hauerwas's disagreement with advocates of "forgetting" for the sake of forgiveness and "no-fault reconciliation" is leveled not only against Forrester, but also against C. Eric Lincoln and more intensely against Miroslav Volf. Volf argues that a certain kind of forgetting or nonremembering is appropriate after certain requirements of truth and justice have been met. Volf argues that final redemption must embody a certain kind of forgetting because "the alternative is: either heaven or the memory of horror." Volf's certain kind of forgetting in relation to those who have committed crimes involves naming, judging, and hopefully transforming the offender, as well as making sure that victims are safe and healing. Volf articulates the theological underpinning of a forgetting-forgiveness as follows: "God, to whom all things are present, will forget the forgiven sin. The God of Israel, who is about 'to do a new thing' and who calls people 'not to remember the former things,' promises to blot their transgressions out of God's own memory (Isaiah 43:18-19; cf. 65:17). 'I will forgive their iniquity, and remember their sins no more' (Jeremiah 31:34)." See Volf's *Exclusion and Embrace: A Theological Exploration of Identity, Otherness, and Reconciliation* (Nashville: Abingdon Press, 1996), pp. 135-36, and in general pp. 131-40. As Hauerwas correctly points out, Volf's comments concerning the "affliction of memory" are in response to Gregory Jones's argument in his *Embodying Forgiveness: A Theological Analysis* (Grand Rapids, Mich.: Eerdmans, 1995) that it is a mistake to forget. Jones argues that "the judgment of grace enables us, through the power of the Holy Spirit, to remember well. When God promises to 'blot out [Israel's] transgressions' and not remember [Israel's] sins' (Isaiah 43:25; see also Jeremiah 31:34), God is not simply letting bygones be bygones. Rather, God is testifying to God's own gracious faithfulness. Moreover, such forgiveness provides a way to narrate the history of Israel's sinfulness with the context of God's covenant of grace. To be sure, such a narration makes it possible, and even necessary, to forget the sin. But the past itself, the history, is and needs to be remembered so that a new and renewed future becomes possible" (p. 147). Quoted in Hauerwas, "Why Time Cannot and Should Not Heal the Wounds of History," p. 266 n. 26. Cf. also C. Eric Lincoln, *Coming Through the Fire: Surviving Race and Place in America* (Durham, N.C.: Duke University Press, 1996), pp. 133-34; 157.

The chief moral obstacle in the path of reconciliation is the desire for revenge. Now, revenge is commonly regarded as a low and unworthy emotion, and because it is regarded as such, its deep moral hold on people is rarely understood. But revenge — morally considered — is a desire to keep faith with the dead, to honor their memory by taking up their cause where they left off. Revenge keeps faith between generations; the violence it engenders is a ritual form of respect for the community's dead — therein lies its legitimacy. Reconciliation is difficult precisely because it must compete with the powerful alternative morality of violence. Political terror is tenacious because it is an ethical practice. It is a cult of the dead, a dire and absolute expression of respect.[45]

Applying Ignatieff's account of revenge to the practice of criminal corrections, instincts that underlie retributive forms of punishment (keeping faith between generations, respect for the community's dead, etc.) can perhaps be said to have at least some positive aspect. At least it can be said that an instinctive goal of retributive punishment, no less than that of more restorative forms of justice, is to vindicate through reciprocity, by "setting things right," so to speak. Indeed, the desire for revenge (or vengeance) may well be a worthy emotion insofar as its motive is to keep faith with, and honor, the memory of individuals, communities, and a society that has been wronged. Moreover, even revenge may contain as a motive the reestablishment (or establishment) of respect for the cohesion and well-being of moral community and society.

All of this notwithstanding, revenge is freighted with serious liabilities. While some of its underlying motives and goals may be morally praiseworthy, revenge fails to right the balances of justice for the sake of victims, offenders, communities, and society at large. Although the goal of criminal retribution (a form of social vengeance) may well be to restore moral balance and safety to communities and societies in which humans dwell, the currency of pain and suffering it employs in the service of "evening the score" will not (in general) fulfill the obligations and right power imbalances perpetuated by acts judged to be criminal. The infliction of pain, suffering, and status humiliation as routine functions of punishment simply will not vindicate in the long run. Nonetheless, as Hauerwas has

45. Quoted in Hauerwas, "Why Time Cannot and Should Not Heal the Wounds of History," p. 145. See also Ignatieff, *Warrior's Honor*, p. 188.

been reminded by his philosopher friend Michael Quirk, "contrary to the liberal assumption that justice and vengeance are opposites, justice is a 'purification' of the moral impetus behind vengeance. Vengeance schooled by justice no longer takes delight in the harm it must do."[46]

Learning to Remember Well

Hauerwas's Christian alternative to vengeance is a form of "justice" which purifies vengeance. The theological content of such justice "is the name and confession: Jesus is the Christ of God. Jesus Christ is the language that ends the silences that threaten to destroy us. Christ is the memory that makes possible the memory of the wrongs we have done as well as that have been done to us."[47] Hauerwas believes that the truth of this form of Christian believing and knowing is but a "simplistic preachment" without some material display of the costs required. The reconciliation of Christ in the face of a criminal breach always happens in communion among the saints, a communion that makes possible a reconciliation of memory otherwise impossible. Drawing somewhat on Ignatieff's account of reconciliation, Hauerwas insists that, "any account of healing of memories is a 'politics.'" From here Hauerwas moves on to the challenge of articulating the form that politics ought to take for Christians. This requires *making explicit the difference God makes in the world.*

In agreement with Gregory Jones, Hauerwas contends that it is in remembering that we find hope of protection from our sin. What protects us from the pain and suffering that issues from our sin becoming the justification for sinning against others all the more "is not the hope that God will forget but rather that we are able to remember forgiven sin."[48] Transgression needs to be remembered, on Hauerwas's view, because God remembers: ". . . because if God does not remember then God is not the timeful God we find in Israel and the cross and resurrection of Christ.

46. Hauerwas, "Why Time Cannot and Should Not Heal the Wounds of History," p. 265 n. 17.

47. Hauerwas, "Why Time Cannot and Should Not Heal the Wounds of History," p. 146.

48. Hauerwas, "Why Time Cannot and Should Not Heal the Wounds of History," p. 150. Here Hauerwas references page 9 of an unpublished lecture by Gregory Jones entitled "Healing the Wounds of Memory." (Hauerwas does not cite the place or date of this lecture.)

That God, the God of Israel, the God that raised Jesus from the dead, is the God who makes time, makes memory, possible."[49] It is in time that a God of "temporal infinity" "makes possible all the time in the world to make our time, our memories, redeemed," according to Hauerwas. The memories of wrongs perpetrated against us in time can be redeemed because time has been redeemed by Christ. And this, for Hauerwas, "is why we do not need to deny our memories, shaped as they are by sin, but why we can trust memories to be transformed by forgiveness and reconciliation. Christian forgiveness is not that our sins no longer matter but that our sins are now made part of the economy of salvation for the constitution of a new community otherwise impossible."[50] It is crucial for Hauerwas that the gift of our forgiveness, of transformed but not forgotten memories of offense, be received in the context of gathered community. Hauerwas drives this point home with the words of Jones:

> Our forgiveness is not a gift that we receive as isolated individuals; it is a gift from the Spirit that is irreducibly particular in terms of the narratives of our pasts, yet that gift calls us into communion. In such communion, we are invited and required to learn to tell the story of each of our pasts, not ultimately in terms of diminutions, of betrayals and being betrayed, of violence committed or suffered, but in terms of the new life that induces us to repent and invites us to become holy in the future.[51]

Drawing on the work of Christian Duquoc, Hauerwas contends that God's work as displayed through Jesus' cross breaks "the link between offense and death and, in so doing, bring[s] to an end history as a history of violence."[52] God upsets the logic and power of violence by forgiving those — i.e., humanity at large — who crucified God's Son Jesus. And it is precisely because this most horrendous of crimes is not forgotten by God that forgiveness is made possible. Once more making the critical point that for-

49. Hauerwas, "Why Time Cannot and Should Not Heal the Wounds of History," p. 150.

50. Hauerwas, "Why Time Cannot and Should Not Heal the Wounds of History," pp. 150-51.

51. Quoted in Hauerwas, "Why Time Cannot and Should Not Heal the Wounds of History," p. 151. Also see Gregory Jones, *Embodying Forgiveness*, p. 173.

52. Hauerwas, "Why Time Cannot and Should Not Heal the Wounds of History," p. 151. See also Christian Duquoc, "The Forgiveness of God," *Concilium* 184 (1986): 40-41.

giveness has nothing to do with nonremembering, Hauerwas quotes favorably from Duquoc: "Forgiveness is not forgetfulness, it maintains the offending past in all its concreteness; nor is it lax, it calls for conversion."[53]

On Hauerwas's view it is through the resurrection of God's "envoy" Jesus Christ that God sows forgiveness in history. Pentecost then becomes the confirmation of this new beginning, a new beginning by which forgiveness is offered to everyone through the church: "The church is quite simply those converted, those made vulnerable, to God's history of forgiveness. They are those who have been given a new history, a new story rather than the world's story."[54]

53. Quoted in Hauerwas, "Why Time Cannot and Should Not Heal the Wounds of History," p. 151; Duquoc, "The Forgiveness of God," p. 42.

54. Hauerwas, "Why Time Cannot and Should Not Heal the Wounds of History," p. 151. Here we begin to see Hauerwas's longstanding tendency to see the contemporary church as a community of "resident aliens" enduring in a "wilderness" called "the world." Jeffrey Stout, in his book *Democracy and Tradition* (Princeton, N.J.: Princeton University Press, 2004) has accurately summarized Hauerwas's rhetorical tendency to view the church as set apart from a corrupt world existing after virtue — thereby intensifying the ugliness of its vices. Moreover, although Hauerwas affirms that the gospel is for the world, his description of the "the world" of "liberal democracy" easily gives the impression that society outside the church is wholly lacking in God's grace. Although Hauerwas views himself as drawing on the best of the traditions of John Howard Yoder and Karl Barth, Stout correctly points out that Hauerwas has neglected critical aspects of both Yoder's and Barth's thoughts regarding the church's relationship to "the world," in terms of the locus of grace. Stout (an atheist, no less) insightfully tries to get Hauerwas to tell the story of God's nondualistic, and gracious, providence over the world: "Notice, however, that Yoder intended his historical narrative as a criticism of the church, not as a criticism of the world. It was therefore possible, in principle, for Hauerwas to develop Yoder's conception of the church in a nondualistic direction, as seems to have been his intention in 1974. All he needed to do was emphasize that the world, like the church, is a realm ordained and ruled by God — an arena in which those with the eyes to see can perceive the working of God's gracious providence. He could reinforce this emphasis by adopting the Barthian view . . . that 'the boundary between Church and the profane still and repeatedly takes a course quite different from that which we hitherto thought we saw.' The main effect that MacIntyre's traditionalism has held on Hauerwas's thinking is to hinder the possibility of taking Yoder's 'politics of Jesus' where he had once wanted to take it. For he seems no longer to be moving in the direction of world-engaging conversation about the biblical injunction to build communities — ecclesial, familial, and national — in which justice and peace visibly embrace. One reason for this is that justice has largely dropped out of the picture. Another is that what Barth saw as an ever-shifting boundary between church and world appears to have hardened in Hauerwas's rhetoric into a rigid and static line between Christian virtue and liberal vice. It is clear that he does not intend to allow the boundary to harden in this way at the level of doctrine. But his

Hauerwas implies in his rhetoric that the distinction between the church and the world is powerfully embodied at baptism, in which sinners receive a new self and name. Baptism is but a reminder that individuals need the whole church to help them understand what the ongoing task of shedding the old self and learning to appropriate a new life of self in community looks like. But unlearning the old self is not the same as forgetting; unlearning the old self involves a critical "restoration of memory by our being given a new story that makes truthful memory possible."[55] This means that Christians must learn to become who they were ideally made to be, "not first by learning how to forgive but by learning to be forgiven." Christians receive their lives as individuals and in community as gifts from God situated in historical time:

> Our lives are constituted by discovering we are part of a history we have not created, a history without which we cannot make sense of what we think we have done as well as what we think has happened to us. Baptism is thereby completed in Eucharist, through which we discover that our lives are constituted by the lifelong project of forgiveness and repentance. God does not forget our sins but rather redeems our sins through eucharistic transformation.[56]

It is the Christian God who makes it possible for the church to be a community of memory; the church is also "God's memory for the world." God's memory for the world, then, involves "not forgetting but having our memories transformed through the discovery that our sins cannot determine God's will for our lives."[57]

Hauerwas contends that Christian reconciliation is a deeply illiberal

---

antiliberal rhetoric can easily give the impression that the boundary has hardened in practice. In practical terms, Barth was engaged in a project quite unlike Hauerwas's. He wanted both to utter an absolutely unequivocal 'NO!' to Nazism and to counteract the tendency of the confessing church to believe that it could have the gospel without progressive politics. Hauerwas utters his 'No!' to liberalism, but there is little in his work that resembles Barth's active commitment to democracy and socialist reform" (pp. 154-55).

55. Hauerwas, "Why Time Cannot and Should Not Heal the Wounds of History," p. 151.

56. Hauerwas, "Why Time Cannot and Should Not Heal the Wounds of History," p. 151. See also Jones, *Embodying Forgiveness*, p. 179.

57. Hauerwas, "Why Time Cannot and Should Not Heal the Wounds of History," pp. 152-53.

idea; it is an "idea" fundamentally at odds with liberal political arrangements.[58] Reconciliation as Hauerwas has outlined it takes slow and painful time. As a forgiving refusal to forget, reconciliation is a counterpolitics to the world's politics. Yet it is a counterpolitics that even makes reconciliation between nations a possibility.

The foregoing theological politics of memory is suggestive for Christian thinking about the practice of punishment and imprisonment insofar as it places the hope of forgiveness firmly within a communal framework guided by obedience to God. Hauerwas thinks that too often attempts to think through and understand the practice of punishment starting with the standard theories renders theological considerations absent. From a theological point of view the *telos* of punishment must be reconciliation and forgiveness. On Hauerwas's view, the absence of hope for forgiveness with memory will reinforce and expand prisons as human warehouses. In such a situation both offenders and criminal justice system administrators will continue to have serious difficulties viewing their experiences and their work as significant and purposeful.[59]

Although Hauerwas views forgiveness and reconciliation as the *telos*

---

58. It could of course be objected here that it depends what "liberalism" one is referring to. Some secular humanist liberal traditions, even on antifoundational grounds, also remember well. Michael Ignatieff has correctly pointed out that "the strength of a purely secular ethics is its insistence that there are no 'sacred' purposes that can ever justify the inhumane use of human beings. An antifoundational humanism may be insecure, but it does have the advantage that it cannot justify inhumanity on foundational grounds. A secular defense of human rights depends on the idea of moral reciprocity: that we judge human actions by the simple test of whether we would wish to be on the receiving end. And since we cannot conceive of any circumstances in which we or anyone we know would wish to be abused in mind or body, we have good reasons to believe that such practices should be outlawed." I would contend that the "good reasons" to believe what Ignatieff is arguing here regarding a basic fact that we generally possess "the faculty of imagining the pain and degradation done to other human beings as if it were our own," points to a liberal-tradition-based human capacity to remember well. This is no less true even for those who choose to, or who have learned to, suppress or remain indifferent to traditions, liberal or otherwise, that tell stories of the empathy most all humans possess within our consciences. See Michael Ignatieff, *Human Rights as Politics and Idolatry*, ed. Amy Gutmann (Princeton, N.J.: Princeton University Press, 2001), pp. 88-89. All of this is to say that Christianity does not have a corner on remembering well; but when conceived of at its best, Christianity can provide humanity some roots for anchoring the flower of moral empathy.

59. Hauerwas, "Punishing Christians," p. 189. See also Forrester, "Priorities for Social Theology Today," p. 30.

of criminal punishment, he is equally sure that appeals to forgiveness and reconciliation ought not hide from us the seriousness of punishment and the legitimate role punishment has for society and the church. It does no good to lift up "forgiveness" if Christians do not live their own lives in ways that demonstrate why punishment is a necessary practice, particularly if the church is to be the church: "Appeals to forgiveness are too easy if we have not first made clear why we think it is wrong to execute people for stock fraud." Hauerwas reminds readers that the church at one time believed that persons convicted of heresy should be killed, a position justified on grounds that heresy was a more serious crime than murder: "A murderer after all only robs us of our life; a heretic robs us of our salvation."[60]

Righteous Retribution? Critiquing O'Donovan's Commentary on *Evangelium Vitae*

In order to further explore the theological issues at the heart of criminal punishment, Hauerwas draws on Oliver O'Donovan's compelling justification of capital punishment, which emerged in the context of O'Donovan's critique of John Paul II's praise in *Evangelium Vitae (The Gospel of Life)* for the limited use or abolishment of capital punishment. O'Donovan, like Hauerwas, was troubled by the Pope's apparent caving in to the "sentimental humanism of our time."

O'Donovan developed his critique of *Evangelium Vitae* in the context of a close reading of the following passage:

> This is the context in which to place the problem of the death penalty. On this matter there is a growing tendency, both in the Church and in civil society, to demand that it be applied in a very limited way or even that it be abolished completely. The problem must be viewed in the context of a system of penal justice ever more in line with human dignity and thus, in the end, with God's plan for man and society. The primary purpose of the punishment which society inflicts is "to redress the disorder caused by the offense." Public authority must redress the violation of personal and social rights by imposing on the offender an adequate punishment for the crime, as a condition for the

60. Hauerwas, "Punishing Christians," p. 190.

offender to regain the exercise of his or her freedom. In this way authority also fulfills the purpose of defending public order and ensuring people's safety, while at the same time offering an incentive and help to change his or her behavior and be rehabilitated.

It is clear that for these purposes to be achieved, the nature and extent of the punishment must be carefully evaluated and decided upon, and ought not go to the extreme of executing the offender except in cases of absolute necessity: in other words, when it would not be possible otherwise to defend society. Today, however, as a result of steady improvements in the organization of the penal system, such cases are very rare, if not practically nonexistent.

In any event, the principle set forth in the new Catechism of the Catholic Church remains valid: "If bloodless means are sufficient to defend human lives against an aggressor and to protect public order and the safety of persons, public authority must limit itself to such means, because they better correspond to the concrete conditions of the common good and are more in conformity to the dignity of the human person."[61]

Hauerwas outlines O'Donovan's criticism of the Pope's position by noting three issues in need of clarification: (1) What characteristics of a society are presupposed by the "steady improvements" to which the Pope refers?; (2) What kind of situation would count as an "absolute necessity"?; and (3) Why does the Pope justify capital punishment in classical retributive categories, but make the possibility for the lessening use of capital punishment turn on remedial considerations?[62]

Hauerwas points out that O'Donovan's most critical challenge to the Pope's position concerns question number three. Hauerwas lifts up for analysis O'Donovan's account of why the late eighteenth- and nineteenth-century consensus that retribution is the final function of punishment can never be disavowed by public authorities. Hauerwas questions why this was a development Christians should applaud and argues that, "I should

---

61. Quoted in Hauerwas, "Punishing Christians," pp. 190-91. See also *The Encyclicals of John Paul II*, ed. J. Michael Miller, C.S.B. (Huntington, Ind.: Our Sunday Visitor, 1996), par. 56.

62. See Oliver O'Donovan, "The Death Penalty in *Evangelium Vitae*," in *Ecumenical Ventures in Ethics: Protestants Engage Pope John Paul II's Moral Encyclicals*, ed. Reinhard Hutter and Theodor Dieter (Grand Rapids, Mich.: Eerdmans, 1998), pp. 220-23.

think the 'reformative' account of punishment was and is the justification most modern people assume justifies punishment."[63] While Hauerwas may well be right in thinking that most people assume reformation to be the justification for punishment, I have endeavored to demonstrate here that whatever the popular assumption(s) may be about the aim of punishment, the actual function of punishment produces little in the way of reformation of those convicted of crime.

On O'Donovan's view, punishment is an expressive act to the extent that "punishment must pronounce judgment on the offense, describing it, disowning it, and refounding the moral basis for the common life which the offense has challenged."[64] Here "punishment" is viewed as "giving back" the offense. Not only can this be understood in terms of vengeance, to "give back" also constitutes a true statement about what has happened. On this view, retribution is rightly considered the primary aim of punishment. Moreover, retribution is not considered to be a synonym for vengeance on this account because vengeance is "private" and, therefore, arbitrary according to O'Donovan.[65] While Hauerwas does recognize the

---

63. Hauerwas, "Punishing Christians," p. 192 n. 14.

64. O'Donovan, quoted in Hauerwas, "Punishing Christians," p. 192; O'Donovan, "The Death Penalty," p. 224.

65. O'Donovan is not alone in arguing that important distinctions between retribution and vengeance ought to be observed. Louis Pojman, a philosophy professor at the United States Military Academy, suggests that retribution expressed as *lex talionis* ("an eye for an eye, a tooth for a tooth, a life for a life," see Exodus 21) "was actually a gesture of restraint on the passion for vengeance." Pojman goes on to argue that, "we must separate retributivism form vengeance. Vengeance signifies acts that arise out of the victims' desire for revenge, for satisfying their anger at the criminal for what he or she has done. . . . But retributivism is not based on hatred for the criminal (though a feeling of vengeance may accompany the punishment). Retributivism is the theory that the criminal *deserves* to be punished and deserves to be punished in proportion to the gravity of his or her crime — whether or not the victim or anyone else desires it. We may all deeply regret carrying out the punishment." Pojman goes on to rightly admit that retributivism and revenge represent "two attitudes [that] are often intermixed in practice," but then retreats back to his main argument: "Revenge is a personal response to a perpetrator for an injury. Retribution is an impartial and impersonal response to an offender for an offense done against someone. You cannot desire revenge for the harm of someone to whom you are indifferent. Revenge always involves personal concern for the victim. Retribution is not personal but based on objective factors: the criminal has deliberately harmed an innocent party and so *deserves* to be punished, whether I wish it or not." See Louis P. Pojman and Jeffery Reiman, *The Death Penalty: For and Against* (New York: Rowman & Littlefield, 1998), pp. 19, 21, 52. I think that Pojman is

distinction O'Donovan wishes to draw between the arbitrariness of private vengeance and the social legitimacy of retribution, he nonetheless finds the distinction to be "a bit forced." Suggesting that retribution is but the public authority's working out of vengeance, Hauerwas summarizes his disagreement with O'Donovan as follows:

> If vengeance is the symbolic way people gesture that order is deeper than disorder, it seems appropriate that retribution serve to provide the vengeance those directly involved in a crime feel they need. That those who have someone close to them violated so often express the need to have the perpetrator of the violence killed and even to see them executed cannot be easily dismissed as "a primitive attitude." That a "public authority" should perform the execution is important, but the execution remains the working out of vengeance.[66]

In this argument, Hauerwas is drawing heavily on a pamphlet written by John Howard Yoder entitled "The Christian and Capital Punishment," in which Yoder maintains that vengeance plays an important role in shaping capital punishment. Hauerwas correctly notes that Yoder's position concerning the role of vengeance in capital punishment "does not necessarily make his view of capital punishment different from O'Donovan's stress on justice because Yoder also observes that 'vengeance is happening; the necessity is that it be controlled.'"[67] Yoder argues that a significant function of

---

most correct in his admission that retributivism and revenge "are often intermixed in practice." Given that this reality is much more intensified today, I contend that retributive justice as practiced today in the U.S. amounts to a form of social vengeance. Given society's fast-paced and ubiquitous participation in the public spectacle of horrendous crime and punishment stories, our manufactured "culture of fear" leaves few people capable of "indifference" or "objectivity" in the face of crime perceived as gone amok. For example, the ferocious and exaggerated pace at which crime is piped into the homes of average U.S. residents via television makes for fewer and fewer people devoid of a personal concern for victims they do not know. Given the ever increasing vicariousness of society's fear and empathy for the victims of crime-gone-wild, a much more public desire to inflict social vengeance on criminals who we feel are a threat to our personal sense of safety and well-being is now fairly common. Today, for all practical purposes, retribution as defined (idealistically) by Pojman and others has been corrupted by the passion of vengeance. Retributive justice now amounts to social vengeance incarnate.

66. Hauerwas, "Punishing Christians," p. 192 n. 16.
67. Quoted in Hauerwas, "Punishing Christians," p. 192 n. 16.

civil order is that it "limit vengeance to a level equivalent to the offense." But, according to Yoder, "Vengeance was never God's highest intent for men's [sic] relations with one another; permitting it within the limits of justice, i.e., of equivalent injury, was never really his purpose."[68] Hauerwas concurs with Yoder's argument that what God aims to do with evil is to "swallow it up, drown it in the bottomless sea of His crucified love."[69] Hauerwas contends that Yoder's understanding of how the civil order "limits vengeance" has "at least resemblance to O'Donovan's understanding of justice."

O'Donovan's account of retribution as giving back the offense (i.e., doing justice) is viewed as the legitimate primary function of punishment, and, as such, retribution is not a means to some other end. The primary goal of punishment is not one of making the offender good; rather the goal of punishment is justice. On this account retribution as the form that justice takes may well produce secondary goods associated with punishment, but this ought not alter our understanding that the end of punishment is justice understood as retribution.

O'Donovan is worried that John Paul II might have come too close to suggesting that capital punishment be abolished in principle. O'Donovan thinks that in paragraph 40 of *Evangelium Vitae* the Pope appears to be moving toward advocacy of a position that would not require capital punishment as a necessary part of a humane justice system. In paragraph 40 John Paul II comments on the prohibition of murder in the Decalogue: "Of course we must recognize that in the Old Testament this sense of the value of life, though already quite marked, does not yet reach the refinement found in the Sermon on the Mount. This is apparent in some aspects of the current penal legislation, which provided for severe forms of corporal punishment and even the death-penalty."[70]

O'Donovan, as Hauerwas correctly observes, believes that the Pope's account of capital punishment severs the necessary link between public safety and the system of retributive justice. This, from O'Donovan's point of view, wrongly makes capital punishment but an emergency provision

68. Quoted in Hauerwas, "Punishing Christians," p. 192 n. 16; Yoder, "The Christian and Capital Punishment," p. 7.

69. Yoder, "The Christian and Capital Punishment," p. 7. Quoted in Hauerwas, "Punishing Christians," p. 192 n. 16.

70. Quoted in Hauerwas, "Punishing Christians," p. 193; O'Donovan, "The Death Penalty," p. 229.

that allegedly is no longer necessary in modern, economically developed, and well-governed societies. O'Donovan believes it a terrible mistake that the coercive powers of the state in matters of criminal justice be derived and justified on grounds similar to the just war perspective of "legitimate defense." The difficulty for O'Donovan here is that, "The right of the state to impose coercive measures against wrongdoers arises 'not from its need to defend itself but from its office of judgment.'"[71]

O'Donovan suggests theologically that death was not part of God's original created order. But death does enter into human history as a judgment upon sin. Here O'Donovan sees a critical link between judgment and death. He contends that Christ is viewed as just another victim of injustice rather than as the one who bore human sins, suffering the death they deserved, whenever the link between judgment and death is severed. Therefore, according to O'Donovan, we "cannot be rid of the symbolic role that the death penalty plays in relating death to judgment. There will always be a death penalty in the mind — if, that is, we are to learn to 'die with Christ,' understanding our own deaths as a kind of capital punishment."[72]

With regard to the Christian understanding and practice of punishment, Hauerwas wants to challenge what he views as the sentimental humanism that currently dominates discussions surrounding capital and other types of punishment. Like O'Donovan, Hauerwas rejects calling for an end to capital punishment on grounds associated with "humanistic" ideologies and practices. Nonetheless he parts company with O'Donovan with his insistence that from a Christian perspective capital punishment must come to an end while retaining nonlethal forms of punishment as a valid social practice. While Hauerwas does believe that punishment has a legitimate social function, "the end of that punishment has been transformed by the cross and resurrection of Christ."[73] Moreover, Hauerwas's account of punishment sees transformation as a possibility for the practice of punishment in both the church and society. Hauerwas rightly understands that any society, and its public authorities and state officials doing the governing, has a responsibility to serve the goods in common. This in-

71. See Hauerwas, "Punishing Christians," p. 194.

72. Quoted in Hauerwas, "Punishing Christians," p. 195; primary source, O'Donovan, "The Death Penalty," p. 235.

73. Hauerwas, "Punishing Christians," p. 195.

cludes the meting out of punishment.[74] For Christians, this meting out of punishment occurs within a particular countercultural narrative always discerning and acting upon the difference the "peaceable" politics of Jesus makes in the world.

Summary

Stanley Hauerwas's Christian ethics of punishment, first and foremost, challenges Christians to a testimony and witness of holiness steeped in the tradition of the peaceable countercultural politics of Jesus. Indeed the church's practice of "punishment" is to be grounded in a vision of faithfulness that does not conceive of human life and social arrangements in terms of liberal, contractual, notions of "freedom," "justice," and "individual autonomy." Rather Christians are memory-bound by (are "slaves" to) one another and to their God.

The end of "good punishment" within the bounds of the Christian moral life is made concrete in the process and form of penance, forgiveness, and reconciliation in the context of self-inflicted sinfulness. Taken together, this process constitutes a politics of healing memory, a form of divine "justice" which limits, purifies, swallows up, and drowns in the bottomless sea of God's crucified love, the understandable human thirst for vengeance, for retribution. For Christians, this represents the foundations of "goodness" in view of which "punishment" is understood and regulated; indeed this anchors "good punishment" in the process of becoming.

In the next two chapters, then, I will, in critical engagement with Hauerwas's very important work, turn toward constructing a Christian social ethics of good punishment as a way forward in Christian discernments

---

74. Hauerwas intentionally distinguishes "public authorities" from the "state" because he means to call into question "the assumption that the 'state as such' is a known entity." He proceeds to explain that, "I assume peoples can exist with structures of authority that are not the same as 'a state' particularly when the state in modernity is identified with the locus of hegemonic power. This may seem an unimportant distinction, but too often the 'state' is simply accepted as a given in a manner that makes it impervious to the gospel. For example, Avery Cardinal Dulles observes that while the church can and does punish, she is also indulgent toward offenders. For example, he observes 'it would be clearly inappropriate for the Church, as a spiritual society, to execute criminals, but the State is a different type of society. It cannot be expected to act as a Church.'" Hauerwas, "Punishing Christians," p. 196.

about U.S. imprisonment and the attending collateral social consequences. I approach this task in Chapters Five and Six respectively, by building upon two important dimensions of Hauerwas's Christian understanding of punishment: namely, his conceptions of "healing memories" and "ontological intimacy." Specifically I will build upon his use of these terms by bringing them to bear on an analysis of U.S. imprisonment practices. In Chapter Five, I will take up the relevance of healing memories as a politics that informs a public Christian practice of "good punishment" in the context of imprisonment and its social consequences. Finally, in Chapter Six, I will take up the relationship between imprisonment practices and what I call a "politics of ontological intimacy." The politics of ontological intimacy is the name I give to the restorative aim of the politics of healing memories. A politics of healing memories (penance, forgiveness, and reconciliation) as the form good punishment takes is a transformative social tributary that moves us toward transformed lives of ontological intimacy. My hope is that my efforts will prove useful for Christians (and perhaps others) who wish to address contemporary U.S. imprisonment practices, their associated collateral social consequences, and the deep-issue human alienations exacerbated by both.

5. Good Punishment:
The Possibility of a Politics of
Healing Memories in the Public Square

Revisiting the Problem

In this book I have tried to demonstrate that the current United States practice of increasingly harsh imprisonment, along with the scale with which imprisonment is imposed, are major obstacles to the transformation of offenders, victims, families, and communities, as well as to the common good of society as a whole. Moreover, I have argued that associated with contemporary prison practices, and in the service of a wider prison-industrial complex, are a variety of (largely unrecognized) collateral social consequences. These consequences include a significant transformation in the nation's family and community dynamics, and the exacerbation of racial divisions, broad-scale economic hardship, and economic and social risk for the most vulnerable of the nation's residents, particularly children. In addition, I have argued that imprisonment on such a large scale poses fundamental questions of justice/fairness and citizenship in a democratic society. Such a state of affairs has worsened a basic and tragic human tendency to become alienated from one another, to turn away from our mutual affections with both neglectful indifference toward and virulent oppression of other human beings — especially the "criminals" among us.

To be sure, incapacitation of dangerous offenders is an important requirement for any society wishing to maintain itself and flourish. My intention here is to be critical of practices of punishment that ironically leave individuals, families, communities, and society less able to realize peace, transforming justice, and common flourishing. Today such goals are routinely sacrificed at the altar of the prison-industrial complex, an interlocking matrix of corporate, governmental, correctional, and media interests that encourage increased spending on imprisonment, regardless of the actual need. As an alternative to this system, I now turn to an argument for the relevance of healing memories as a politics that informs a public Christian practice of "good punishment" in the context of imprisonment and its attending collateral social consequences.

A Politics of Healing Memories as Good Punishment

Stanley Hauerwas views the Christian understanding of punishment (of which reconciliation and forgiveness are the *telos*) as a politics of healing memories. The proper name given by Christians to punishment understood as a politics of healing memory is "excommunication" or "binding and loosing," according to Hauerwas. To have our offense confronted by our sisters and brothers because of our sin is a call to reconciliation. For Hauerwas, penance and forgiveness are critical components of reconciliation. When offenders refuse to respond positively to hearing the call to reconcile, they condemn themselves. To be excommunicated is not the same as being thrown out of community; rather, offenders already stand outside community on account of their offense. Excommunication, then, "is a call to come home by helping us locate how we have alienated ourselves from God and those that gather to worship God."[1] A practice of holiness commensurate with the Christian desire to be a people called to witness to God, the only forgiver of sins, is the background before which excommunication makes sense.

From Hauerwas's point of view, to say that "Christians punish" necessarily means that practices exist in which it is possible to recognize sins. Such practices include lying, stealing, rape, adultery, killing, and so forth. A question that fascinates Hauerwas, and that needs exploration, "is the relation between what Christians call sin and what is understood as crime." According to Hauerwas, "Christians who commit crimes may sin, but criminals who are not Christians may not be sinners."[2] Yet because

1. Stanley Hauerwas, "Punishing Christians," in *Performing the Faith: Bonhoeffer and the Practice of Nonviolence* (Grand Rapids, Mich.: Brazos Press, 2004), p. 199.

2. Hauerwas, "Punishing Christians," p. 199 n. 33. Lee Griffith helpfully reminds us of the attempts of Luther and Calvin ("and other Christians before and since") to undo the un-

Christians have contributed so heavily to current understandings of crime, it is difficult to distinguish between sin and crime. Hauerwas apparently believes that since liberal society cannot, with any measure of certainty, name the common goods allegedly injured by crime, arguments about crime tend to be waged randomly.

> In social orders as fragile as those in the so-called first world, one of the few places the language of the common good works is in agreements about what constitutes crime. But to recognize a crime requires an account of the positive goods that crime injures. It is not clear that liberal social orders can confidently name such goods, which makes their presumed arguments about crime increasingly arbitrary.[3]

Hauerwas argues that the Christian practice of punishment must necessarily "resist being confined by the various theories of punishment." What Christians offer the wider society is not a better theory of punishment, but a practice of punishment based on the peaceable narrative of Je-

---

fortunate Christian tendency to equate "crime" with "sin." Griffith is worth quoting at length on this issue: "The equation falls apart when we recognize that many crimes are not sins and many sins are not crimes. Some young men, for example, have justifiably committed the crime of refusing to register for the draft in order to renounce war. On the other hand, even though the prophets railed against the sins of those who cast widows out of their homes, modern bankers can do precisely that without committing any crime at all. Even though sin and crime may coincide at some points, the laws of society often pick the specks while ignoring beams. There is an incongruity to punishing petty theft when the middle-class life-style of Americans represents a grand-scale theft from the planet. There *are* enough resources to provide all people with food and shelter on the planet, but it would simply be impossible to provide six billion people with a middle-class American life-style. What remains of the natural integrity of the creation is already under severe strain. We cannot continue to view the earth as one giant 'resource' from which we may extract at will. We share the planet with other creatures that have also been given the gift of life, and we share the planet with other people. We have limits, and today those limits mean that the acquisition of possessions invariably *dispossesses* others. Climbing up the social ladder is stealing. It is stealing from the earth and from those sisters and brothers who are currently living on the fringes of survival. It is an example of how some of the most deadly sins are perfectly legal. The point is not to criminalize sin but to stop pretending that law-abiding citizens are holier than common criminals. Quite literally and directly, climbing the social ladder is stealing — and it is time for us to climb on down." Lee Griffith, *The Fall of the Prison: Biblical Perspectives on Prison Abolition* (Eugene, Ore.: Wipf and Stock, 1999), pp. 186-87.

3. Hauerwas, "Punishing Christians," p. 199 n. 33.

sus. Hauerwas raises what is for him a very serious concern regarding whether a societal imitation of the difference Jesus makes in the world can be achieved abstracted from the worship of God. It is in the context of the worship of God that Christian action gains its intelligibility.

Hauerwas suggests that there was a time in the past when civil/state authorities were willing to pursue a practice of punishment in imitation of a Christian "better hope." But once the religious/theological backdrop of the prison faded the result has been the miserable practice of punishment we know today. Drawing on the work of Mennonite theologian John Howard Yoder, Hauerwas argues that, "prisons were once called 'penitentiaries' because they were understood as places to repent. Once the background practices that make repentance the *telos* of punishment were missing, prisons could not help but become the hell holes they are today."[4] (And of course it can be said, given the observations of numerous commentators who were present to witness and experience the beginning experiments in modern penology, that prisons were basically "hell holes" from the start.)

As stated above, "excommunication" is the name Hauerwas gives to the "good punishment" that Christians practice. Excommunication as he articulates it is guided by a politics of healing (or reconciled) memory, which counts reconciliation and forgiveness as its goals. Although Hauerwas's articulation of a politics of healing memories is primarily addressed to Christian communities, I believe that such a politics holds promise as an important goal in the context of public debates over imprisonment.

It is apparent on a theological level, i.e., at the level of faith seeking understanding, that Hauerwas's ethics of punishment is helpful in laying down virtue-dependent principles that could appropriately be applied (for example) to society's routine reliance on vengeance and status humiliation in its practice of imprisonment. Rather than vengeful status humiliation (retributive degradation) as a function of imprisonment, Hauerwas's Christian vision of reconciliation and forgiveness could be extended beyond the church and be brought to bear within a wider society struggling with the crisis of imprisonment and its allied collateral social consequences.[5]

---

4. Hauerwas, "Punishing Christians," p. 200.

5. This kind of active, expressive hope for a "better relevance" of Christian concern for society at large is (for example) an expression of Reinhold Niebuhr's important challenge in *Moral Man and Immoral Society* (New York: Charles Scribner's Sons, 1932).

A politics of reconciled memory is the positive dimension Hauerwas gives to the Christian practice of reconciliation, and it is a salient dimension of Hauerwas's understanding of good punishment. I, too, think a notion of reconciled memory is critical, because of its insistence that Christians understand that *memories of sin cannot be denied or forgotten.* Hauerwas wisely acknowledges that the elimination of what Christians might call punishment must never seek forgetfulness in the name of forgiveness and reconciliation.

Since I will employ Hauerwas's principle of memory as a politics which redeems our memories of criminal offense, it is worth repeating here, in summary, what I said in the preceding chapter about the important aspects of Hauerwas's ethics of punishment on the matter of memory in the context of reconciliation. Recall that Hauerwas thinks it wrong to suggest that the Christian practice of forgiveness "wipes out memory." On the contrary, according to Hauerwas, forgiveness is a power that makes memory possible. It is fair to say that with Hauerwas's politics of healing memory the link between offense and death is broken, bringing to an end the history of violence. God upsets the logic and power of violence by forgiving humanity for its sins, including that of the execution of God's Son Jesus. Tied to both a theology meant to address distortions in the grammar of the faith and as virtue-dependent Christian practice, Hauerwas's Christian ethics of punishment offers promise to the extent that it challenges Christians to imagine and perform "good punishment" that heals and reconciles. Such a politics is a witness to Christian faith and obedience to the God of Israel.

Hauerwas's basic theological argument is that the church best exemplifies its witness to the world when it *remembers* itself as a tradition committed to being a living testimony to the difference Jesus' life, death, and resurrection makes in the world. Against societal convention the church is to embody peaceableness. As a holy people, the church understands its gift to society as that of modeling suffering love and endurance. Christians are not to be triumphalistic seekers of "justice" who think they must control history. It is in such a context that Hauerwas understands the Christian politics of healing memory.

An Assessment

Much of the content and function of Hauerwas's politics of healing memory (or reconciled memory) is useful as a guide for Christian discernment regarding good punishment. Indeed, not only does Hauerwas view good punishment as a process of penance, forgiveness, and reconciliation in obedience to Jesus Christ, he rightly understands the refusal to forget as an important dimension of such a politics. For Christians, the pain and suffering associated with remembering well is rightly linked to the hope of transformed memory as a result of God's self-unveiled forgiveness and reconciliation in the person of Jesus Christ.

However, despite its merits, Hauerwas's explication of a Christian politics of healing or reconciled memory is unconvincing on a number of important levels, both as politics for the Christian community itself and for a wider society struggling with imprisoning its residents at an unprecedented rate. The first difficulty I have concerns Hauerwas's use of the term "excommunication." While I do understand what I take to be Hauerwas's intention to be faithful to an allegedly peaceable Anabaptist communal sanction, which has long meted out excommunication as a church discipline, the term, far from being an "invitation" back into community, contains connotations of cruelty, furthering the cause of human alienation, which is an affront to Hauerwas's own politics of healing memories within gathered community. I believe this to be the case notwithstanding the distinctive content and function given to the term by Hauerwas. I would argue that in the minds of contemporary Christians, and in the wider society, excommunication as a term conjures up notions of being thrown or cast out, exiled, or banished from the geopolitical space and affections of one's community or nation. While much of the content of Hauerwas's understanding of excommunication may be appropriate, the term itself does not sound quite like the invitation of "welcoming back" he hopes the church will communicate to those who have transgressed against the community.

In my hope of bringing to bear on the problem of imprisonment something of Hauerwas's understanding of penance, forgiveness, and reconciliation, I would suggest recasting Hauerwas's contention that excommunication constitutes the proper term for Christian punishment. For example, without changing the content, instead of employing the term "excommunication" as an expression of good punishment, we might understand community sanction in terms of an expression already being used in some peace church circles, namely, "care-fronting." Though some may dismiss it as sentimental, this term brings a less alienating emotional tenor to corrective, transforming punishment and communal good will. The use of the term care-fronting, or some other like it, would avoid excommunication's negative sense of being rejected, ostracized, and stigmatized, which are feelings already experienced by most prisoners. Here a community signals to an offender, "We care about you, you are still one of us, even as we must now insist that you take serious responsibility for your offense." Here an offender might still feel a sense of excommunication, but the experience of isolation would be self-imposed (as Hauerwas understands) and would not be meted out by the grammar of Christian sanction.

Whatever terms one may choose to communicate the means of good punishment to offenders, such terms ought not deepen the waters of alienation already experienced by most prisoners. Writer and broadcaster David Cayley has rightly contended that "prison is the world of those who feel themselves to have been rejected and ostracized."[6] He goes on to imply, quite correctly, that because prisoners feel themselves to be outcasts, the prison "tends to develop a defensive counterculture — it is an upside down world, a demonic parody of conventional society in which rules are reversed."[7] Finally Cayley, summarizing an observation made by Monty Lewis, argues that "prisons and the world of crime they anchor must be understood as counterfeit communities: a place to belong for people who have not belonged anywhere else."[8]

It needs to be made abundantly clear that I am not meaning to suggest that Hauerwas intends his vision of excommunication to be applied to social problems in the society or "the world," or in particular to social problems related to the practice of imprisonment. Excommunication, as Hauerwas understands the term, points to a practice of particular Christian churches, which ought to be practiced by Christians in general. Yet, as I see things, the content of good punishment (penance, forgiveness, reconciliation) and its function (restoring/reconciling offenders to community) can be applied to the social practice of imprisonment. A question that immediately arises in what has been said in this chapter up to now concerns

6. David Cayley, *The Expanding Prison: The Crisis in Crime and Punishment and the Search for Alternatives* (Cleveland: Pilgrim Press, 1998), p. 107.

7. Cayley, *The Expanding Prison*, p. 107.

8. Cayley, *The Expanding Prison*, p. 107.

the extent and manner to which Christians ought to involve themselves in the cultivation of good punishment (as expressed in practices associated with a politics of healing memories) within society at large. In particular, can Hauerwas's understanding of what constitutes "good punishment" for the Christian community adequately be brought to bear on the societal problem of imprisonment and its collateral social consequences? I now turn to a critical exploration of these important questions.

Christian Witness in the Public Square

Hauerwas contends that, although "the world" does not share the Christian faith and therefore cannot be expected to live as Christians ought to live, this in no way means that a sectarian demarcation should be established indicating what Christians cannot ask of the societies in which they find themselves as "resident aliens." Hauerwas's reasoning here draws heavily (once again) on the thought of Mennonite theologian John Howard Yoder. Although Hauerwas's rhetoric is very critical of the moral limits of liberalism, he is not in my judgment a true sectarian, at least not all the way down.

Hauerwas himself vigorously argues against being labeled a sectarian, if by "sectarian" one means regard only for the faithfulness of the church with no concern for the common good of society at large. Hauerwas argues that Christians are never faced with the option of "either *complete* involvement in culture or *complete* withdrawal." Indeed, Hauerwas sees "no reason why such a stark alternative is necessary." "The issue," he contends, "is how the church can provide the interpretative categories to help Christians to better understand the positive and negative aspects of their societies and guide their subsequent selective participation."[9] Christians must decide upon their selective participation contextually,

> Insofar as the church can reclaim its integrity as a community of virtue, it can be of great service in liberal societies. Moreover, the fact that I have written about why and how Christians should support as well as serve the medical and legal professions, Christian relations with Juda-

9. Stanley M. Hauerwas, *Christian Existence Today: Essays on Church, World, and Living In Between* (Grand Rapids, Mich.: Baker Books, 1995), p. 11.

ism, how we might think about justice, as well as an analysis of the moral debate concerning nuclear war seems to have no effect on those who are convinced I am a "withdrawn" sectarian. To be sure, I have made no secret of my indebtedness to John Howard Yoder . . . but I do not understand why that association is sufficient to make me a sectarian, unless one assumes uncritically that a Mennonite must be a sectarian. At the very least those making that charge should attend to Yoder's arguments concerning the Christian's positive duties to wider society and the state.[10]

Hauerwas affirms that the resurrection and ascension of Christ is relevant for the church and world, hence no societal situation exists in which Christians should think that nothing can be done. On this point Hauerwas is again deeply indebted to Yoder's teachings:

The world can be challenged, one point at a time, to take one step in the right direction, to move up one modest notch in approximation to the righteousness of love. To challenge capital punishment no more undermines government than does rejection of the oath (Matthew 5:33-37, James 5:12) undermine truth telling; no more than does the consent of the governed destroy the authority of the state. The civil order is a fact. That [the state] might be done away with by pushing the

10. Hauerwas, *Christian Existence Today,* p. 7. See also the following by Stanley Hauerwas: on the church as a positive influence on society, *Vision and Virtue* (Notre Dame, Ind.: University of Notre Dame Press, 1974), pp. 222-60, and *A Community of Character: Toward a Constructive Christian Social Ethic* (Notre Dame, Ind.: University of Notre Dame Press, 1981); on a Christian relationship to the medical and legal professions, *Suffering Presence* (Notre Dame, Ind.: University of Notre Dame Press, 1986); on Christian relations with Judaism, *Against the Nations* (Minneapolis: Winston-Seabury, 1985), pp. 61-90; reflections on justice, "Should Christians Talk So Much About Justice?" *Books and Religion* 14, no. 6 (May-June 1986): 5ff, "On the Right To Be Tribal," *Christian Scholars Review* XVI, 3 (March 1987): 238-241, *Truthfulness and Tragedy: Further Investigations into Christian Ethics* (Notre Dame, Ind.: University of Notre Dame Press, 1977), pp. 132-47, and "Postscript: A Response to Jeff Stout's *Democracy and Tradition,*" in *Performing The Faith,* pp. 215-42; esp. pp. 229-32; on the moral debate concerning nuclear war, *Against the Nations,* pp. 132-208. Cf. with Yoder on church society/state relations, *Christian Witness to the State* (Newton, Kans.: Faith and Life Press, 1964). It is also worth reading, with regard to Hauerwas's alleged sectarianism, Nigel Biggar's essay "Is Stanley Hauerwas Sectarian," in *Faithfulness and Fortitude: In Conversation with the Theological Ethics of Stanley Hauerwas,* ed. Mark Thiessen Nation and Samuel Wells (Edinburgh: T&T Clark, 2000), pp. 141-60.

critique of love "too far" is inconceivable. Thus the Christian (and any believer in democracy) will be concerned to restrain the violent, vengeful potential of the state. That potential for violence does not need our advocacy: it is already there.[11]

Hauerwas points out that there is an objection to what Yoder has said above that misses the point in the context of criminal punishment. According to Hauerwas it could be argued that, "the issue is not whether the state exists or, even, whether we have a justification to sustain the legitimacy of the state. The issue is justice."[12] In responding to this assertion Hauerwas leans on a rebuttal offered by Yoder himself, who questions the assumption that there is any univocal "concept of justice, having the same meaning in all times and places, consisting in an exact logical or mathematical equivalence of offense and retribution, and that such 'justice' must (or can) be either wholly respected or fundamentally rejected."[13]

In fundamental agreement with Yoder concerning the historical flexibility of defining "justice," Hauerwas contends that there is no such thing as a culturally invariant understanding of what equivalent punishment should or does require in terms of responding to similar criminal cases. For example, the presumption that a murderer's life is required in return for the life that has been taken is not some sort of common sense. Similarly, one might argue that the presumption that criminal punishment must necessarily issue in a justice that is retributive, and only retributive, is not written in stone. If it were really true that life for life is required by justice, then there is no reason why the mentally handicapped should be spared the death penalty, according to Hauerwas: "The character or 'freedom' of the murderer should not be taken into account if all that matters is that justice be served. Yoder rightly uses all the anomalies created by capital punishment — it can result in killing the innocent, it falls disproportionately on the poor and African American, its infrequency ironically makes it more arbitrary — to call into question its use."[14]

---

11. Quoted in Hauerwas, "Punishing Christians," p. 197. Primary source, Yoder, "Against the Death Penalty," in John Howard Yoder and H. Wayne House, *The Death Penalty Debate* (Dallas: Word, 1991), p. 142.

12. Hauerwas, "Punishing Christians," p. 197.

13. Quoted in Hauerwas, "Punishing Christians," p. 197. Primary source, Yoder, "Against the Death Penalty," p. 143.

14. Hauerwas, "Punishing Christians," p. 197 n. 27.

Hauerwas concurs with Yoder that justice is a "direction" not an "achievement." By this Hauerwas means to emphasize what he thinks to be true of all classical accounts of justice, "namely, that justice depends on the practices of a people that embody the hard-won wisdom of the past tested by the challenges of the present in the hope of a better future."[15] In agreement with those who might sympathize with the notion that punishment is an "enacted language" (e.g., Oliver O'Donovan, and perhaps Yoder), Hauerwas believes that as a language, punishment can and must continually evolve. The symbolic meaning of social acts changes over time given the particular context of social expectation.[16]

Given the improvisational quality of social symbols and practices, Hauerwas, like Yoder, wants to force questions about the "context of social expectation" in a way that accounts for the difference that Christ's cross and resurrection make on social practice. From Yoder's point of view, if it is inappropriate for the church to execute criminals, it is equally the case for the public officials of any society. Summarizing Yoder in this regard, Hauerwas contends, "If the shedding of blood is meant to expose the killer to killing in expiation in the name of justice or the cosmic order, it is Yoder's contention that Christ is the end of expiation."[17] This means, on Hauerwas's view, that at the very least, Christians must be willing to challenge accounts of justice that assume the only way to restore the injustice of murder is by taking the life of the murderer. To the extent that murderers' self-understanding ought not be allowed to be determined by them, refusing to kill those who kill may actually be a sort of punishment itself.

> The refusal to kill those who kill can be seen as a kind of cruelty just to the extent such a refusal refuses to allow those that kill to determine their own self-understanding. To kill another human being can be the ultimate act of self-assertion, the claim of ultimate autonomy, and thus an act that creates an extraordinary loneliness. Murder is not an act to be shared. The refusal to kill others is the refusal to let them de-

---

15. Hauerwas, "Punishing Christians," p. 197.

16. Cf. O'Donovan, "The Death Penalty in *Evangelium Vitae*," in *Ecumenical Ventures in Ethics: Protestants Engage Pope John Paul II's Moral Encyclicals,* ed. Reinhard Hutter and Theodor Dieter (Grand Rapids, Mich.: Eerdmans, 1998), p. 225.

17. Hauerwas, "Punishing Christians," p. 198; House and Yoder, *The Death Penalty Debate,* p. 128.

termine that meaning of their lives. The refusal to kill them is the refusal to let their loneliness determine who they are.[18]

In an important theological move, Hauerwas argues that while
Christ is indeed the end of expiation (that is, he pays the ultimate punishment for human sin, hence no more atonement is necessary), this does
not mean that Christians and society at large do not reach out to each
other in a manner that some may call punishment, notwithstanding the
fact that we ought not kill. Hauerwas maintains that the Christian understanding of punishment must start with the recognition that we humans
are not punished for our sins; "sin is our punishment." Hauerwas says
that on this point he is in agreement with two theologians who are not
usually considered allies, John Howard Yoder and John Milbank. Milbank
argues in *Theology and Social Theory* that God's will is not to punish sin
because "punishment is not an act of a real nature upon another nature,
and God always remains within his nature. Punishment is ontologically
'self-inflicted,' the only punishment is the deleterious effect of sin upon
nature, and the torment of knowing reality only in terms of one's estrangement from it."[19]

In agreement with Milbank, Hauerwas understands Jesus' trial and
punishment as a judgment of all other trials and punishments just to the
degree that the latter cannot help but be "alien." Hauerwas quotes Milbank
to make the point that the notion of the "tragic necessity" of such "alien
punishment" cannot be a sign of God's justice if God's justice is the cross:

---

18. Hauerwas, "Punishing Christians," p. 198.

19. Quoted in Hauerwas, "Punishing Christians," p. 198. Primary source, John
Milbank, *Theology and Social Theory: Beyond Secular Reason* (Oxford: Basil Blackwell, 1990),
p. 420. Hauerwas furthers the argument that God is not required to punish humans for sin
by appealing to the work of Herbert Fingarette: "In an extraordinary essay on the book of
Job, Herbert Fingarette argues that 'the Book of Job shatters, by a combination of challenge
and ridicule and ultimately by direct experiential demonstration, the idea that the law
known to human beings reflects law rooted in the divine or ultimate nature of being, and
the idea that the divine or ultimate nature of being is in its essence lawlike.' Fingarette argues
that if God were required to punish us for disobedience to God's law, then we could control
God by forcing God to punish us. That is a bargain decisively rejected by Job." See "The
Meaning of Law in the Book of Job," in *Revisions: Changing Perspectives in Moral Philosophy*,
ed. Stanley Hauerwas and Alasdair MacIntyre (Notre Dame, Ind.: University of Notre Dame
Press, 1983), pp. 269; cf. pp. 249-86.

The only finally tolerable, and non-sinful punishment, for Christians, must be the self-punishment inherent in sin. When a person commits an evil act, he cuts himself off from social peace, and this nearly always means that he is visited with social anger. But the aim should be to reduce this anger to a calm fury against the sin, and to offer the sinner nothing but good will, so bringing him to the point of realizing that his isolation is self-imposed.[20]

One sees from this Hauerwas's view that punishment is not to be confused with sin itself. Punishment is understood by Hauerwas to be certain social consequences of sin. These consequences (or assaults upon the social peace) are what make sin punitive, not God's judgment or wrath. It appears from my reading of Hauerwas that both sin (as a spiritual separation from God and holiness) *and* the social consequences of sin constitute punishment. Sin-in-itself can be viewed as the spiritual, dispositional, precondition leading to the concrete social-historical manifestations of sin.

Hauerwas contends that Milbank's position "does not commit him to the absurd position that we know that we are being punished for our sin." As a matter of fact, observes Hauerwas, a frightening reality is our apparent happiness with our unrighteousness. Even some forms of "happy living" may constitute self-inflicted punishment. In light of this observation, Hauerwas contends that it is a good thing that we should suffer for our sins: "To suffer for our sins is a great gift that makes possible the identification as well as the appropriate penance for our sin."[21]

Penance, in Hauerwas's estimation, is the means by which Christian hope makes reconciliation with God possible. Penance also makes reconciliation possible with one's self as well as with the neighbor against whom one has sinned. In agreement with Milbank, Hauerwas maintains that the result of sin "estranges us from ourselves creating a loneliness that cannot be overcome."[22] The positive thing about punishment from a Christian perspective is that an offender is to be called home, to be reunited with the community, all of whose members are sinners, called the church.

---

20. Quoted in Hauerwas, "Punishing Christians," p. 199. Primary source, Milbank, *Theology and Social Theory*, p. 421.
21. Hauerwas, "Punishing Christians," p. 199.
22. Hauerwas, "Punishing Christians," p. 199.

A Christian Ethics of Good Punishment in the Public Square

So how *practically* useful within the wider society is Hauerwas's ethics of punishment for dealing with social problems associated with contemporary imprisonment practices? Is Hauerwas's understanding of healing memory adequate for addressing the collateral social consequences fostered by the prison-industrial complex? Can his ethics of punishment assist society in the development of a view of justice that moves us in the direction of "purifying" the vengeance we seek? Might his view of punishment be brought to bear beyond the church, challenging Christians to model for society "correctional" practices that do not (for example) rely on retribution and degradation or become entangled with corporate profit? Can Hauerwas's Christian ethics of punishment serve as a useful compass for those wanting to reject the idea that race, gender, and/or class should serve as primary determinants of the severity of punishment? These are some of the questions that might be posed by Christians wanting to participate in an "effective" public and peaceable witness against current U.S. imprisonment practices and their social consequences.

Hauerwas acknowledges that Christians are right to be concerned with prison reform. Christians are right to work for societies that no longer employ the death penalty, but which, nonetheless, participate in corrective practices that may be characterized as "punishment." Christians, particularly those committed to nonviolence, fail both their non-Christian neighbors and themselves if they act as if punishment is a problem unrelated and alien to contemporary Christian existence. What Christians must first learn to give the world, however, is a better model of how to be a community that can punish. "Only then will the world have an example of what it might mean to be a community that punishes in a manner appropriate for a people who believe that we have been freed by the cross of Christ from the terror of death."[23] It is here, according to Hauerwas, that Christian community becomes good news for the world, the kind of "permeable boundary" that the Christian God desires.

Hauerwas's articulation of a politics of Jesus that is good news for church and world, at first glance, seems fine enough in terms of being a narrative tradition inside of which Christians think about and practice punishment. Indeed, I have no difficulty with Hauerwas's assertion that

23. Hauerwas, "Punishing Christians," p. 200.

"since there is literally nothing outside God, he makes the entirety of the finite realm *ex nihilo,* through an act of purest and gentlest generosity." All things therefore "participate in the power of God's being, which means all that is is related through bonds of ontological intimacy. . . . All that is exists in communion because all that is is rooted in a more primordial communion with God."[24] This is a confession of profound interrelatedness that represents just one of many possible grounds on which human commonality amidst difference can be conceived. While the relationship between imprisonment practices and ontological intimacy will be taken up more extensively in the next chapter, I will simply suggest for now that the idea of a primordial interrelated human communion inaugurated by the Christian God happens to be a foundation for the unity-in-difference epistemology Christians ought to keep in mind in public debates about imprisonment practices. My agreement with Hauerwas here is a "decision of faith" and not an act of certainty. While I confess that there is never complete empirical certainty or access to "Truth with a capital T" in a decision of faith, there are possibilities for arguing and supporting the relative adequacy of a decision grounded in faith soaked in the memory-tradition of a healing and just incarnate God. My decision here is grounded in an argument that Christian faith's notion of ontological intimacy holds great promise for Christian practice vis-à-vis a society of largely counterproductive and alienating punishment and prisons. The character of ontological intimacy modeled in the radically interrelational and gracious politics of Jesus helps Christians to engage imprisonment and the resultant alienations from a fresh and powerful perspective.

Hauerwas is right to insist that within the larger economy of salvation forgiveness (an important dimension of a politics of healing memories) is not a gift to be understood or received as isolated individuals. Hauerwas's theological affirmation is indeed correct, that all things participate in God's being and, therefore, must be understood as related through the bonds of ontological intimacy, which challenge Christians to work against the very types of alienations I have identified earlier: atomism,

---

24. Here Hauerwas is drawing on Archbishop Francis Cardinal George's "Catholic Christianity and the Millennium: Frontiers of the Mind in the 21st Century," p. 2, which is a manuscript copy of the archbishop's speech he received from a friend. See Hauerwas, *A Better Hope: Resources for a Church Confronting Capitalism, Democracy, and Postmodernity* (Grand Rapids, Mich.: Brazos, 2000), pp. 11-12.

(vulgar) individualism, and racism. Understanding humanity in terms of ontological intimacy amidst difference could help Christians to see humanity's inextricable and complex interrelatedness as we participate in society's debates about imprisonment.

If Christians could see that contemporary imprisonment practices and their collateral social consequences generally reinforce human alienation, then perhaps they could better see their way clear to imagine practices of criminal corrections that comport to a restorative testimony of necessary human interrelatedness. Such a restorative testimony of interrelatedness is, from a Christian perspective, deeply rooted in the difficult, agonizing, and hopeful memory of God's bottomless love. Hauerwas reminds Christians that the active ontological intimacy of humanity ought to be expressive of Christian participation in the faith, hope, and love of God's being. This theological affirmation should help Christians argue for better attitudes, institutions, and policies related to punishment and imprisonment. Theologically, one could reasonably presume in all of this that Hauerwas is affirming that God's grace is indeed operating in the church *and* society. Yet my assumption about Hauerwas on this point may not be wholly justifiable if one closely considers his attitudes regarding the church's relationship to the wider society. This is so because Hauerwas appears to privilege the workings of God's gracious ontological intimacy in the church against a liberal society seemingly deserted by the ontological intimacy powered by God's grace in and for the world. This is not to say that Hauerwas has not been hard on Christian churches that have forsaken truthful memory for the idolatrous worship of liberalism in one form or another. But at least the church, unlike liberalism(s), has the better hope of recovered memory on its side.

This notwithstanding, I would concur with Hauerwas, when considering the legitimate function of punishment, that all categories of social arrangements and practices depend on and emerge out of the actual societies in which Christians (and all others) live. Indeed the virtues (the good) and principles (the right) that guide human ways of being-in-the-world are not developed in the abstract, out of thin air. Every human virtue and principle of truth and justice are bound by a bone-deep historicity from which we can never escape. As Hauerwas knows well, within any society Christians, like everyone else, will try, "through the study of history and social and political thought, to gain wisdom about how societies, the law, and government best work." But Christians must recognize, according to Hauerwas, that, "Such knowledge, however, lacks the status of 'gospel truth,' as we are too much the product of accidents of geography, climate, and history to speak with certainty about what society ought to look like." Hauerwas correctly observes that, "Every society has its strengths and weaknesses which change through time. How Christians relate to those strengths and weaknesses will and should also change through time."[25] Given that human social location is "too much" a product of geographic, climatic, and historical accident, according to Hauerwas, human beings can only develop virtues befitting the common life in the context of living narratives, or stories. (Yet the assertion that "we are too much the product of accidents" is dubious in relation to so many who suffer; it seems neither helpful nor accurate to describe the "situations" of peoples repressed by racism, xenophobia, sexism, poverty, corporate greed, imperial globalization, and the like as "accidents."[26])

It is on the same Christian ground that Hauerwas stands that I affirm the common communion, the "ontological intimacy," of all to be an act of God's grace in the world. The implications of this theological understanding may be useful to the wider society's discernments about punishment. But there are important implications for the church's assessment of itself as well. Philosophical and religious ethicist Jeffrey Stout has correctly observed that "the actual church does not look very much like a community of virtue, when judged by pacifist standards." Stout pointedly notes with regard to Hauerwas's illiberal call to Christian virtue that "[a] large percentage of those who call themselves Christians favor capital punishment, the possession of nuclear weapons, and using force to defend their nation

---

25. Hauerwas, *Christian Existence Today,* pp. 11-12.

26. I say this notwithstanding the common and "technical" broad use of the term "accident" by historians, philosophers, and natural and social scientists, which refers to the historical variety of phenomena that are thought to occur without intentionality. Perhaps this is the sense in which Hauerwas is using the term "accident." That is, perhaps he means to suggest, descriptively, not so much that social phenomena have no intentionality but rather that there are varying aspects of human situations. Nonetheless, given the common understanding of "accident," and given the pervasiveness and intentionality of many "nonaccidental" and oppressive social phenomena, I think it problematic to say, "we are too much a product of accidents." This way of describing human situations obscures what is really going on. For an excellent essay related to the way language can be exploited, particularly by those "authorities" holding and wielding the great powers of language "knowledge" packaged in an air of impartiality, see George Orwell's "Politics and the English Language," in *A Collection of Essays* (New York: Harcourt, 1946), pp. 156-71.

against terrorists."[27] In light of the obvious truth of Stout's observation, Hauerwas is right to call Christians to more ideal expressions of Christian virtue. Specifically with regard to the issue of punishment, Hauerwas's politics of healing memory which calls the wrongdoer home is one of the forms of theological imagination that pacifist Christians offer the society at large.

Yet problems arise for Hauerwas when he claims that, unlike the church or other tradition-based communities, "liberalism," or "liberal democracy," or "America" cannot provide for a measure of certainty regarding a view of the common goods allegedly injured by crime. Hauerwas suggests that to the extent that liberal society is void of a common story sufficient to bind its residents to common virtues that make social agreement possible, to just that extent attempts to practice good punishment will fall short. The practice of punishment in the form of penance, forgiveness, and reconciliation works for Christians precisely because of their common commitment to the difference "crucified love" makes in the world. Because liberal society cannot give an account of common virtues that undergird practices that comport to the common good, even past attempts made toward a "Christian" institutionalization of punishment have failed. For example, drawing on the work of Andrew Skotnicki, Hauerwas suggests that a reason why the Quaker-led development of penitentiaries failed is because practices of silent penance (e.g., prayer and Bible study) were divorced from the tradition of faith and holiness that the practices were supposed to serve. In other words, the practice of silent penance by offenders living in a societal ethos that privileges autonomy and individuation is necessarily divorced from a practice of holiness commensurate with a communal Christian desire to be a people called to witness to God.

From Hauerwas's point of view, the background narrative before which Christian punishment made sense was largely absent in the modern penitentiary, with quite destructive results for prisoners. Hauerwas draws on Skotnicki's work on the history of Christian reform movements to make his point: "History suggests that the absence of a clearly defined moral organizational principle, one that articulates the justification and meaning of

27. Jeffrey Stout, *Democracy and Tradition* (Princeton, N.J.: Princeton University Press, 2004), p. 161. Going beyond what Hauerwas perhaps wishes to admit, not only doesn't the contemporary church (on the whole) look much like a community of peaceable virtue, it also cannot, in any comprehensive way, model community for the world because it possesses neither the social or institutional complexity to be an analogous setting to that of "the world."

punishment, and to which each element of the penal environment is held accountable, is at the heart of the decisive problems in American correctional experience."[28] In my judgment it is highly debatable that punishment practices in the United States were ever "defined," and therefore governed, by a "moral organizational principle" existing outside of other political dynamics that have always been at work: e.g., racism, classism, and xenophobia together with the economic exploitation of labor by capital. In any case, Hauerwas goes on to suggest that at least the religious language once utilized in modern penal institutions gave such institutions some purpose, no matter how inadequate. By "purpose," I take Hauerwas to mean, for example, that at least Christian penance and regeneration (or holiness), rather than punishment qua punishment, was the goal of imprisonment. The situation today, however, is worse, on Hauerwas's view, because "there is now no clear sense that we know what we do when we punish."[29]

To the extent that "liberal democracy" (as a particular sociopolitical expression in "the world") finds itself divorced from "truthful" traditions of memory that foster communities of character, which therefore makes understandings of and agreements about the common good impossible, Hauerwas's primary objective is "to remind Christians that we are in a life-and-death struggle with the world."[30] And in this life-and-death struggle with the world Christians must be "nonviolent terrorists."[31]

28. Quoted in Hauerwas, "Punishing Christians," p. 200 n. 35. See also Andrew Skotnicki, *Religion and the Development of the American Penal System* (Washington, D.C.: University Press of America, 2000), pp. 141-42.

29. Hauerwas, "Punishing Christians," p. 200 n. 35.

30. Stanley Hauerwas, "The Christian Difference; or, Surviving Postmodernism," in *A Better Hope*, p. 36.

31. Stanley Hauerwas, "The Non-Violent Terrorist: In Defense of Christian Fanaticism" and "No Enemy, No Christianity: Preaching between 'Worlds'," in *Sanctify Them in the Truth* (Nashville: Abingdon, 1998), pp. 177-200. For an excellent summary of Hauerwas's theology as a thoroughly apocalyptic activity see Douglas Harink, "Apocalypse: Galatians and Hauerwas," in *Paul among the Postliberals: Pauline Theology Beyond Christendom and Modernity* (Grand Rapids, Mich.: Brazos Press, 2003), pp. 67-103. In strong opposition to Hauerwas's view that "liberalism" is *necessarily* anathema to Christian tradition, some contemporary Christian ethicists, among them Max Stackhouse, counter that "Christianity has a liberal element at its core. Following Jesus, Christians have been willing to challenge tradition when it becomes too legalistic, ethnic or impervious to prophetic insight." Stackhouse thinks that the "liberal" impulse of Christianity has historically made good use of resources from beyond itself in the service of a socially engaged theology. The critical use of philosophy, ethics, and social theory play important roles in the Christian understanding of just

Given Hauerwas's understanding of liberalism's inability to provide for a common understanding of tradition-based virtue and practice, it follows for him that, as a "theory of society," liberalism cannot respond well to the social problems associated with punitive imprisonment practices as I have delineated them in this work. Hauerwas's peaceable Christian ethics of good punishment will find it difficult to take root to a liberal society devoid of a tradition of common virtue. In the name of *foundational* ahistorical, metaphysical, and abstract natural laws and principles like "freedom," "autonomy," and "justice," liberalism is hostile to the historical particularity of a counterculturally peaceable Christian tradition. This poses a dire challenge to Christian holiness, on Hauerwas's view. Refusing to cooperate with such a state of affairs, and with all of its promise, Hauerwas's account of Christian good punishment — excommunication, penance, reconciliation, forgiveness — refuses to offer much in the way of concrete possibilities and proposals in the service of dealing effectively with the problem of punitive large-scale imprisonment. As a matter of fact, and as he himself readily admits, Hauerwas is not at all concerned with being "effective" by society's (or "the world's") standards. His concern, rather, is with faithful obedience to a God whose gracious gift to a liberal democracy is peaceable Christians of character who get a pass on making the society come out right. Providing something of a definition of liberalism in his introduction to *Against the Nations,* Hauerwas argues that

> In the most general terms I understand liberalism to be that impulse deriving from the Enlightenment Project to free all people from the chains of their historical particularity in the name of freedom. As an epistemological position liberalism is the attempt to defend foundationalism in order to free reason from being determined by any particular tradition. Politically liberalism makes the individual the supreme unit of society, thus making the political task the securing of cooperation between arbitrary units of desire.[32]

In view of Hauerwas's characterization of liberalism in terms of a metaphysical understanding of freedom which trumps historical particu-

---

social-political arrangements. See Stackhouse, "Liberalism Dispatched vs. Liberalism Engaged," in *Christian Century,* October 18, 1995, p. 962.

32. Hauerwas, *Against the Nations,* p. 18.

larity, his ethics of punishment does not allow for any practically useful and countercultural consideration of alternatives to imprisonment. This is so notwithstanding the potential for alternatives to imprisonment in light of his politics of healing memory. It is almost as if Hauerwas is saying, if you do not accept a particular tradition (preferably the Christian one) as the "foundation" of a good society, you must (in general) withdraw from public debates and practices regarding criminal justice — that is, beyond simply saying that society ought not kill offenders and that police officers as peace officers should refrain from the use of lethal force.

Although I believe that I am correct here about the general implications of Hauerwas's rhetoric for Christian participation in the public square, I am of course not totally right about what I am implying: namely, that Hauerwas wishes to empty the public square of *all* Christian participation. After all, Hauerwas's own countercultural Christian rhetoric is carried out in public from the perch of a leading American institution with the aid of leading publishing houses and media outlets. Yet he would still contend that the presence of his voice in these very public domains is meant *primarily* to address Christians who have embraced a kind of sinister master and have strayed away from the true holiness taught to them in the politics of Jesus. This dimension of Hauerwas's thought is concerned that liberal democracy in America necessarily calls Christians to idol worship, to ultimate allegiance to a democratic society whose capitalist spirit produces "shitty people."[33] Hauerwas cautions Christians against believing

> That democratic societies and states by being democratic are any less omnivorous in their appetites for our loyalties than non-democratic states. Indeed exactly because we assume that democracies protect our freedoms as Christians we may well miss the ways the democratic state remains a state that continues to wear the head of the beast. For example, democratic societies and states, no less than totalitarian ones, reserve the right to command our conscience to take up arms and kill not only other human beings but other Christians in the name of relative moral goods.[34]

---

33. Princeton University professor Jeffrey Stout occasionally recounts this sentiment by Hauerwas when giving talks about Hauerwas's work.

34. Hauerwas, *Against the Nations,* p. 127.

Given Hauerwas's understanding of the perils of Christian conformity to the ethos of liberal democratic regimes, and his subsequent refusal
to offer examples of the possible concrete social practices, policies, and/or
institutions, that might embody more effective approaches to punishment,
charges of provincialism (even tribalism) have been levied against him. It
is often presumed that Hauerwas is calling for Christian obedience to a
tribal God who supervises Christian withdrawal from the world. Yet
Hauerwas appears to view himself as something of an apostle *to* the nations. Hauerwas understands that the meaning of the crucifixion of Jesus
is for the sake of the nations. But he also contends that the gospel of the
slain and resurrected Jesus Christ is "imperial in its demands" and "om-
nivorous in its appetite." Jesus ushers in a kind of "totalizing" universalism.
Yet, unlike liberalism or Americanism, "[Christian] universalism is not
based on assumed commonalities about humankind; rather it is based on
the belief that the God who has made us his own through Jesus Christ is
the God of all people. Christian universality is too often based on a high
view of the human, rather than a high view of Jesus."[35] Hauerwas's high
view of Jesus, which informs the very limited social usefulness of his ethics
of good punishment in the context of the problem of imprisonment,
should not be judged as an indication of sectarianism on Hauerwas's part;
he is actually an advocate of a certain form of (reconfigured) Constantinianism. Douglas Harink offers a good summary of Hauerwas's high
view of the universal and nonsectarian meaning of Jesus Christ for the
world:

> Ultimate allegiances must, therefore, be declared, enemies identified,
> battles engaged, territory taken, in the task of declaring the name Jesus
> Christ to every tribe and nation, calling them to confess Jesus as Lord
> and to become obedient to him through the church in the power of the
> Holy Spirit.[36]

Certainly if Harink's summary is correct, and I believe it is, one
could easily get the impression, despite his own sure protestations to the
contrary, that Hauerwas, like John Milbank, wants to effect victorious

---

35. Hauerwas, "Remembering as a Moral Task: The Challenge of the Holocaust," in
Against the Nations, p. 77.
36. Harink, "Apocalypse: Galatians and Hauerwas," p. 101.

Christianity's triumph over the world. And Hauerwas is willing to work hard (though allegedly peacefully) to secure such a victory. Regardless of whether Hauerwas wants Christians to realize victory over the world or is employing the rhetoric of Christian endurance against the encroachment of the world, Harink is right to say that, "Hauerwas has never disavowed a certain kind of Constantinianism."[37] Regarding Hauerwas's theological agenda in relationship to a certain version of Constantinian Christendom, Harink maintains that Gerald Schlabach's summary of Hauerwas's position has been one which Hauerwas himself has endorsed:

> Hauerwas has discovered a dirty little secret — Anabaptists who reject historic Christendom may not actually be rejecting the vision of Christendom as a society in which all of life is integrated under the Lordship of Christ. On this reading, Christendom may in fact be a vision of shalom, and our argument with Constantinianism is not over the vision so much as the sinful effort to grasp at its fullness through violence, before its eschatological time. Hauerwas is quite consistent once you see that he does want to create a Christian society (polis, societies) — a community and way of life shaped fully by Christian convictions. He rejects Constantinianism because "the world" cannot be this society, and we only distract ourselves from building a truly Christian society by trying to make our nation into that society, rather than be content with living as a community-in-exile.[38]

Yet Hauerwas never simply retreats quietly into exile. He confronts liberal democracy and its institutional practices by evoking a form of Constantinianism that is both nonviolent and ecclesiocentric. Unfortunately, this posture will not help us with an adequate response to the prob-

---

37. Harink, "Apocalypse: Galatians and Hauerwas," p. 101. Cf. John Howard Yoder, "Constantinianism: The Constantinian Sources of Western Social Ethics," in *The Priestly Kingdom: Social Ethics as Gospel* (Notre Dame, Ind.: University of Notre Dame Press, 1984), pp. 135-47.

38. Quoted in Harink, "Apocalypse: Galatians and Hauerwas," p. 102. Harink himself is quoting from "Christian Difference," in *A Better Hope*, p. 44. Harink tells us that, "In a footnote to [the Schlabach] quotation Hauerwas speaks of 'what might be described as my lingering longing for Christendom' (227 n. 39). At the 1999 meeting of the Society of Christian Ethics, Hauerwas, in positioning himself vis-à-vis John Howard Yoder, declared, 'I am much more Catholic, more Constantinian, than John.'"

lem of retribution and degradation in our prisons. Nor can this posture help free society of the collateral social consequences associated with the problem of punishment and imprisonment on a large scale. Although Hauerwas knows that the good news of the gospel is for the world, there is a powerful indication that the Lord's grace has no (or minimal) power outside the confessing community of "saints." God's grace is operative (principally) in the church, not in the world, or so it appears with Hauerwas. Where Hauerwas does confess the power of God's grace in and for the world, he can offer little more than to tell us with concern to criminal justice, "do not kill," "do not employ lethal force."

Hauerwas's view of Christian punishment cannot really imagine the legal, public policy, institutional difference, or profound societal self-evaluative questioning, that Jesus Christ, as God's grace in and for the world, makes in the societal practice of good punishment. In other words, as central as Hauerwas's pacifism and ecclesiocentrism are to his understanding of punishment he cannot or will not say what these demand, practically speaking. By "practically speaking" I mean to say that Hauerwas's politics of healing (or reconciled) memory — i.e., the process of penance, forgiveness, and reconciliation — cannot be translated into private and public institutions or public policies that address concrete problems associated with imprisonment. Given Hauerwas's hostility toward a "worldly ecclesia," he apparently will not entertain telling us the roles that (for example) neighborhoods, unions, political parties, schools, voluntary organizations, cultural institutions, or social movements might play in inching society in the direction of "good punishment."[39] His advo-

---

39. Hauerwas's refusal to "compromise" the gospel in order to achieve practical social "successes" is also demonstrated when, for example, he deals with the issue of militarism. In the absence of military conscription, for example, Hauerwas's pacifist contempt for liberal democracy often comes across, as Jeffrey Stout has argued, "more as a quixotic gesture than as the demanding doctrine he intended it to be." Stout implies that Hauerwas could learn a lesson or two from Princeton Seminary theologian George Hunsinger: "The core of Hauerwas's anti-Constantinian teaching is absolute pacifism, justified on biblical grounds as a vocation of discipleship to Christ. Most of his readers have found this commitment hard to swallow, but they have often been prepared to treat it as a side-issue, while focusing instead on his critique of liberalism. Hauerwas, to his credit, has long insisted on the centrality of pacifism to his outlook. He has not, however, made clear what his pacifism demands, practically speaking. Given that military conscription is no longer the law of the land, his followers face no governmental pressure to serve in the armed forces. He does not, as Hunsinger does, hold up Pax Christi, World Peacemakers, and the sanctuary movement as

cacy of healing memory is never given real concrete organizational, structural, or public policy form in society at large. Thus Hauerwas cannot ultimately deal effectively with the deleterious social consequences of the prison-industrial complex's tightly held grip on the nation. In the final chapter, then, I try to imagine beyond where Hauerwas appears willing to take his own promising work. I now invite us all to consider the public struggle toward a "politics of ontological intimacy" as the social aim of a politics of healing memories in the service of a Christian social ethics of good punishment.

---

exemplary concrete practices. To my knowledge, he has advocated neither the withholding of taxes that finance the military, nor participation in costly acts of civil disobedience, nor refusal of communion to soldiers and their commanders." See Stout, *Democracy and Tradition,* p. 159.

6. Good Punishment:
Toward a Politics of Ontological Intimacy

In the last chapter I introduced the notion of "ontological intimacy" as a name Christians may give to the profound human and natural interrelatedness that is rooted in a primordial communion with God. Such a profound interrelatedness of intimacy, even while celebrating the gifts of discrete individuality, is the Christian context that makes a politics of healing memories possible. In this final chapter, and in continued conversation with Stanley Hauerwas's work, I return to the notion of "ontological intimacy" in order to imagine how this expression of radical human bondedness amidst difference might be developed to take Christians to a fuller, more dynamic, and more socially responsible practice of good punishment. Since racism is one of the most intractable features of U.S. imprisonment practice, I will also be giving significant attention to the problem of racism and imprisonment in the context of ontological intimacy as a "politics" concerned with the manner in which our common lives are arranged. In addition to considering the problem of racism, the social relevance of a politics of ontological intimacy will also be demonstrated in a review of representative social practices where signs of such a politics in the making are already apparent, namely, in restorative justice and in representative systemic alternatives. Finally, I will offer an assessment of what peaceable Christians might learn from "the liberals" in the service of their social participation in "good punishment."

"Good Punishment" Beyond Hauerwas

In the previous chapter I tried to suggest that there are aspects of Hauerwas's ethics of "good punishment" that at first glance appear promising in terms of addressing the social problems associated with the manner in which imprisonment is practiced in the U.S. Indeed, Hauerwas's articulation of a politics of healing memories (which includes the concepts of penance, forgiveness, and reconciliation) provides a useful way of naming the transformative practice of good punishment from a Christian perspective. The name I give to the ultimate restorative relationships in support of which "good punishment" aims is the politics of ontological intimacy. Recall Hauerwas's suggestion that "ontological intimacy" refers to the Christian understanding that literally nothing exists outside God since God makes the entirety of the finite realm *ex nihilo,* through an act of purest and gentlest generosity. Therefore all of creation should be understood as participating in the power of God's being. This means that all that is related through bonds of ontological intimacy should aim to exist in communion because all that is is rooted in a more primordial communion with God as modeled in history by Jesus Christ.[1]

As suggested in the previous chapter, even though much of the theological grammar that supports Hauerwas's understanding of "good punishment" is promising for realizing the goal of ontological intimacy, his ethics of punishment offers very little, *practically speaking,* to a "liberal" society largely unsympathetic to, or apathetic with regard to, his anti-foundationalist and illiberal vision of Christian community. But then Hauerwas feels that Christians have no obligation to be "practical," at least as far as practicality entails submission to liberal notions of social effectiveness. On Hauerwas's view, Christians are not called to be "effective," "successful," "victorious," or "heroic" because the pursuit of such ends would mean participation in social habits of "justice" that are contrary to the Christian "peaceable kingdom." Christian effort in pursuit of such a peaceable kingdom is a mark of holiness. As a matter of faithful obedience, Christians are called to participate in a particular story, one that is not

---

1. Please be reminded that Hauerwas himself is drawing on the work of Archbishop Francis Cardinal George, "Catholic Christianity and the Millennium: Frontiers of the Mind in the 21st Century," p. 2, which is a manuscript copy of the archbishop's speech Hauerwas received from a friend. See Hauerwas, *A Better Hope: Resources for a Church Confronting Capitalism, Democracy, and Postmodernity* (Grand Rapids, Mich.: Brazos Press, 2000), pp. 11-12.

based on a politics of death. Indeed, on Hauerwas's view Christians are not called to be heroes, "[w]e are called to be holy."[2]

We can appreciate Hauerwas for his challenge to all Christians to embody and perform a politics of healing memories as the model of "good punishment." An understanding of good punishment is a gift to the wider society and world. Indeed, the pursuit of ontological intimacy in our practice of criminal justice should favor penance, forgiveness, and reconciliation as means to that end. A salient challenge, then, is to begin to imagine the possible attitudinal, institutional, public policy, and social advocacy reforms that could emerge if Hauerwas's Christian ethics of punishment were brought to bear on the problem of imprisonment and its collateral social consequences.

Ontological Intimacy and Imprisonment

Participation in a politics of ontological intimacy guides Christians toward undoing practices and consequences associated with vengeful and humiliating large-scale imprisonment and other social aspects of the prison-industrial complex. A politics of ontological intimacy makes God's love of all creation the story in view of which Christians pursue good punishment. Building on Hauerwas's understanding of ontological intimacy, I am casting a politics of ontological intimacy as the restorative goal employing a politics of healing memories. Paul Tillich might have called what I am suggesting here an "ontology of love," which essentially drives humanity toward "the reunion of the separated."[3]

Clues about what such an intimacy entails for Christians can be discerned in God's self-unveiling as the lowly-born, tortured, spat-upon,

2. Hauerwas articulated this sentiment in the wake of the tragedy visited upon the United States on September 11, 2001 when he argued that, "Christian nonviolence is not a strategy to rid the world of violence, but rather the Christian must live in a world of violence. In short, Christians are not nonviolent because we believe our nonviolence is a strategy to rid the world of war, but rather because faithful followers of Christ in a world of war cannot imagine being anything else but nonviolent." See Stanley Hauerwas, "September 11, 2001: A Pacifist Response," in *Dissent from the Homeland: Essays After September 11*, ed. Stanley Hauerwas and Frank Lentricchia (Durham, N.C.: Duke University Press, 2003), pp. 183, 188.

3. Paul Tillich, *Love, Power, and Justice: Ontological Analyses and Ethical Applications* (Oxford: Oxford University Press, 1954), p. 57.

beaten, and crucified Jesus Christ of Nazareth. It is crucial to note here that these sufferings were not ends in themselves, but the misery-filled consequences of Jesus' living toward the restorative end of ontological intimacy. The way of this humiliated Jesus has been demonstrated for us in a gospel tradition that aims at the restoration of grace in human relationships. The grace modeled for Christians in the Jesus tradition is a profound love and concern for others that speaks of our primal interrelatedness, our radical mutuality for the cause of liberation from the wages of what many Christians know as "sin." Some Christians and others might want to point out, in the context of considering the relationship between the retributive humiliation meted out on Jesus the crucified God and that meted out on today's average criminal, that Jesus was innocent while most criminals are guilty. Yet the Jesus of the Good Friday story provides Christians with one of history's most profoundly radical displays of the place of criminals within a politics of ontological intimacy: *They crucified him with criminals, one on either side* (Luke 23:33). Karl Barth offered Christians everywhere a provocative summary of the social implications of Jesus' crucifixion alongside criminals in his 1957 Good Friday sermon entitled "The Criminals with Him":

> 'They crucified him *with the criminals.*' Which is more amazing, to find Jesus in such bad company, or to find criminals in such good company? As a matter of fact, both are true! One thing is certain: here they hang all three, Jesus and the criminals, one at the right and one at the left, all three exposed to the same public abuse, to the same interminable pain, to the same slow and irrevocable death throes. Like Jesus, these two criminals had been arrested somewhere, locked up and sentenced by some judge in the course of the previous three days. And now they hang on their crosses with him and find themselves in solidarity and fellowship with him. They are linked in a common bondage never again to be broken, just as the nails that fasten them to the piece of wood would never break. It was as inescapable for them as it was for him. It was a point of no return for them as for him. There remained only the shameful, painstricken present and the future of their approaching death. (Strangely enough, there are many paintings of Jesus' crucifixions where the two criminals are lost to sight. It would perhaps be more appropriate not to present Jesus' death at all. But if it is done, then the two thieves on the right and the left must not be left out. In

any painting or representation where they are absent, an important, even an essential, element is missing.)

They crucified him with the criminals. Do you know what this implies? Don't be too surprised if I tell you that this was the first Christian fellowship, the first certain, indissoluble and indestructible Christian community. Christian community is manifest wherever there is a group of people close to Jesus who are with him in such a way that they are directly and unambiguously affected by his promise and assurance. These may hear that everything he is, he is for them, and everything he does, he does for them. To live by this promise is to be a Christian community. The two criminals were the first certain Christian community.[4]

Here Barth provides a commentary on the Good Friday story that at least begins to challenge Christians to move in the direction of seeing the implications of ontological intimacy in the formation of Christian community in relation to those societal authorities condemn as criminals. Yet, by later suggesting that "[Jesus] was the principal actor, the hero of Good Friday, the head of the first Christian community," Barth does a disservice to the important companionship and comfort offered the human Jesus himself as he suffered the same abuse, the same pain, and the same death throes as the criminals with him.[5]

Like Barth, Rita Nakashima Brock rightly calls Christians to a reconsideration of the gospel narratives, which offer Christians a model of the mutuality, self-awareness, openness, and caring that characterized Jesus' life. The church, as the Body of Christ in history, is to disciple its followers in the way of the radical mutuality seen in the narratives of Jesus. Brock's advocacy of human ontological relational existence hopes to undo the various social consequences associated with a historical Christian fixation on original sin, pride, blame, guilt, alienation, and punishment over against the better ontological intimacy that "original grace" implies. The aim of life, on Brock's view, is to restore our "original grace," that is, our basic intimate ontological connection to one another and to all of existence. Our damage, our "brokenness," is a consequence of our

---

4. Karl Barth, *Deliverance to the Captives: Sermons and Prayers by Karl Barth* (New York: Harper and Brothers, 1961), pp. 76-77.

5. Barth, *Deliverance to the Captives*, p. 78.

relational existence; healing comes with active focus on "original grace" rather than "original sin." On this view sin is not something to be punished, but something to be healed.[6] Brook's movement toward better ontological intimacy is to be striven for not only within the more intimate relationships of family, but also in the social arrangements and institutions of society at large. How we deal with one another in our most intimate social arrangements mirrors our wider sociopolitical arrangements — for better or worse.

A particularly important reason why Christians might think in terms of a politics of ontological intimacy as the goal that good punishment supports is that such thinking aids us in our own self-understanding that we share, with all other residents of society, a shared criminality. Not only are persons rightly to be called upon to take responsibility for the crimes they commit; society as a whole is also to view itself as a significant cause of crime. Lee Griffith has gone so far as to suggest that, "At the most fundamental level, it is only society that creates crime, by empowering elected representatives to define what is or is not crime."[7] All societies create crime through some form of legislative process and definition. And given the widespread social implications of such a power to define every aspect of individual, civil, and political responsibility, legislators along with the lay citizenry must carry on a vigorous, rigorous, and continuous self-inventory of the agreed-upon definitions of what constitutes crime and a just meting out of punishment.

Continued evaluation is always necessary since the legislative process inside of which definitions of crime emerge never occurs in an atomistic or objective way, detached from our various cultural prejudices, biases, and stereotypes about "the other" in our midst.[8] Griffith offers salient examples of just why it is that continued evaluation is so necessary in society: "Our definitions of crime outlaw the inner city crack house but not the Wall Street cocktail lounge. They make killing a crime in some circumstances and not in others. Legislative bodies have as their very purpose the creation of crime via definition. It is illusory to assume that the business of

6. Rita Nakashima Brock, *Journeys by Heart: A Christology of Erotic Power* (New York: Crossroad Publishing Company, 1993), p. 7.

7. Lee Griffith, *The Fall of the Prison: Biblical Perspectives on Prison Abolition* (Eugene, Ore.: Wipf and Stock, 1999), p. 181.

8. The same thing needs to be said of the Christian churches' assessments of what constitutes "sin" and "guilt."

defining crime occurs in a vacuum."[9] Griffith goes on to cite a report by the American Friends Service Committee in support of the contention that the content and practice of criminal law is more often weighted against the poor and (more or less) despised than against the wealthy:

> The selection of candidates for prosecution reflects inequality in the larger society not only because of bias on the part of police or prosecutors, but because the substantive content of the law affects those who are not social equals in quite different ways. A wealthy industrialist has little difficulty in having his opinions on political questions heard at the highest levels of government. . . . But who speaks for the unemployed, the welfare mother, the habitual drunkard, the inmate, the drug addict, the recidivist? Laws forbidding armed robbery and burglary have very different impact for a millionaire and for an unemployed twenty-year-old black male in a ghetto where the unemployment rate is 25 percent.[10]

This excerpt from the Friends Report on Crime and Punishment is suggestive of my argument that the workings of society itself are a cause of crime, and therefore must seek the same process of *non-forgetful* penance, forgiveness, and reconciliation (indeed healing memories) called for by Hauerwas in the service of positive expressions of our ontological intimacy.

In support of the contention that society itself is a significant cause of crime through its creation and advocacy of the very conditions that make crime possible, T. Richard Snyder has asserted, "Certainly the one who has committed a criminal act is in need of forgiveness from the victim and the larger society that has been harmed. But so too is the society in need of forgiveness for having created and permitted crime-generative communities to exist."[11] If Snyder is correct here, then one must pay attention to the distinction between the habilitation of prisoners verses the rehabilitation of offenders: "If the lack of habilitation is a reality, then those

9. Griffith, *The Fall of the Prison*, p. 181.

10. Quoted in Griffith, *The Fall of the Prison*, p. 182. See also *Struggle for Justice: A Report on Crime and Punishment in America*, prepared for the American Friends Service Committee (New York: Hill and Wang, 1971), p. 15.

11. T. Richard Snyder, *The Protestant Ethic and the Spirit of Punishment* (Grand Rapids, Mich.: Eerdmans, 2001), pp. 110-11.

responsible for this condition are as much in need of forgiveness as is the perpetrator of any specific crime."[12]

By routinely meting out retributive degradation in the context of an excessively large-scale regime of imprisonment tied to a host of collateral social consequences, society re/produces crime. By normalizing the vengeful status-humiliation of offenders over significant periods of time, and on an increasingly large scale, a perpetually high level of inferiority and humiliation clings to those subjected to punishment. It is an affront to a Christian conception of ontological intimacy whenever persons are routinely subjected to physical, psychological, and emotional retribution and degradation. By routinely assigning to offenders the fairly resilient status of social inferiors as they serve out their time within largely overcrowded warehouses of confinement, which feed them a steady curriculum of violence and humiliation, society commits a significant crime against itself. That is, society undermines itself by committing a crime against its own potential for better expressions of human civilization. In general, imprisonment fosters and/or intensifies criminal conduct in inmates. Moreover, it tends to re/habituate cynical and vindictive dispositions in both the people meting out the punishment and in society at large.

To be sure, I do not deny that many criminal acts are indeed the actions of individuals. Within the nation's prisons and jails are many persons who disrupt ontological intimacy by virtue of crimes they *chose* to commit. Indeed, significant numbers of persons who involve themselves in proscribed behaviors possess *agency*. But at a deeper level so many of these individual actions need to be seen as destructive reactions to wrongs committed against them, though this in no way means they lack responsibility. Crime constitutes a negative expression of our ontological intimacy. It is so often alienating behavior powerfully influenced by lifetimes of destructive intimacies: "The child who is battered, sexually abused, provided with second-rate education and no employment opportunities not surprisingly may turn to battering and abuse as an adult."[13] When such an adult eventually reaches the prison a further denial of a better ontological intimacy

12. Snyder, *The Protest Ethic and the Spirit of Punishment*, p. 111.

13. Snyder, *The Protestant Ethic and the Spirit of Punishment*, p. 111. Cf. the strong exploration and general affirmation of this point in James Gilligan, M.D., *Violence: Our Deadly Epidemic and Its Causes* (New York: Grosset/Putnam, 1996). For a very good summary concerning treating violence as the public health epidemic that it is see Jane Ellen Stevens, "Treating Violence as an Epidemic," *Technology Review*, August/September 1994, pp. 23-28.

takes the form of retributive degradation. An irony here is that retributive degradation in overcrowded prisons and jails might be understood as an alienating-intimacy, a form of social death, which reinforces an inmate's alienation from "law-abiding" humanity, and in some cases, humanity itself. For example, and with regard to the irony of alienating-intimacy, with the numbers of persons imprisoned continuing to rise, double and triple bunking has become more prevalent. Snyder reports on one prisoner's experience of the conditions that routinely accompany prison overcrowding, and which I contend is a routine example of alienating-intimacy in the nation's prisons and jails:

> I am a nonsmoker with a medically documented history of respiratory problems. . . . I have now been in double bunking status for two weeks, yet in all that time, I have spoken to the other guy in here with me not more than 20 minutes combined . . . the other guy is a heavy chain smoker . . . my lungs are giving me serious chest pains.
>
> This double bunking is the most inhumane, humiliating, degrading, stressful, and unsanitary condition that I have ever been exposed to through my 25 years of incarceration. . . . I cleaned particles of feces (not mine) from inside the toilet with my hand wrapped only in toilet tissues (there is no toilet brush). . . . I turned my head one night and witnessed the other guy in the cell with me masturbating, only two feet away. I've smelled a thousand farts and smoked at least a thousand cigarettes of second hand smoke.
>
> The sink is only one inch from my bed, which constantly sprays water on the bed. The toilet is only 17 inches from my bed. . . . The space between my bottom bunk and top bunk is only 32 inches, which prevents me from being able to sit up in the bed. . . . I can't last much longer under these conditions.[14]

The foregoing example of an inmate's life that is alienating in the midst of its very intimacy is not unusual; it can rightly be considered more typical than atypical. Although some will no doubt claim that inmates "deserve what they get" while serving time, the routine performance of the kind of vengeful humiliation retold by Snyder above occurs without much regard for the collateral "ripple effects" that will be experienced by com-

---

14. Reported in Snyder, *The Protestant Ethic and the Spirit of Punishment*, pp. 7-8.

munities and society at large once inmates are released. And of course the alienating violence of the prison is often more intensely vile than Snyder's aforementioned example. Indeed, the alienating-intimacy of misery, humiliation, isolation, and shame can be seen in an anonymous young inmate's "Story of a Black Punk." This individual was a victim of the all-too-common violence and humiliation of sexual abuse in what the now deceased former prisoner and prison reform activist Stephen "Donny" Donaldson contends is "[t]he prisoner subculture [which] fuses sexual and social roles and assigns all prisoners accordingly."[15] The following is an extensive excerpt from "The Story of a Black Punk," a series of summaries of letters sent by "Anonymous" to Donaldson, who was himself brutally raped while incarcerated. (Let me warn the reader that this account is particularly graphic):

October 7, 1982

I haven't done too much thinking about these things and to my surprise, they are still painful. It's hard to put them down on paper and to tell someone who is a stranger to me (even though you have suffered the same things).

I got busted on a silly theft rap (stole a toy . . .) and they sent me to the . . . Youth Facility for ten days. The first night three older teens raped me for two hours. The second night the three dudes came back with three friends and they all took turns raping me again. It was the first experience I ever had with white folks and the other Black kids didn't lift a finger to help me out. They just turned away. The next day I was accosted by two custodians who told me they had heard I was turned into a girl by some of the other dudes — they raped me orally. I spent the rest of my time there servicing the three dudes that took me off the first night and depending how they felt, their buddies as well. I remembered how my insides hurt but I was too ashamed to even report it, and then when I finally got out I was too scared to even go to a doctor.

When I was 14 I got busted for "joy-riding" in a "borrowed" car (smile) and sentenced to a year at [a reform school]. The first day there

15. Stephen Donaldson, "A Million Jockers, Punks, and Queens," in *Prison Masculinities,* ed. Don Sabo, Terry A. Kupers, and Willie London (Philadelphia: Temple University Press, 2001), p. 118.

I was put into a dorm and one of the three dudes who initially took me off in the youth house was on the same dorm. He told the rest of the inmates that I got turned out and then beat me badly in front of the other guys. He topped his beating off by raping me and established my identity in the dorm as the "nigger punk." I spent that year servicing the boys in the dorm and any of their friends that wanted sex. Donny, that was when I realized that my position wasn't too different from my ancestors and that for the rest of the year I wasn't any different from a plantation slave.

Would you believe that as I typed the above I started to get all choked up and actually felt like crying? Talk about actual catharsis (smile).

When I was about 15½ years old I ran away from home. . . . My sex with girls was terrible and I couldn't always get hard. Lots of times, if I got hard then I couldn't cum. This scared me and I began to think that I really got turned into a freak or something. So, I ran off. . . . [I] tried to call home but I didn't have any money. So I broke into a car and stole a camera and some petty shit that was in the glove compartment. Got busted and did a year in . . . county jail. I remembered the second night when a Puerto Rican dude paid the hack to leave my cell door unlocked.

Donny, this dude was BIG and he just walked right into my cell and told me he was going to fuck my sweet ass. I got up real fast and tried to run out of the cell but he grabbed me by the hair and punched me in the face. I remembered that I was bleeding from the nose and suddenly I was on the bunk, pants off and my legs were on his shoulders.

He told me that he liked his girls Black and that he wanted me to be his girl. I agreed to the arrangement and was his punk for the whole year I was there. He was into s & m, which was my first experience with that shit. It was my first experience with "ride the whip" too. He would invite his buddies (Whites and Puerto Ricans) to his cell where I would be forced to sit on his lap with his dick up my ass. Then he would masturbate me while his friends would take turns raping my mouth. God, even now I'm humiliated telling anyone about that. . . . I learned that I had to do everything a wife did and my existence depended on his contentment. If I resisted his little torture scenes, he would beat me and I would wind up doing it anyway.

Donny, you wrote . . . about how you couldn't escape the sense that they . . . had conquered you and I could relate to that feeling too. This Puerto Rican jock just walked up and there wasn't anything I could do to stop it. He just took possession of me and for one year I belonged to him. This again took on the aspects of slavery which I guess is what all of us punks experience. Still, with a Black punk it takes on certain connotations. . . . I felt totally humiliated when my rapists were White and terribly sad when Blacks took me off.

My bids at the State level were for armed robbery. . . . My first night out of quarantine I was gang raped in the shower and the word went into population that I was fully turned out. I got raped a few more times until a Black Brother offered to be my man, which I accepted right away to avoid getting killed. He wasn't too bad but he got into heavy debt and "sold" me to this other Black dude for swag to get him off the hot seat. By this time, Donny, I was beginning to identify with slaves and took it with a grain of salt. I became terribly depressed suddenly and my new man ignored my feelings and moods. It got real bad and I began to withdraw into a fantasy world. It was this time that I started to get psychotherapy which helped me deal with my self-conflicts.

I met my wife when I was back on the streets and she helped me out sexually. Thank God for her patience, Donny. I got back some of my old confidence thanks to her. Still, in a short period of time I was back in prison. My reputation as a punk before was still fresh in the minds of the men who raped me earlier, and before long I was getting offers. Two Italian dudes raped me in very much the same way. I started to get depressed again and the way they treated me (and all the other punks too) began to mess with my head. I was terribly scared all the time and humiliated by the things they would yell as I walk by. . . .

My first year back . . . they had the riot and that probably did the trick. I remember it like it was only one minute ago — a straight dude (also Black) and I were walking near the school when a huge gang of crazy cons came running up the stairs screaming and yelling. They saw us and started yelling "Get the queers" (at this time I didn't know what was jumping off). They grabbed us and dragged us into the t.v. room, stripped us and draped us side by side over the back of a sofa. They took turns raping us anally and orally simultaneously. I don't know how many there were but they were lined up all the way to the stairs to get at us. I passed out and woke up in the hospital with both my arms broken. As soon as I got out of the hospital one of the Italian dudes that raped me came up and offered to be my man and I accepted. I was thankful for the protection and greatful [sic] that he didn't force me to wear drag. However, I played the total woman and for three years I became the perfect punk in every way. The young man that was raped with me in the t.v. room went on a shooting spree two years ago and was shot to death by the police.

This has proven to be weird and I'm not too sure that I've actually dealt with my feelings as well as I originally thought. I feel very humiliated that you should know what happened to me, even though I know you understand.[16]

As has already been suggested, our nation's current large-scale practice of imprisonment is socially corrosive; and there is a basic failure to connect the manner in which inmates are (formally and informally) punished to the numerous social consequences that get injected back into families, communities, and society at large. Whenever a society produces such a large prison population, living under conditions of routinized vengeance and (often violent) status humiliation, the negative social effects will "bend back" into society, as the above story powerfully and painfully illustrates. Negative social effects will also bend back again into the prison. In short, our present "cure" for crime contains abundant amounts of the very poison that re/produces it.

One of the latest "innovations" in contemporary American corrections presents a clear example of the kind of correctional poison that I am speaking of. Today increasing numbers of inmates are being held in what are called "special housing units" (SHUs), or what prisoners and others know as "The Box." Columbia University professor of history, political science, and public policy Manning Marable described the unique design of SHUs, which function as months- or sometimes years-long, twenty-three-hours-a-day solitary confinement, as follows:

SHU cell blocks are electronically monitored, prefabricated structures of concrete and steel, about 14 feet long and 8½ feet wide, amounting to 120 square feet of space. Two inmates who are confined to each cell, however, actually have only about 60 square feet of usable space, or 30 square feet per person. All meals are served to prisoners through a thin

16. Anonymous, "The Story of a Black Punk," in *Prison Masculinities,* pp. 128-30.

slot cut into the steel door. The toilet unit, sink, and shower are all located in the cell. Prisoners are permitted one hour of "exercise time" each day in a small concrete balcony, surrounded by heavy security wire, directly connected with their SHU cells. Education and rehabilitation programs for SHU prisoners are prohibited.[17]

Related to this, Marable also correctly notes that as of 1998 8 percent (or 5,700) of New York State's total prisoner population was confined to SHUs. Concurrent with this, a new 750-cell maximum-security SHU facility was being constructed in upstate New York costing state taxpayers some $180 million. The fact that Amnesty International and various human rights organizations and groups in the United States have widely decried SHUs on the grounds that such forms of imprisonment violate prohibitions in international law on the use of torture has not stopped other states from following New York's lead. Arguing that the introduction of SHUs "reflects a general mood in the country that the growing penal population is essentially beyond redemption," and thus, "convicted felons cease to be viewed as human beings," Marable reports that "as of 1998, California had constructed 2,942 SHU beds, followed by Mississippi (1,756), Arizona (1,728), Virginia (1,267), Texas (1,229), and Florida (1,000). Solitary confinement, which historically had been defined even by correction officials as an extreme disciplinary measure, is increasingly becoming the norm."[18]

Today the nation continues to cram more and more offenders into prisons to face the retributive violence and humiliation of prison life. Concurrently, there has been a retreat from what Elliott Currie, a professor of Legal Studies at the University of California Berkeley, argues was "the already minimal commitment to help [prisoners] reenter productive society."[19] Currie goes on to contend that, "Indeed, many states have moved beyond their traditional indifference to rehabilitation and now embrace what some criminologists call 'penal harm' — the self-conscious use of 'tough' measures to inflict pain and deprivation on inmates in the name of retribution and deterrence."[20]

17. Manning Marable, *The Great Wells of Democracy: The Meaning of Race in American Life* (New York: Basic Civitas Books, 2002), p. 156.

18. Marable, *The Great Wells of Democracy*, pp. 156-57.

19. Elliott Currie, *Crime and Punishment in America* (New York: Henry Holt and Company, 1998), p. 165.

20. Currie, *Crime and Punishment in America*, p. 165.

To be sure, the habitual infecting of the nation's prisoners with retributive degradation ought to make it a surprise to no one that the overwhelming majority of inmates will be returned to prison for one offense or another within a few short months or years of their release. Vengeful status humiliation (physical, emotional, and /or psychological) represents a kind of "soul murder" that will make it difficult for the average prisoner to contribute positively to the common good upon release. (By "soul murder" I am referring to the death of the metaphorical dimension of the human self, perhaps the "psyche,"[21] that inspires and animates.) The guards (and other prison personnel) who enforce this murder of the human soul will also poison society, communities, and families with a cynicism and vindictiveness inspired by intimate and habitual participation in retributive degradation practiced on a large scale.

An example of the consequences of such vindictiveness and cynicism by guards was caught on videotape being meted out on New Mexico prisoners who were being held in a Virginia prison. A number of New Mexico inmates who were shipped in 1999 to Wallens Ridge, a Virginia supermax prison designed for the "worst of the worst," were videotaped being assaulted by prison guards. These inmates, whose cases, according to their lawyer, Paul Livingston, involved nonviolent offenses (and who therefore had no business in a supermax prison), were beaten, shot with stun guns and rubber bullets, slammed against walls and floors, chained to their beds for days at a time, subjected to racist verbal abuse, and threatened with sodomy and vicious dogs. Livingston alleges that all of this was done as a matter of policy.[22] And of course the international expression and reach of this sort of vindictiveness and cynicism against prisoners has come to us live and in color in the photographs and videotapes of American soldiers and civilian interrogators performing the worst kinds of violent humiliation and torture on Iraqi prisoners of war and other "detainees": killing, rape, electric shock, and various other forms of cruel and unusual punishment.[23] This display of vindictiveness

21. Cf. Richard K. Fenn, *The Return of the Primitive: A New Sociological Theory of Religion* (Burlington, Vt.: Ashgate Publishing, 2001), pp. 110-11, 123.

22. Laura LaFay, "Abu Ghraib in Farmville: Mistreatment of Iraqi Prisoners Mimics Abuse in Virginia Prisons," *Style Weekly*, May 19, 2004. Available online at http://styleweekly.com/article.asp?idarticle=8431.

23. See, for example the "Report of the International Committee of the Red Cross (ICRC) on the Treatment by the Coalition Forces of Prisoners of War and Other Protected

and cynicism by guards, whom prison researcher Gordon Hawkins has referred to as "the other prisoners," points to a twist of tragic irony manifested in the words of a prison guard: "We're all doing time, some of us are just doin' it in eight-hour shifts."[24]

As if the goings-on inside the prison were not enough, the problems get intensified for the majority of prisoners who are returned to the streets. Once most prisoners are (inevitably) returned to communities, society then routinely enforces policies that contribute to leading ex-prisoners straight back to prison. For example, the denial of civil liberties like voting rights, access to public housing, and federal and state educational assistance to large numbers of ex-felons simply undercuts any good thoughts they may harbor about their full participation, for the good of all, in transforming communities in the service of a better democratic and just society. In my judgment such policies (in effect) constitute social crimes and are an affront to a Christian politics of ontological intimacy.

Since African Americans make up the largest population of felons and ex-felons, the denial of an important civil liberty like voting leaves them with less potential opportunity and incentive to participate well in practices that benefit the interconnected good of all. With so many young Black men being disenfranchised, whole communities in some cases lack the potential of public representation that otherwise could voice their communities' needs and concerns. Moreover with the massive increase in the numbers of female prisoners, most of them Black, Latina, and poor, the situation for many of the nation's most vulnerable children is desperate as the nation's prisons and jails make social orphans of many of them. Most children of incarcerated parents find little in the way of official resources and care; due to so much official societal neglect many of our children inevitably become "prisoners once removed" and the next generation of "criminals." Indeed, the generalized refusal of the "justice" system and public policymakers to consider non-alienating views and forms of good punishment contributes significantly to the negative expressions of ontological intimacy that surround contemporary imprisonment.

To the extent that we as a society continue (for all practical purposes)

Persons by the Geneva Convention in Iraq During Arrest, Internment and Interrogation," February 2004, and Seymour M. Hersh, "Torture at Abu Ghraib," *The New Yorker*, May 10, 2004, pp. 42ff.

24. Quoted in Richard Hawkins and Geoffrey Alpert, *American Prison Systems: Punishment and Justice* (Englewood Cliffs, N.J.: Prentice Hall, 1989), p. 337.

to view prisoners as *only* discrete subjects who choose crime in a social vacuum, we (from a Christian perspective) deny the (very difficult to achieve) peaceable ontological intimacy that Jesus Christ has ushered into human history. There is indeed a powerful conflict between a politics of ontological intimacy and imprisonment practices that routinely assault such a politics. The societal struggle for ontological intimacy in the context of the way we punish is not at all easy or without excruciating pain. For Christians such a politics is to be pursued informed both by the story and model of communal tragedy *and* celebration symbolized by the narrative of a bloodstained cross that had company, as well as by the Christian confession that after Good Friday, Easter came. As most Christians anticipate celebrating the promised return of Christ they might, when thinking about punishment and imprisonment, want to think about what kind of people they wish to be in the context of their politics of living. Perhaps we ought to remind ourselves that Jesus' cross is a bloody mess that stands as a monument to the alienation between both humanity and God and humanity and itself. When Jesus' people remove him from the cross, bury him, and later witness his resurrection, we see an Easter monument to the active hope of ontological intimacy. Indeed, with the model of his life, death, and resurrected return we see the communal dimensions of salvation that has been ushered into human history by a convicted criminal believed by Christians to have saved the world. What does it mean for society's criminals when Christians ask society to punish in a manner that testifies to Christian participation with God in the flesh, a victim of Rome's arbitrary defining of crime and who most Christians confess has saved the world?

As I suggest in the Introduction to this book, a politics of ontological intimacy refers to the binding and dynamic way of being-there-with-and-for-others that should characterize a Christian faith seeking to participate in the being of God. The possibility of such participation is affirmed by many Christians to be a product of the "image of God" *(imago dei)* etched in every human personality (Gen. 1:26-27).[25] The Christian conception of *imago dei* is profoundly egalitarian and universal and means that all people — the criminals with Jesus and with us included — have equal dignity and value in the eyes of God.

---

25. See, for example, Martin Luther King Jr., "The Ethical Demands for Integration," in *A Testament of Hope: The Essential Writings of Martin Luther King, Jr.*, ed. James M. Washington (New York: Harper and Row, 1986), p. 119.

On my view, a primary model for a politics of ontological intimacy is supremely self-revealed by God in the concrete politics of Jesus Christ. Indeed, the manner in which Christians understand criminal justice ought to reflect our participation in the being of God as Christ *(participatio Christi)*. It is Jesus who provides the primary moral compass for understanding "persons-in-bonded-community" as participants in the divine life.[26] Such participation, however, never lifts human communities, including the church, up to a place of ontological sameness or oneness with the Trinitarian communion of Beings. Human participation in the divine life, even when at its sublime best, can never represent more than a creaturely correspondence, a shaky, unsteady, and provisional witness to the moral vision modeled supremely in the life-affirming communal testimony of Jesus Christ. Such a shaky, unsteady, and provisional communal witness to human moral bondedness, to radical intimacy, renders all of society responsible when struggling with crime's causes, consequences, and discernments in the name of what Christians know as our ontological intimacies even with the "criminals" among us.

As I have insisted repeatedly, none of what I am saying is to deny that offenders are individuals who ought to regulate their actions in the service of responsible citizenship and basic human rights. Rather, I am suggesting that the economic, political, and social context in which crime takes place must be understood as sharing equally the weight for producing crime. (Hauerwas's understanding of "excommunication" apparently makes a similar mistake just to the extent that he views the offender as having separated him- or herself from Christian community as a result of some sinful action. He does not explore the community's responsibility in the assigning of labels like "sin" and or "crime" to an individual's actions. The very act of authoritative assigning of categories like "sin" serves as an active prelude to the political act of "excommunicating.")

A Christian understanding of peaceable ontological intimacy knows that offenders always act within thick networks of social interconnectedness. Not to acknowledge this salient reality further exacerbates the human alienation that is an affront to Christian participation in the being of God. Such participation does not mean that the sins of individuals, which become demonstrative in the crimes they commit, nor the sins of a society

---

26. See Stanley J. Grenz, *The Social God and the Relational Self: A Trinitarian Theology of the Imago Dei* (Louisville, Ky.: Westminster John Knox Press, 2001), p. 305.

that produces "crime," are to be forgotten. God does not forget our alienation from God or one another. Yet any legitimate practice of "punishment" from a Christian perspective must ultimately be in remembrance of *forgiven* sin and with regard to the image of God that resides in every human being. Christian passion (tied to Jesus' death on a cross) and hope (tied to the resurrection of Jesus Christ) is the communal reality in view of which Christians relate the question of good punishment to that of imprisonment for the sake of a politics of ontological intimacy.

Racism and Imprisonment

As I reviewed the prospects of drawing on the work of Stanley Hauerwas as a resource for constructing a social ethics of good punishment as a way forward in Christian discernments about U.S. imprisonment practice, I was surprised by his general omission of a discussion of the relationship between punishment, White racism (especially its anti-Black dimension), and imprisonment. I have already pointed out that racism constitutes a particularly vicious and alienating phenomenon infecting the United States prison system. No racial or ethnic community in the nation (with the possible exception of Amerindians) experiences the brutality of retributive degradation on a scale as extensive as that experienced by African Americans. With about one half of all U.S. prisoners classified as African American (or "Black"), a vast institution like the American criminal justice system cannot help but reinforce systemic anti-Black White racism. The racism embedded in the nation's imprisonment practice constitutes a form of social alienation opposed to the kind of ontological intimacy Hauerwas would surely want to embrace. The criminal justice system perpetuates White racism in the context of (for example) the excessive national anxiety, fear, hate, vindictiveness, cynicism, and profit motive that often accompanies the very thought of "Blackness."

Recall from Chapter Three my suggestion that certain philosophical developments in the modern age have contributed to a conception that Black peoples needed to be controlled because they (to an unusually high degree) were devoid of requisite reason to well regulate their natural excess of uncontrolled passion, appetite, and desire. Such "empirical" deficiencies were thought to contribute to the baseness of the Black criminal disposition in an era of "scientific revolution" which highlighted observation and evidence as two of its foundational ideas.[27] Such perceptions of Black people by White people were intensified after the Civil War as Black folks stood at the dawn of emancipation. "Progressive" and "scientific" myths about inchoate Black people contributed significantly to the alienating racism infecting penal practice in the United States. Subtle yet common beliefs about Black people's inability to regulate their naturally and hopelessly carnal dispositions continue to influence the construction of hierarchical racial images, attitudes, and identities that are intimately bound to the creation, development, and maintenance of the dogma of White supremacy, economic wealth, and social-political power.[28] Indeed race matters greatly in the matter of who is likely to suffer most — and least — from the practice of retributive degradation. So it has been surprising to me that Hauerwas's theological ethics of good punishment has yet to confront the racism of the U.S. prison system as a towering breach of the goal of Christian ontological intimacy.

As I reflect in my less optimistic moments on the situation of Black misery within the nation's prison system, I wonder just how many White people in America (due to an excess level of irrational anxiety and fear) feel paradoxically grateful for the imprisoned Black presence among them insofar as the Black prisoner provides them a stark representation of what providence has spared them from becoming.[29] Perhaps it can be said fairly that a dimension of the dogma of White supremacy is institutionalized in the

27. I will not here rehearse once again all that I already said about this issue in Chapter Three. For a brief summary outline of the modern historical developmental stages in the evolution of race "science," and the racism and dogma of White supremacy that ultimately issues from it, see (for example) Cornel West's "A Genealogy of Modern Racism," in *Race Critical Theories*, ed. Philomena Essed and David Theo Goldberg (Malden, Mass.: Blackwell Publishers, 2002), pp. 90-112. Indeed, many of the most prominent philosophers of the Western world are coming under careful philosophical scrutiny for their roles in the development and philosophical maintenance of racism: for example, the "barbarian" versus Greek oppositions articulated by Plato and Aristotle, the existence of racial categories in "social contract" and "Enlightenment" thought (e.g., Hobbes, Locke, Rousseau, Kant, Hegel), the post-Enlightenment (e.g., Nietzsche, Mill, Carlyle), and the twentieth century (e.g., Heidegger, Dewey, Sartre, Beauvoir). See Julie K. Ward and Tommy Lee Lott, eds., *Philosophers on Race: Critical Essays* (Malden, Mass.: Blackwell, 2002).

28. See and cf. Mark Kline Taylor's insightful theorization of anti-Black White racism in *Remembering Esperanza: A Cultural-Political Theology for North American Praxis* (Maryknoll, N.Y.: Orbis Books, 1990), pp. 135-49.

29. Cf. Mark Lewis Taylor, *The Executed God: The Way of the Cross in Lockdown America* (Minneapolis: Fortress Press, 2001), p. 28.

form of the prison, which continually seeks to reinforce racism as a therapy — and economic boon to boot — for dealing with a White sense of existential dread. After all, is it not true that when Black men, in particular, look into the eyes of any number of White people they will see the images of themselves which White souls mirror back at them: for many, many, White people Black men are still like "that spook who haunted Edgar Allan Poe." Black men are still the "boys" who incite skepticism and suspicion in those anxious for personal safety. Black men are still Black as death, compilations of flesh and bone, fiber and liquids, which represent a continual challenge and menace to others. Black men are still niggers. When Black men see their distorted reflections through the collective White gaze they will see why homicide, suicide, and prison have so overwhelmingly become the Black man's burden: our humanity is invisible, we are beasts.[30]

I am drawing here of course on that wonderfully crafted prologue to Ralph Ellison's *Invisible Man*. And, while I am on the issue of the boundary between Black invisibility and Black presence, I have been stunned by the utter dearth of writings and active concern by Stanley Hauerwas (and the overwhelming majority of White theologians) regarding the American democratic and Christian church struggle with the sin (and crime) of anti-Black racism.[31] I have wondered aloud elsewhere, how an issue so divisively and horrendously present in the bone marrow of the society and church remains so invisible in Hauerwas's work? In Hauerwas's single significant essay on the struggle for African American rights since writing an article entitled "The Ethics of Black Power" for his college newspaper back in 1969 (the same year James Cone wrote *Black Theology and Black Power*), he argues that "for me to 'use' Martin Luther King Jr., and the church that made him possible, to advance my understanding of 'Christian Ethics' seems wrong."[32] Then, in an astounding breach of the very ontological intimacy which characterizes the peaceable Christian tradition, he calls on the faithful to recover, Hauerwas claims, with regard to the Black struggle that produced King, that "that story is not my story, though I pray that

---

30. See Ralph Ellison, *Invisible Man* (New York: Vintage Books, 1989), pp. 3-14.

31. See James Cone's still salient, still fresh discussion of this troubling reality in *Black Theology and Black Power* (Minneapolis: Seabury Press, 1969), pp. 62-90. Also see the important "Preface to the 1989 Edition" of this book, published by Orbis Books.

32. Stanley Hauerwas, "Remembering Martin Luther King, Jr.," in *Wilderness Wanderings: Probing Twentieth-Century Theology and Philosophy* (Boulder, Colo.: Westview Press, 1997), p. 225.

God will make that story my story, for I hope to enjoy the fellowship of the communion of saints."[33]

Hauerwas goes on to say that, "I have written about the South, which obviously involves race, but I have not written about 'the struggle.'" He also notes that, "I am . . . a white southerner from the lower-middle classes who grew up in the practices of segregation." "Segregation was so 'normal,'" confides Hauerwas, that "[I] did not even notice that there were no black people either in the schools I attended or where I went to church."[34] Since Hauerwas appears to understand that the habits of racism and White supremacy have been deeply written into the story of his life, he ought to also know, then, that the story of "the struggle" is as much his story as it was King's story. An important dimension of ontological intimacy includes knowledge of a historical social ontology that bonds humanity together. King's insistence that the peoples of the United States and world wore a "single garment of destiny," and that all of life is inextricably connected in an "inescapable network of mutuality," has been most intensively true for the relationship between U.S. Black and White peoples who must struggle together (along with many other U.S. peoples) under the weight of the dogma of White supremacy. The story of Hauerwas's education and habituation in White racism (at home, school, and church) and "the struggle" fronted by King against this most dismal of horrors *is one and the same social story,* albeit interpreted and experienced from very different positions around the Christian table. It *is* Hauerwas's story, too, because even Christian disunity is part of a common story.

The story of the Jim (and Jane) Crow South in which Hauerwas was raised routinely displayed a paradoxical and ironic politics of ontological intimacy. Consider, for example, historian Tim Tyson's *Radio Free Dixie,* a biography of the Black power activist Robert Williams (1925-1996), author of *Negroes With Guns.* Regarding what can be described as a strange-union-within-segregation (or a kind of "alienating-intimacy") between Black and White peoples in the very South in which Hauerwas was nurtured, Tyson argues that

> The power of white skin in the Jim Crow south was both stark and subtle. White supremacy permeated daily life so deeply that most peo-

33. Hauerwas, "Remembering Martin Luther King, Jr.," p. 225.
34. Hauerwas, "Remembering Martin Luther King, Jr.," p. 225.

ple could no more ponder it than a fish might discuss the wetness of water. Racial etiquette was at once bizarre, arbitrary and nearly inviolable. A white man who would never shake hands with a black man would refuse to permit anyone but a black man to shave his face, cut his hair, or give him a shampoo. A white man might share his bed with a black woman but never his table. Black breasts could suckle white babies, black hands would pat out biscuit dough for white mouths, but black heads must not try on a hat in the department store, lest it be rendered unfit for sale to white people. Black maids washed the bodies of the aged and infirm, but the uniforms they wore could never be laundered in the same washing machines that white people used. It was permissible to call a favored black man "Commodore" or "Professor" — a mixture of affection and mockery — but never "mister" or "sir." Black women were "girls" until they were old enough to be called "auntie," but could never hear a white person, regardless of age, address them as "Mrs." or "Miss." Whites regarded black people as inherently lazy and shiftless, but when a white man said he had "worked like a nigger," he meant that he had engaged in dirty, back-breaking labor to the point of collapse.[35]

Although born about a decade apart, King (b. 1929) and Hauerwas (b. 1940) were raised, from different yet profoundly interrelated perspectives, deep within the story of "the struggle" that Tyson gives us a glimpse into. Why Hauerwas refuses to risk writing constructively about "the struggle," and why he views the potential for unity and peace regarding this issue as hopelessly "eschatological," given his insights into the politics of ontological intimacy, is a real puzzle.[36]

35. Quoted in Craig Werner, *A Change is Gonna Come: Music, Race & the Soul of America* (New York: Plume Books, 1999), pp. 56-57. Cf. also C. Van Woodward, *The Strange Career of Jim Crow: A Commemorative Edition* (Oxford: Oxford University Press, 2002), pp. 7; passim.

36. Hauerwas, "Remembering Martin Luther King, Jr.," p. 237. It is obvious in this essay that Hauerwas is using the memory of King as a launching pad for still another attack upon liberalism. Hauerwas makes a similar error to the one he makes with the story of King and "the struggle" when he claims that "[Malcolm X's] story cannot be ours, however — if we are white, Christian and American or even European — for the evil he had to recognize is not the same as ours." See Stanley Hauerwas with Richard Bondi and David B. Burrell, *Truthfulness and Tragedy: Further Investigations into Christian Ethics* (Notre Dame, Ind.: University of Notre Dame Press, 1977), p. 97.

In any case, when the perception of Blackness today is seen in the eyes of too many White folk one gets clues as to why masses of Black men, women, and children live in ever more concentrated and isolated pools of poverty and despair, just waiting, waiting, in the antechamber of hell: Black-is-the-color-of-the-beast-the-color-of-death-and-the-color-of-crime. It is the Blackness of African Americans that is to blame for the *Fall* of their divine image (if they ever really had one). For the sake of their own self-identity, White people have too often — not every single one of them, but as a collective Body — enshrined the American civil religion of blame and shame on Black men in particular. (And all of this in spite of a relatively law-abiding, well-integrated and substantial Black middle class.)

Lest one view what I have been saying here as simple-minded rhetorical anger and frustration, consider a recent enough *New York Times* article that cites a University of Michigan study of 328 criminal cases over the last 15 years in which persons convicted mainly of rape and murder have been exonerated. The study is suggestive of the strong probability that today there are thousands of innocent people, especially Black men, doing time in prison. Among other discoveries the *Times* piece contends that

Some 90 percent of false convictions in rape cases involved misidentification by witnesses, very often across races. In particular, the study said black men made up a disproportionate number of exonerated rape defendants. The racial mix of those exonerated, in general, mirrored that of the prison population, and the mix of those convicted of murder. But while 29 percent of those convicted of rape are black, 65 percent of those exonerated are. Interracial rapes are, moreover, uncommon. Rapes of white women by black men, for instance, represent just 10 percent of all rapes, according to the justice department. But in half of the rape exonerations where racial data was available, black men were falsely accused of raping white women. "The most obvious explanation for this racial disparity is probably the most powerful," the study says. "White Americans are much more likely to mistake one black person for another than to do the same for their own race."[37]

37. Adam Liptak, "Study Suspects Thousands of False Convictions," *New York Times*, April 19, 2004.

The study goes on to say that the leading causes of wrongful convictions for murder in particular were false confessions made mostly by the mentally retarded, the mentally ill, and juveniles — in other words, groups most vulnerable to suggestion and intimidation. And given the racial disparities within the prison system it is safe to say that a disproportionate percentage of those from the most vulnerable groups "just happen" to be black.[38]

All of this reasonably suggests that a far disproportionate number of innocent Black men (a number in the thousands) are being subjected to imprisonment. Critical numbers of these Black men (and increasingly Black women, through their imprisonment) have become valuable economic commodities for the benefit of industry and communities in need of an economic fix. Black men also make up a significant proportion of those U.S. residents (discussed in Chapter One) who are members of "surplus populations" disproportionately represented in the nation's prisons and jails. Many Black inmates, while in prison and upon their release, face what Cornel West argues is "a kind of 'Good Friday' state of existence in which one is seemingly forever on a cross, perennially crucified, continuously abused and incessantly devalued." Yet there remains a hope that the Black prisoner (and all others) will be "sustained by a hope against hope for a potential and possible triumphant state of affairs."[39]

In dialectical tension with what I am arguing here — and this too

---

38. Paul Street has argued that the prison system negatively affects Black lives more, and this is tied to wider socioeconomic, political, and institutional interests little bothered by expressions of overt public bigotry against Black persons in America. In the context of noting Stanley Aronowitz's contention that more than thirty years after the heroic civil rights movement. "The stigma of race remains the unmeltable condition of the black social and economic situation," Street goes on to argue that the seemingly insoluble persistence of the social and economic situation of Black people in America "is seen in an inequitably funded educational system that 'just happens' to provide poorer instruction for blacks than whites, an electoral system whose voting irregularities and domination of Big Money 'just happens' to disproportionately disenfranchise blacks, and job, housing, health care, and financial labor markets that 'just happen' to especially disadvantage and segregate African-Americans. It is evident in a political economy whose tendency toward sharp inequality 'just happens' to especially impoverish and divide black communities. And it is evident in the glaring injustices of the U.S. prison system." Paul Street, "Color Blind: Prisons and the New American Racism," *Dissent*, Summer 2001, p. 30. Cf. also Stanley Aronowitz, "Race and the Continental Divide," *The Nation*, March 12, 2000.

39. Cornel West, "Prophetic Christian as Organic Intellectual: Martin Luther King, Jr," in *The Cornel West Reader* (New York: Basic Civitas Books, 1999), p. 427.

must be said — is the reality that there are a critical mass of Black men who have come to believe and internalize many of the hurtful and savage images of ourselves that are part of the popular national imagination. Addison Gayle was right when in his essay "Beyond Nihilism" he argued that "Bigger Thomas," the tragic antihero of Richard Wright's novel *Native Son*, "is still present in modern day America, goading and pushing each Negro across the nihilistic brink where, in one transcendent moment, he is lifted above his predetermined state, gaining a sense of manhood, identity, and social worth, through the only means possible, in an oppressive society — the medium of violence."[40] Indeed, the question asked by the poet Nikki Giovanni more than three decades ago is still relevant for us Black men today as we struggle against a spiritual and psychic death that often lands us in somebody's prison or jail: "Can you kill the nigger in you? . . . Can you kill your nigger mind?"[41]

Racism and the Culture of Violence and Materialism

The foregoing comments concerning White anti-Black racism as a salient dimension of U.S. imprisonment practice are not meant to suggest that there is a single comprehensive explanation affecting the nation's reliance on imprisonment as a response to crime. While one is indeed justified in judging racism as a real problem associated with the active misery of the prison-industrial complex,[42] racism must be viewed as intimately bound to at least two other deep-issue dimensions of the American ethos. The American appetite for racism and the excessive incarceration of its residents is inextricably tied to a *mutually reinforcing* and generalized idolatry of materialism and violence that holds considerable sway over the nation.

40. Quoted in Margaret Walker, *Richard Wright, Daemonic Genius: A Portrait Of The Man A Critical Look At His Work* (New York: Warner Books, 1988), p. 154.

41. Nikki Giovanni, "The True Import of Present Dialogue: Black vs. Negro" in *Black Feelings Black Talk: Black Judgment* (New York: Morrow Quill Paperbacks, 1979), pp. 19-20. For a more comprehensive account of African American and African "spiritual death" (nihilism) see Amos N. Wilson, *Black-on-Black Violence: The Psychodynamics of Black Self-Annihilation in Service of White Domination* (New York: Afrikan World Infosystems, 1990).

42. Of course the prison-industrial complex is also interlaced with highly sexualized masculinities and high levels of classism and xenophobia against various "low-status" working peoples.

The materialist aspect of the prison-industrial complex supports the production and maintenance of steady supplies of predominantly Black cheap labor. This is part of the "affirmative action" that disproportionately metes out retributive degradation on Black bodies and psyches. This "labor force" serves the corporate thirst for profit, a thirst that will never be satiated. And of course this materialist dimension of imprisonment constitutes a violence that undermines Christian ontological intimacy as human beings are transformed into capital and commodities.

With regard to the issue of violence in general, Griffith correctly argues that "America is possessed by the spirit of violence, that violence has become an idol more palpably real than any golden calf. Violence is worshiped; it is glorified as the divine source of security, and sacrifices both material and human are offered up to it. Any who doubts this can check the national military budget or explore the desk drawers and gun cabinets of millions of American homes or (simplest of all) turn on the television."[43]

If one harbors any doubts that an idolatry of violence pervades criminal punishment in the United States, one need only observe the common communicative and performative rituals that accompany state-sponsored executions. Snyder correctly notes in this regard that, "The return and increase of capital punishment have been welcomed by many of our citizens. Reminiscent of the bloodthirsty crowds at the ancient gladiatorial arenas, advocates of capital punishment gather outside the prisons to celebrate with parades, flags, banners, music, cheering, and fireworks as the hour of execution strikes."[44] Even professed Christians routinely join in on these celebrations of violence and death. Instead of lamenting executions of the condemned, many Christians welcome these carnivals of bloodlust.

Not only is the nation swayed by an idolatry of violence, its general idolization of material culture is an additional affront to a Christian politics of ontological intimacy. Not only do most prisoners learn to value violence as a way of life, but "materialism is another American icon that many offenders have learned to value," as Griffith correctly notes.[45] While it is true that material well-being is a critical and necessary dimension of human life, Griffith is right to insist that, "Too much importance is loaded onto material when it is viewed as the source of happiness or the

43. Griffith, *The Fall of the Prison*, p. 183.
44. Snyder, *The Protestant Ethic and the Spirit of Punishment*, p. 9.
45. Griffith, *The Fall of the Prison*, p. 185.

sign of success."[46] The economic powers-that-be routinely generate discontent by manufacturing a culture of continuous material need that can never be satiated. There is very little in the culture that advocates for "enough is enough" in terms of material possessions. The pursuit of material possessions often becomes inextricably bound to our sense of self-worth, meaning, and purpose. It is perhaps correct to say then that robbers and thieves do not rebel against American materialism when they steal; they are affirming it.[47] From a Christian perspective that favors societal cohesion while celebrating and embracing difference, the twin American icons of violence and materialism are towering breaches of ontological intimacy. They are also powerful backdrops against which racialized aspects of imprisonment exist.

Restorative Justice, Systemic Alternatives, and Imprisonment

I now turn to offering a trajectory of what a Christian politics of *ontological intimacy in the making* might look like when practically applied as countercultural to contemporary imprisonment practices.

Moving beyond our reliance on counterproductive regimes of punishment towards a politics of ontological intimacy means focusing some attention on examples of practical restorative practices that move us toward addressing wrongdoing while reducing reliance on current imprisonment practice. In the discussion of imprisonment and ontological intimacy that follows, I will give attention to a specific countercultural model of criminal justice, namely "restorative justice." I will then highlight examples of existent countercultural activism that speaks to contemporary imprisonment practices and the hope for societal well-being.

Restorative Justice and Imprisonment

One of the best contemporary social experiments bringing a deep concern about crime and punishment together with the cultivation of better Christian (and "non-Christian") participation in efforts toward ontological in-

46. Griffith, *The Fall of the Prison*, p. 185.
47. Griffith, *The Fall of the Prison*, p. 185.

timacy can be seen in the work being done under the name "restorative justice." Several Christian communities since the 1970s, including a proportionately sizable Mennonite population, have brought a peaceable faith perspective to bear on the vengeful and degrading world of imprisonment. Beginning in Ontario, Canada, and later in the state of Indiana, experimental cases with victim-offender encounters have led to programs throughout Canada and the United States. The early "case experiments" in restorative justice in Canada and the U.S. "later became models for programs throughout the world," according to Howard Zehr, one of the founding architects and advocates of restorative justice as an alternative or supplement to official criminal justice processes.[48] Zehr (self-described as "a white, middle-class male of European ancestry, a Christian, a Mennonite," and who happens to be the first White graduate of Morehouse College) correctly acknowledges that the restorative approach to justice "owes a special debt to the Native peoples of North America and New Zealand." Moreover, he notes, "The precedents and roots of restorative justice are much wider and deeper than the Mennonite-led initiatives of the 1970s. Indeed, they are as old as human history."[49]

Although the term "restorative justice" is a phrase used to encompass a variety of programs and practices, Zehr contends that at its core restorative justice "is a set of principles, a philosophy, an alternative set of guiding questions. Ultimately, restorative justice provides an alternative framework for thinking about wrongdoing."[50] Restorative justice is community-based and deals with offenders through a victim-oriented process of restoration in the form of restitution. At their core, restorative justice approaches to wrongdoing seek to undo society's prevailing and morally restrictive understanding of who constitutes the legitimately concerned in matters of criminal justice. Restorative justice expands the circle of persons who have a standing in the event or case of wrongdoing beyond the boundaries of the government and the offender. The approach aims to give more voice and control to victims and community members as well.[51] In a society where crime is understood as occurring "against the

---

48. Howard Zehr, *The Little Book of Restorative Justice* (Intercourse, Pa.: Good Books, 2002), p. 11.

49. Zehr, *Little Book of Restorative Justice*, pp. 11-12.

50. Zehr, *Little Book of Restorative Justice*, p. 5.

51. Zehr, *Little Book of Restorative Justice*, p. 13.

state," restorative justice approaches work for increased victim empowerment and the restitution of actual losses.

With the provision of restitution comes recognition that an offender is seriously accountable for his or her crime, a recognition that removes the dangerous possibility of blaming the victim. Restitution recognizes the basic need of victims for vindication without making the pain and humiliation of punishment the final word. Offenders are to face squarely the harms resulting from their actions within a process that encourages empathy and hopefully transforms shame. Restorative justice also encourages offenders to experience personal transformation by addressing the harms that contributed to their offending behavior. This includes seeking treatment for addictions and/or other problems and enhancing their more positive personal competencies. Ideally, encouragement and support for integration into the community will also be provided for within restorative justice programs. However, most advocates of restorative justice approaches to crime and punishment recognize that some offenders will need at least temporary restraint to ensure community and self-safety.[52]

Restorative justice approaches try to understand and work toward a community's need for justice by giving attention to their concerns as victims; this enhances opportunities to build a sense of community and mutual accountability. Communities are encouraged to take seriously their responsibility for the welfare of all community members, including victims and offenders. In general communities must recognize their obligation to foster the conditions that promote and expand their collective health; indeed communities are invited to take appropriate responsibility for building the kinds of people they wish to produce. It is in the context of this community involvement that restorative justice understands what Zehr names as the three pillars of restorative justice: (1) restorative justice focuses on harm, (2) wrongs or harms result in obligations, (3) restorative justice promotes engagement or participation by all "stakeholders."[53]

Although I would claim that restorative justice approaches to crime and punishment are useful as a politics of healing memories in the service of ontological intimacy, restorative justice on the whole is not viewed by its

52. Zehr, *Little Book of Restorative Justice*, p. 17.
53. Zehr, *Little Book of Restorative Justice*, pp. 22-24. Zehr has been appropriately ambivalent about the word "stakeholder" in the field of restorative justice, arguing that, ". . . the term 'stakeholder' is problematic; it may in fact originate from white settlers driving their stakes into the ground to mark what was originally Native land" (p. 70).

most prominent Christian advocates primarily as a vehicle for forgiveness or reconciliation. Restorative justice does not aim to encourage or coerce victims of crime to forgive or reconcile with offenders, though the process "does provide a context where either or both might happen."[54] This is important to note. Nonetheless, restorative justice does foster the fertile soil where forgiveness and reconciliation might take root. Zehr suggests that in the context of restorative justice "some degree of forgiveness or even reconciliation does occur much more frequently than in the adversarial setting of the criminal justice system. However, this is a choice that is entirely up to the participants. There should be no pressure to choose to forgive or to seek reconciliation."[55] This aspect of restorative justice notwithstanding, restorative justice does comport toward a Christian politics of ontological intimacy with its insistence that certain underlying (root) values be embraced if restorative justice is to function properly: *interconnectedness, particularity/individuality, respect.* Zehr insists that, "to apply restorative justice principles in a way that is true to their spirit and intent, we must be explicit about our values. Otherwise, for example, we might use a restoratively-based process but arrive at non-restorative outcomes." With regard to the critical importance of making explicit the core values he thinks are too often understated and taken for granted, Zehr contends that

> Underlying restorative justice is the vision of interconnectedness. . . . We are all connected to each other and to the larger world through a web of relationships. When this web is disrupted, we are all affected. The primary elements of restorative justice — harm and need, obligation, and participation — derive from this vision. But this value of interconnectedness must be balanced by an appreciation for particularity. Although we are connected, we are not the same. Particularity appreciates diversity. It respects the individuality and worth of each person. It takes seriously specific contexts and situations. Justice must acknowledge both our interconnectedness and our individuality. The value of particularity reminds us that context, culture, and personality are all important. . . .
>
> Ultimately, however, one basic value is supremely important: respect. If I had to put restorative justice into just one word, I would

54. Zehr, *Little Book of Restorative Justice*, p. 8.
55. Zehr, *Little Book of Restorative Justice*, p. 8.

choose respect: respect for all, even those who are different from us, even those who seem to be our enemies. Respect reminds us of our interconnectedness but also of our differences. Respect insists that we balance concern for all parties. If we pursue justice as respect, we will pursue justice restoratively. If we do not respect others, we will not do justice restoratively, no matter how earnestly we adopt the principles. The value of respect underlies restorative justice principles and must guide and shape their application.[56]

Though Zehr is a Christian, and though that fact may indeed root his particular embrace of the underlying values of restorative justice, he never suggests that one needs to be a Christian to affirm the values of interconnectedness, particularity/individuality, and, most of all, respect. Human beings may come to embrace such values from any number of cultural or religious contexts. And I would contend from the perspective of a Christian narrative that the possibility of such a common *human* embrace constitutes the grace of God in the service of ontological intimacy.

In any case, in addition to not aiming primarily at forgiveness or reconciliation, restorative justice is not mediation, nor is it primarily designed to reduce recidivism or repeat offenses. In fact, restorative justice is not any particular program or blueprint — it is "more a compass than a map."[57] Restorative justice is not mediation because the parties involved may not be willing or able to meet. In addition, the fact that parties in the dispute are not assumed to be on a level moral playing field with equal shared responsibility rules out viewing restorative justice as a form of mediation. Victims of rape and/or other serious crimes do not want to be known as "equal" disputants in the violence perpetrated against them. Indeed, many victims already struggle to not blame themselves.[58] And although reduced recidivism might be (and sometimes is) a byproduct of restorative justice in some cases, the approach is employed simply because "victims' needs *should* be addressed, offenders *should* be encouraged to take responsibility, those affected by an offense *should* be involved in the process, regardless of whether offenders catch on and reduce their offending."[59]

56. Zehr, *Little Book of Restorative Justice*, pp. 35-36.
57. Zehr, *Little Book of Restorative Justice*, pp. 9-10.
58. Zehr, *Little Book of Restorative Justice*, p. 9.
59. Zehr, *Little Book of Restorative Justice*, p. 10.

Restorative justice is not primarily intended for comparatively minor offenses or for first-time offenders. This is because programs that address so-called "minor" cases find it easier to get community support. Experience has shown that restorative justice approaches may have the greatest impact in more severe cases, although domestic violence is probably the most problematic area of application. It should go without saying that great caution is an utmost necessity when restorative justice is brought to bear on such cases.[60] Finally, it must be admitted that restorative justice is not a panacea. It is not necessarily a replacement for the legal system, nor is it necessarily an alternative to prison. Restorative justice is primarily a process of restitution; Christians may embrace the process because it is guided by a legitimate need for vindication through a peaceable approach to reciprocity. This approach takes justice seriously as it inches society in the direction of ontological intimacy grounded by values of interconnectedness, particularity/individuality, and especially respect.[61]

Systemic Alternatives to Prisons

Not only are Mennonites and other peaceable Christians actively concerned with the issues of crime, prisons, and restorative justice; non-Christian communitarians concerned with systemic alternatives to imprisonment also model movement toward a politics of ontological intimacy. In direct confrontation with contemporary imprisonment practices these justice-seekers give critical voice to better social expressions of our collective intimacies of being.[62] For example, Christian Parenti and Angela Y.

---

60. Zehr, *Little Book of Restorative Justice*, p. 11.

61. While this very brief and basic outline of the salient features of restorative justice approaches to crime and punishment cannot be expanded upon here, readers wanting to engage the literature on restorative justice further should see Howard Zehr's *Changing Lenses* (Scottdale, Pa.: Herald Press, 1990). This text is one of the most influential books on restorative justice. Other very good sources on this issue include an edited volume by Gordon Bazemore and Mara Schiff entitled *Restorative Community Justice: Repairing Harm and Transforming Communities* (Cincinnati: Anderson Publishing Company, 2001) and Michael L. Hadley's edited volume entitled *The Spiritual Roots of Restorative Justice* (Albany, N.Y.: State University of New York Press, 2001).

62. In general, alternative justice movements may well assist Christians with a deeper understanding of their own vision of ontological intimacy by tilting Christian allegiance toward viewing the world through the eyes of those who work at creating solidarities attentive

Davis offer some possible ways forward in terms of providing concrete alternatives to current U.S. criminal justice practices. Parenti, a Justice Fellow at the Soros Foundation in New York City, recommends, as regards criminal justice, "less." Specifically he recommends, "[l]ess policing, less incarceration, shorter sentences, less surveillance, fewer laws governing individual behaviors, and less obsessive discussion of every lurid crime, less prohibition, and less puritanical concern with 'freaks' and 'deviants.'"[63]

According to Parenti nonviolent offenders currently make up two thirds of all people entering prison. It follows for him that "there are literally hundreds of thousands of people in prison who pose no major threat to public safety." "These minor credit card fraudsters, joy-riders, pot farmers, speed freaks, prostitutes, and shoplifters should not rot in prison at taxpayer's expense."[64] Of course, there are those who disagree with this assessment of the situation; more hard-line advocates of the "broken window" theory of criminal justice would claim that it is just these very "minor" nonviolent offenders who create (and are responsible for) the very atmosphere in which more serious violent crimes breed. In fact, according to many "hard-liners," a high percentage of petty criminals are also potential or actual violent felons.

In any case, "decarceration" is Parenti's recommendation. Decarceration of the prison-industrial complex entails the following specific recommendations:

> We need a commitment to limiting incarceration and then a policy of "harm reduction" in which we could decriminalize drugs, give junkies their dope, decriminalize sex work, and subsidize prostitute organizing efforts; we could cut off the retail supply of cheap guns and tax other firearms at 500 percent, while at the same time eliminating draconian gun penalties [and] "sentencing enhancements," which mete

---

to struggles against all social-political arrangements that re/produce economic exploitation, racism, patriarchy, homophobia, and xenophobia. See, for example, Angela Y. Davis, *Abolition Democracy: Beyond Empire, Prisons, and Torture* (New York: Seven Stories Press, 2005). Peter Linebaugh and Marcus Rediker, *The Many Headed Hydra: Commoners and the Hidden History of the Revolutionary Atlantic* (New York: Beacon Press, 2000), and Robin D. G. Kelley, *Freedom Dreams: The Black Radical Imagination* (New York: Beacon Press, 2003).

63. Christian Parenti, *Lockdown America: Police and Prisons in the Age of Crisis* (New York: Verso, 2002), p. 242.

64. Parenti, *Lockdown America*, p. 242.

out excessive punishment for firearms possession and use. And since the need for work is at the heart of any real war on crime, we could create jobs that pay a living wage and meet human needs. To achieve anything like this we need more popular resistance and more economic justice.[65]

Philosopher, activist, and social critic Davis would agree with much of what Parenti has said, but also recommend the even more radical step of abolishing prisons (nearly) altogether as a means of solving the nation's most entrenched social problems. Davis's abolitionism has been inextricably tied to her concerns about the American problematics of race, sex, and class. In a 1994 closing address given at a conference entitled "Black Women in the Academy: Defending Our Name" at the Massachusetts Institute of Technology, Davis told the gathered audience that

In the area of the war against drugs, black women comprise the faster growing imprisoned population. The war against drugs serves as the pretext for police and military campaigns and an obscene proliferation of prisons and jails. The only alternatives to imprisonment are those managed by correctional systems. In defending the name of Surgeon General Joycelyn Elders, we acknowledge the courage she displayed in attempting to place the issue of decriminalization of drugs on the political agenda. Because she suggested a national conversation on a reasonable alternative to the present expansion of police and penal institutions — which tend to reproduce crime more than they deter it — she has been harshly rebuked by the White House, as have Lani Guinier and Johnnetta Cole.

In response to Elders' call for conversation on decriminalization, I want to offer a further suggestion about potential research and organizing agendas. I want to ask you to consider the prospect of abolishing jails and prisons for a substantial percentage of the imprisoned population. We might begin with a strategy of decarceration for women prisoners, the vast majority of whom are black women convicted of nonviolent crimes, such as drugs, prostitution and welfare fraud. I am suggesting that we theorize and organize a new abolitionism, an approach that would propose institutions other than prisons to address the social

65. Parenti, *Lockdown America*, p. 243.

problems that lead to imprisonment. I use the term "abolitionism" because of its historical resonance with nineteenth-century struggles against slavery.

Moreover, when slavery was constitutionally abolished by the Thirteenth Amendment, a clause permitting the continued enslavement of people convicted of crimes was retained. Thus, structures of domination associated with slavery have survived, hidden away, behind prison walls. The vast majority of states do not even allow inmates to vote. As a matter of fact, Massachusetts, the site of this conference, is one of the few states, along with Maine and Vermont, that do allow inmates to vote. At least four million current and former prisoners in this country do not have the right to vote. A disproportionate number of them are black and Latino.[66]

In her book *Are Prisons Obsolete?* Davis argues for "abolitionist alternatives" to prisons; abolitionist alternatives to prisons constitute a foreshadowing of the better society people of goodwill hope to build. Davis contends that hope for the future of justice-making requires an abolitionist approach that would eventually "remove the prison from the social and ideological landscape of our society." Davis's abolitionist perspective insists that society not search for prisonlike substitutes for the prison, "such as house arrest safeguarded by electronic surveillance bracelets." Rather, she invites us to imagine a constellational continuum of alternatives to imprisonment: e.g., the "demilitarization of education at all levels, a health system that provides free physical and mental care to all, and a justice system based on reparation and reconciliation rather than retribution and vengeance."[67]

Davis's recommendations are a good example of how the Christian grammar of "good punishment" could be expanded into public debates about imprisonment. Davis's recommendations comport with a Christian politics of healing memories and a politics of ontological intimacy. Her vision of reparation and reconciliation is a salient embodiment of the ontological intimacy sought by peaceable Christians in the service of human participation in the being of God in history; and this is despite the fact she

---

66. Angela Y. Davis, "Marxism, Anti-Racism, and Feminism," in *The Angela Y. Davis Reader,* ed. Joy James (Malden, Mass.: Blackwell, 1998), p. 230.

67. Angela Y. Davis, *Are Prisons Obsolete?* (New York: Seven Stories, 2003), p. 107.

is not a Christian (as far as I know). Davis's abolitionist approach to criminal justice, as well as Parenti's call for decarceration, are imaginative alternatives that model the kinds of transformation that serve the promise of ontological intimacy, even if all Christians cannot embrace every aspect of their proposals.

My own recommendations for addressing problems associated with the current U.S. prison system include much of what has been suggested by Parenti and Davis. In the spirit of what they have suggested, I would argue that the large-scale retributive degradation, economic exploitation, and "surplus population control" routinely employed by the U.S. prison system does not truly "correct." In addition to this, we fail to reform most prisoners because we fail to deal with the systemic social and economic causes and inequities which contribute to large-scale imprisonment. In addition to addressing various levels of individual deviance of one sort or another, the social, economic, and political factors contributing to the disproportionate jailing of the least fortunate among us must be reconsidered, and deeply. Society must deeply reconsider why it is, in the wealthiest nation in human history, a person can work full-time and more and not earn enough to care for even a small family, including receiving adequate family health care benefits. Society must also give serious moral reconsideration to issues such as the legislating of penalties up to ten times more severe for possession of crack cocaine than for powder cocaine, as well as the continued expansion of private prisons. A major national re-envisioning is needed of the relationship between advanced capitalist progress and the economic need to, in turns, exploit the labor of and then jail the nation's "surplus populations." As suggested in Chapter One, many of these *human beings* — poor youths, unemployed and underemployed young adults, the mentally ill, drug addicts, lonely and frayed drifters, alcoholics, and cast-off and impoverished elders — are apparently in the way of the nation's economic prosperity; hence, prisons and jails provide waystations for their regulation and control.

With all of this in mind, I would concur with Parenti that there ought to be an all-around effort at decarceration, with a cornerstone being the decriminalization of drugs — or at least a serious, open, and public debate regarding the matter. Rather than putting massive amounts of our national resources into large-scale retributive degradation, federal and local governments could regulate the distribution and taxation of narcotics much as they do with alcohol and tobacco. This would significantly reduce the level of profit-motivated street carnage that currently surrounds illicit drug use. One could object here arguing that increased accidents from neglect speak against legalization. This counterargument is based partly on reasonable concerns about a presumed increase in the number of users if drugs were decriminalized. But the nation should already know from vast painful experience that widespread neglect as a result of illegal drug use is already ubiquitous throughout society, and the hourly bloodletting related to it is endemic throughout the nation.

Drug abuse ought to be dealt with as the public health issue, even epidemic, that it is. (Of course the collective role of society in creating a social atmosphere in which crime can breed also constitutes a very serious public health threat.) Drug abuse should not be thought of primarily as a criminal justice issue. Public policy reform ought to take tax revenue generated by legal drug use and approach drug addiction in a manner similar to (perhaps in some cases, even better than) the ways in which we approach AIDS, lung cancer, alcoholism, and increasingly obesity (or any other deadly social disease). Society should provide the resources for the creation of massive networks of "free" comprehensive treatment centers for those suffering the ravages of drug abuse. While I suggest, at the very least, conducting a serious national debate on the legalization of drugs like marijuana and cocaine, I would be willing to concede that some drugs may be so dangerous that only under prescription should they be dispensed. But while the particulars may be open to debate, let us at least consider the matter seriously.

Of course all that I have just said puts me in agreement with Angela Davis who, like Parenti, recommends decarceration with a foundation based in the decriminalization of drugs and certain other nonviolent criminal offenses like prostitution. Davis notes, for example, that the "[d]ecriminalization of drugs would greatly reduce the numbers of incarcerated women, for the 278 percent increase in the numbers of black women in state and federal prisons (as compared with the 186 percent increase in the numbers of black men) can be largely attributed to the phenomenal rise in drug-related and specifically crack-related imprisonment. According to the Sentencing Project's 1995 report, the increase amounted to 828 percent."[68]

68. Angela Y. Davis, "Prisons, Repression, and Resistance," in *The Angela Y. Davis Reader*, p. 70.

I agree with Davis on the issue of drug decriminalization. I also agree with her recommendation that serious consideration be given to the abolition of jails and prisons "for a substantial percentage of the imprisoned population."[69] I am thinking particularly of those convicted of "nonviolent" crimes involving (for example) drug use, prostitution, and welfare fraud. Yet notwithstanding my recommendation that fewer behaviors be judged as requiring imprisonment, incapacitation of some kind or another will still need to be reserved for society's most violent and unrepentant felons. Although incapacitation will still be required for some felons, serious effort should be given to transformative practices that, to the extent it is possible, restore. All of society is helped whenever guards, prison administrators, and the general public treat even the most ruthless of prisoners like human beings.[70] Yes, violent restraint and control will be inevitable for some prisoners, but prison officials would serve society better if, in the name of basic human dignity, this most unfortunate of tasks were approached in a spirit of lament and hope.

I do acknowledge that even with the best intentions, resources, and efforts, there will be some offenders that society cannot risk putting back on the streets. But the most violent among us can be housed in a correctional system a fraction of the size we have now. Thinking in terms of (relative) prison abolition, the humanity of those convicted of crime (and those convicting them) would be enhanced by housing them in something other than cages or increasingly in the fortress-like palaces known as supermax prisons. Resorting to the large-scale imprisonment of its residents should not be the primary answer to solving society's social disorders.

Unfortunately, it must sadly be said that most of the aforementioned discussion appears moot since the national appetite for imprisoning ever increasing numbers of its residents only shows signs of continuing unabated. Today there are too few jurisdictions seeking to reduce the numbers of those imprisoned. It should be remembered that critical numbers of Christians are supportive of the current imprisonment frenzy, or of what Parenti sometimes refers to as "the science of kicking ass." Sadly, it appears that a serious conversation about the decriminalization of drugs

69. Davis, "Marxism, Anti-Racism, and Feminism," p. 230.

70. According to an excellent study done by Yale University comparative and foreign law professor James Whitman, European prisons generally succeed in this. James Q. Whitman, *Harsh Justice: Criminal Justice and the Widening Divide between America and Europe* (New York: Oxford University Press, 2003).

(to say nothing of prostitution and welfare fraud) will continue to be staunchly resisted. This despite evidence that a drug like marijuana is one of the safest known in the world, according to much scientific study.[71] Given this reality, I wish to offer some more "realistic" recommendations, relatively speaking — but recommendations that will still be difficult for a "nation of jailers."

A serious difficulty affecting contemporary imprisonment practices is the widespread refusal of many public officials and private residents (whether Christian or otherwise) to truly care much about the humane treatment of prisoners. Tied to this is a general national unwillingness to care about, design, and implement programs aimed at preparing inmates to become contributing members of the communities to which they are released and society at large. In the context of this national unwillingness the prison system tends to focus on retribution, degradation, and control rather than on transformative and restorative alternatives reflective of Christian ontological intimacy. Therefore the prison system generally reinforces the very criminality it wants to deter. And all of this contributes heavily to the high rate of criminal recidivism.

The practice of large-scale retributive degradation presents a real problem for Christians. We must affirm the ontological intimacy of victims and offenders even as we acknowledge a societal responsibility to se-

---

71. Biko Agozino, *Black Women and the Criminal Justice System: Towards the Decolonisation of Victimisation* (Brookfield, Vt.: Ashgate, 1997), p. 174. Agozino correctly summarizes what can happen to a top public health official when they call for a serious national discussion/debate on decriminalizing drugs: "For example, the black US Surgeon General, Joycelyn Elders told a conference on 8 December 1994 that the government should seriously study the experience of countries that decriminalised drugs and thereby reduced drug addiction and violent crimes. This prophetic statement cost her the job as President Clinton, who allegedly smoked but did not inhale, dismissed the messenger with the message even though all available evidence indicates that the war on drugs was yet, 'another lost war' (Chambliss, 1995: 101). That the war is lost was partially conceded by the black man known as President Clinton's 'drug czar,' Lee Brown, former New York and Houston Police Chief (Cockburn, 1993). Brown's rhetoric is said to give the impression that the government had declared the war on drugs over and moved on to rehabilitation whereas the reality remained that simple possession was still increasingly being punished with imprisonment. Lee Brown was continuing the two agendas from the new right and the new left. Congressman Charles Rangel of Harlem called legalisation 'the moral equivalent of genocide of black people.' This agrees with Mr. Clinton's favoured option of increased enforcement and Mr Brown underlined this option when he echoed the Nixon-Carter-Reagan-Bush-Clinton promises of increased military aid for tackling drugs trafficking at source, that is, waging the war abroad" (p. 176).

cure justice. With regard to victims in particular, a politics of ontological intimacy in the context of the most unspeakably anguished and gruesome experiences of crime takes much patience and time. It will take time for families and communities to participate in anything like forgiveness and reconciliation when forced to confront episodes like the one that occurred to friends of my own family in November of 1993:

> Oliver Morgan's rampage began at 8 a.m. Monday when he confronted his ex-girlfriend, Darlene Boyd, 27, outside her mother's Bronx apartment and told her: "We gonna settle this once and for all," investigators and family friends said. Boyd had left him after he allegedly assaulted her in August. Police said Morgan entered the two story brick row house at 2956 Morgan Ave. in Baychester, brandishing a .25-cal. automatic pistol. In front of four small children, including his 20-month-old son, Morgan allegedly ordered Boyd's 54-year-old mother, Shirley, out of the bathroom and shot her in the head, police said. Three of the four children were Darlene Boyd's while the fourth was her sister Natalie's. "Darlene said her mother fell but she didn't die right away," said Olive Matura, 51, a longtime family friend who was with Boyd yesterday. "He told Darlene 'Your mother must be a ghost because bullets can't kill her.' Then he shot her again and again and covered her with a blanket." As Shirley's two daughters and four grandchildren — ages 1 to 7 — watched, Morgan reloaded and pumped a total of 13 bullets into the woman's head and back, investigators said. Matura said Darlene told her that Morgan went into the kitchen and raped Boyd's 23-year-old sister, Natalie. He raped Natalie again on a sofabed in the livingroom with Darlene forced to lie next to him, Matura said. "Say goodbye to Natalie," Matura said Darlene quoted Morgan, who she said then put a pillow over Natalie's head and shot her. "He took the pillow off and shot her again," Matura said. Matura said, Natalie Boyd had at least 6 gunshot wounds to the head, according to the medical examiner. After the killing, Morgan abducted Darlene Boyd and the four children, possibly taking them to a courthouse in an attempt to get a marriage license, police said. He then took them to a cousin's house on Washington Avenue in Morrisania, were he was arrested at 4 a.m. yesterday and the woman and children were found unharmed.[72]

72. Ray Sánchez, "Slaughtered — Cops: Jilted Lover Kills 2 Women in Murder Spree,"

It cannot be denied that this episode of horrendous crime is indeed sensational. And it is critical that any Christian contemplating the radical nature of Christian penance, forgiveness, reconciliation, or restoration in the service of ontological intimacy faces the memory of such acts head-on. We Christians, who are all too human, with trembling rage, fear, and anxiety, must stare into the pale dead face of our misery on account of such an act and confront our understandable blood-thirst for revenge with the memory of the executed God, Jesus Christ, to guide us. Indeed, we must face "the mother who can't sleep, tormented by wondering if her slain daughter's last cry was 'Mama'"; "the jogger who can't forget the crack of her nose breaking just before her rapist beat her into unconsciousness"; "the devoted Catholic who can't quite shed his rage — 'that's hate with a lot of chili sauce poured on it' — at the man in cowboy boots who stomped his elderly mother to death nearly thirty years ago"; or "the woman who goes away each Christmas because that's the season when her ex-husband stabbed their son and daughter, then killed himself."[73] These are the real memories that cry out for a difficult justice that is soaked in a revolutionary love that heals but does not forget. Indeed, such healing in the service of ontological intimacy must deal seriously, yet transformatively, with those who commit violent and death-dealing crime. But a society that creates the Oliver Morgans of this world must also deal transformatively with itself.

Any politics that fosters transformative healing of such memories in the service of ontological intimacy will benefit all concerned. Christian striving toward a politics of ontological intimacy in our punishment practices is indeed a "utopian" goal we must strive for; Christians ought to hope that deeply while living lives at the crossroads of Good Friday and Easter. The goal of ontological intimacy is a profoundly spiritual quest because (as has already been suggested) it is a politics expressive of human participation in the divine life. Such participation is a politics because it is concerned with the manner in which human beings better arrange and manage our common lives together across wide-ranging differences, including our competing versions of happiness. Indeed, a politics of ontological intimacy

New York Newsday, November 3, 1993. Natalie Boyd was a close friend of my own family and a best friend to my youngest sister Wendy, who is now a New York City police officer.

73. Cindi Lash, "Emotional Struggles of Crime Victims Showcased in New Play," Pittsburgh Post-Gazette, May 2, 2004, p. 1. Cf. Howard Zehr, Transcending: Reflections of Crime Victims (Intercourse, Pa.: Good Books, 2001).

is expressive of a political order the "essence" of which, drawing on Sheldon Wolin's discussion of Plato, is the existence of fairly settled institutional and social arrangements "designed to deal in a variety of ways with the vitalities issuing from associated life: to offset them when necessary, to ease them where possible, and, creatively, to redirect and transmute them when the opportunity allows."[74] Politics (at its best) manages our associational lives as we human beings work to gain and act upon the knowledge we need to act wisely in contexts of conflict, ambiguity, and continuous change.[75]

To reiterate what I have already suggested, although a politics of ontological intimacy is bound to a spiritual narrative, even when at its sublime best it can never represent more than a creaturely correspondence, a shaky, unsteady, and provisional witness to the moral vision modeled supremely in the life-affirming communal testimony of Jesus Christ. Such a shaky, unsteady, and provisional communal and societal witness to human moral bondedness, to radical intimacy, is spiritual precisely because it is profoundly shaped by an "outside" story. As Wolin reminds us, even Plato understood the importance of the "outside" to political orders struggling for stability, harmony, unity, and beauty: "Political order was produced by an informing vision which came from the 'outside,' from the knowledge of the eternal pattern, to shape the community to a pre-existent Good."[76] Working toward ontological intimacy is a struggle Christians take on because we seek faithfulness to the Christian God (our "Good"), both outside and inside the world. We celebrate, are ecstatic and joyous about, our participation in the political life of this God self-revealed in Jesus Christ. And to pursue a public witness to a supremely difficult vision of good punishment, as an expression of participation in God's ontological intimacy, is a concrete gift Christians offer society — and themselves.

Epilogue: Learning from "The Liberals"

In the context of examining U.S. imprisonment and various associated collateral social consequences, I have begun an engagement with Stanley

74. Sheldon Wolin, *Politics and Vision*, expanded edition (Princeton, N.J.: Princeton University Press, 2004), 41.

75. Cf. Wolin, *Politics and Vision*, p. 40. Cf. Hauerwas, "Democratic Time: Lessons Learned from Yoder and Wolin," *CrossCurrents*, Winter 2006, p. 544.

76. Wolin, *Politics and Vision*, p. 41.

Hauerwas, one of the most important and provocative Christian theologians writing today. Specifically, I have constructed and engaged what I have termed Hauerwas's Christian ethics of good punishment as a resource for Christian thinking and action. Indeed, how and why the United States punishes those convicted of crime and deals with the social aftermath is (or should be) of pressing concern for Christians living in a society that predominantly claims Christian allegiance. Christians should wonder why a "Christian nation" with just 6 percent or so of the world's population, a nation which views itself as a moral role model for freedom and democracy, incarcerates some 25 percent of the world's prisoners. My constructive agenda has ended up moving beyond Hauerwas by advancing a reconstructive critique and sort of "redeployment" of his Christian ethics of "good punishment." That exercise has been my entryway into responding to the deleterious function of contemporary U.S. imprisonment practice and its allied social consequences.

I have endeavored to move beyond Hauerwas by expanding the social implications of his understandings of "healing memories" and "ontological intimacy" beyond where he himself may think wise. Specifically, it is in the context of a politics of healing memory towards a politics of ontological intimacy that I express a Christian social ethics of good punishment in the service of inching Christians toward a more (yes) "effective" response to the nation's reliance on locking up unprecedented numbers of its residents. This is something Hauerwas himself does not do. In the context of my articulation of the politics of healing memories and ontological intimacy, I offer examples of where I see movement and struggle toward these interrelated politics already occurring in relation to imprisonment practice and its negative social effects: restorative justice and systemic alternatives. I want to conclude my efforts here by returning to the problem of "liberalism," a central issue informing the inability (or at least very limited ability) of Hauerwas's ethics of good punishment to influence a better Christian vision of healing memories and ontological intimacy in the public square.

Hauerwas insists that the corporate witness of Christian faith comes to represent the lived truthfulness of the gospel only through the development of common virtues that dispose Christians to desire rightly. Related to this is the last sentence of the first book he ever wrote, originally published in 1975: "The task of Christian ethics is to keep the grammar of the language of faith so pure that we may claim not only to speak the truth but also to embody that truth in our lives."[77] Hauerwas contends that we as Christians betray our non-Christian neighbors when we rob them and ourselves of "exemplifications of truthful speech forged through the worship of God."[78] As William Werpehowski has correctly observed, Hauerwas's use of the word "'pure' indicates for some critics an ethic that is ecclesiologically sectarian, ethically tribalist, and epistemologically fideist."[79] (Hauerwas now concedes that perhaps the language of "purity" was regrettable.) While his Christian vision does contain strong elements of tribalism and fideism,[80] I have argued that the common charge of sectarianism leveled against Hauerwas can reasonably be viewed as actually obscuring one of Hauerwas's true underlying aims, namely, agitating for a re-envisioned Constantinianism (or Christendom). Hauerwas's version of

---

77. Stanley Hauerwas, *Character and the Christian Life* (San Antonio, Tex.: Trinity University Press, 1985), p. 233.

78. Stanley Hauerwas, "On Being a Christian and an American," *A Better Hope* (Grand Rapids, Mich.: Brazos Press, 2000), p. 24.

79. Werpehowski, *American Protestant Ethics and the Legacy of H. Richard Niebuhr*, p. 72. See Hauerwas's direct response to his critics regarding these charges in his essay, "On Being a Christian and an American," in *A Better Hope*, pp. 23-34. I note that the title Hauerwas first thought to give this essay, "Why Christians Will Never Work in America," displays a powerful and fundamental ambivalence in Hauerwas's thinking about Christian participation in the public square. This ambivalence often comes across as advocacy of Christian withdrawal, hence the charge of sectarianism.

80. Hauerwas's "fideism" is of a sort which paradoxically claims that the teleological (against the *a priori*) character of narrative Christian existence does display "metaphysical" claims. Christians do not give up claims of universality if the bases of our particular, contextual, "universalism" comes about "by first being initiated into a particular story and community." Yet, according to Hauerwas, "Christianity is no 'worldview,' not a form of primitive metaphysics, that can be assessed in comparison to alternative 'worldviews.' Rather, Christians are people who remain convinced that the truthfulness of their beliefs must be demonstrated in their lives. There is a sense in which Christian convictions are self-referential, but the reference is not propositions but lives." While Hauerwas does indeed want to emphasize the distinctiveness of Christian ethics, he does not deny that there can be points of contact between Christian ethics and other forms of moral life. This notwithstanding, Hauerwas argues that while such points of contact frequently exist, "they are not sufficient to provide a basis for a 'universal' ethic grounded in human nature per se." Instead, the moral "foundation" that Christians witness to is Jesus' life, which constitutes the "heartbeat of the Christian life." It is in the narrative of Jesus, inside of which Christians are dependent, where the meaning and form of Christian existence becomes intelligible (and rational) on Hauerwas's view. See Hauerwas, *A Community of Character*, p. 93; *Christian Existence Today*, pp. 9-10; and *The Peaceable Kingdom*, pp. 60-61; 68.

Christendom (he often claims to be a theocrat) rejects its current expression, which identifies the church's mission (along with the whole meaning of history) "with the function of the state in organizing sinful society."[81]

Hauerwas insists that church, as the Body of Christ, must be itself (holy, faithful, peaceable) in a liberal society that refuses to confess and live out the peaceable politics of Jesus. The practical implication of this is that Hauerwas's better vision of "good punishment" is not generally transferable to society; or at least it is just barely transferable. I believe that I am essentially right about Hauerwas here notwithstanding his ostensive openness to other traditions which understand themselves in the context of a common set of tradition-dependent virtues adequate for making a praxis of the common good possible. For example, in his book *Suffering Presence* Hauerwas is, in fact, more than willing (as he has said elsewhere) to "do justice to the contingent 'points of contact' between Christian convictions and the world" on the issue of medical ethics.[82] Werpehowski correctly summarizes Hauerwas's views in *Suffering Presence* as follows:

> Much of the book's argument presupposes an appreciation of the moral practices of medicine, according to which practitioners teach the "wisdom of the body" to the sick while also never abandoning them in their illness and accompanying them in their aloneness. Clearly, this analysis is based on Hauerwas's vision of charity-informed virtues as they arise in the life of discipleship; but it is just as clear that it also depends on a positive view of the goods proper and available to God's human creatures as such. He holds that the practice of medicine needs the church to bring it (by moral osmosis?) something of the faithfulness to the suffering that it requires; the external condition of this holding, however, that is some notion along the lines that human creatures are made for this kind of fidelity in the relevant medical relationships.[83]

---

81. Quoted in Werpehowski, *American Protestant Ethics*, p. 96. Hauerwas is drawing here on John Howard Yoder; see Yoder, *The Original Revolution* (Scottdale, Pa.: Herald Press, 1971), p. 83. See also Hauerwas, *In Good Company* (Notre Dame, Ind.: University of Notre Dame Press, 1995), p. 231 n. 15.

82. See "Epilogue," in Paul Ramsey, *Speak Up for Just War or Pacifism* (University Park, Pa.: Pennsylvania State University Press, 1988), p. 176. See also Hauerwas, *Suffering Presence: Reflections on Medicine, the Mentally Handicapped, and the Church* (Notre Dame, Ind.: University of Notre Dame Press, 1986).

83. Werpehowski, *American Protestant Ethics*, p. 106.

With regard to Hauerwas's Christian vision for the practice of "suf-fering presence," Werpehowski has been right to challenge Hauerwas's ap-positional view of medical ethics and Christian faith by suggesting that there be the requirement of "a substantive reference to human creaturely life, to forms of human relationships that cut across the distinctions be-tween Christians and non-Christians. *They involve shared goods and soli-darities in areas of human activity that obtain even while that distinction is appropriately maintained*" [emphasis mine].[84]

Werpehowski's concern is just the right one and it also has been mine as I have examined the usefulness of Hauerwas's theological ethics in the service of a better Christian response to current imprisonment prac-tices. If society *were already* in the habit of what Hauerwas could confirm as *tradition-bound* nonviolent alternatives to the violence and degradation of imprisonment, then I suppose Hauerwas would allow for more concrete Christian involvement. But since our criminal justice system is violent and degrading at its core with no common tradition to appeal to for better al-ternatives, Hauerwas's ethics of punishment cannot, or will not, really sug-gest what a sociopolitical vision of good punishment might look like in terms of (for example) better public policies and institutions, voluntary community and civic organizations, forms of social protest, etc. Indeed, Hauerwas wants to warn Christians away from sociopolitical agendas that would spoil the purity of the allegedly peaceable Christian community, which sits on a hill and views its life of virtue as a gift to society.

Ultimately, it seems that Hauerwas makes of the body of Christ an idol, holding to a faith that might be called "churchianity," a privileged so-cial movement that must rely on something that Kathryn Tanner rightly warns Christians against being: namely, a dogmatic embodiment of the idea of being a closely guarded and readily defined boundary-marking and boundary-making people.[85] In a vein that builds on Tanner's sentiments, Scott Holland, writing for the *Conrad Grebel Review,* has criticized the se-verity of Hauerwas's boundary-making rhetoric, arguing that

[Hauerwas's] Wittgensteinian, pure narrative approach to theological discourse, which demands a clean self-referential consistency if theo-

84. Werpehowski, *American Protestant Ethics*, p. 106.
85. See Werpehowski's very good summary of Tanner in relation to Hauerwas on this issue in, *American Protestant Ethics*, p. 194. See also Kathryn Tanner, *Theories of Culture: A New Agenda for Theology* (Minneapolis: Fortress Press, 1997), p. 56.

logians are to play by the rules of this proposed language game, fails to address the fact that the entire vocabulary of Christian community, including central signifiers like God, revelation, faith, love, and justice are ordinary terms grounded in the language and culture of general experience. Because no community is an island in the contemporary world, there is no language of revelation or peoplehood that does not have its beginning in broader human experience.[86]

In general Hauerwas fails to account for what Christians can "truthfully" (with a small "t") understand as manifestations of God's grace outside the church. This is particularly true with regard to moral concerns that the church lacks the communal resources to deal adequately with on its own. Christian ethicist Max Stackhouse summarizes this concern as follows:

> Today, many of the decisive ethical problems facing the people in our churches have to do precisely with social institutions and intellectual developments outside the church at levels for which there is no corresponding political order and for which the church is not fully competent within itself. They are issues that more frequently have to be dealt with in "civil society" by "community organizations" and "voluntary associations" in relation to various spheres of the social order. Matters such as good schools, excellent and accessible medical care, quality movies and music and TV offerings, responsible corporations and unions, and enduring, loving families are not matters that can be built from the top down by any regime, nor from the bottom up from the formation of virtue within the churches alone. Rather they have to be formed, and repeatedly reformed, from the center (*their* center) out, and take shape in law, cultural expectation, educational curriculum, corporate policy, and physical architecture. This requires a public theology able to engage them with an ethic that aids them to clarify how they live in the world. A certain expansive scope, thus, is required along with a personal conversion and socio-institutional savvy if anything like sanctification, holy living, viable communities, care for the neighbor or a relatively just society is to be sustained.[87]

86. Scott Holland, "The Problems and Prospects of a 'Sectarian Ethic': A Critique of the Hauerwas Reading of the Jesus Story," *Conrad Grebel Review* 10 (1992): 166.

87. Max L. Stackhouse, "In the Company of Hauerwas," *Journal for Christian Theological Research* 2, no. 1 (1997): 4. While Stackhouse and I may disagree on the root theological

Whatever one might think about the theological "center" that grounds Stackhouse's understanding of social institutions and intellectual developments, his challenge to Hauerwas correctly implies that God's grace is apparent in the world outside the strict boundaries of the church.

Perhaps better than most other American religious and/or philosophical ethicists, Jeffrey Stout has done the best job of trying to get Hauerwas to see the good potential in "liberalism." Stout understands well that much of society's current expression of liberal democracy is indeed corrupted with vice. Yet he would reject the argument that all liberal democratic ideas, by necessity, produce the opposite of a virtuous society. Hauerwas sees the church as a kind of ethical aristocracy that is essential to the production and expansion of a community of character. Hauerwas's hope is that such a community of character, because of the kind of instruction given by the ethical aristocrats of Christian faith contained therein, must be "antidemocratic." But Stout rightly challenges this view as he works to recover the more hopeful and humane possibilities of liberal democracy as a tradition:

> I agree with Hauerwas's claim that an ethical aristocracy is essential to the maintenance of a virtuous community, assuming that "aristocracy" is here being used metaphorically. But in that case, the claim is hardly antidemocratic — not, at any rate, if Emerson, Whitman, and Thoreau qualify as paradigmatic democratic thinkers. Democracy, in their view, is not an attempt to level qualitative distinctions in the various domains of human life. They all believed that the excellence of "representative" individuals raises them above the mediocre mean, and confers on them a high vocation of awakening others to virtue.
>
> Say if you like, that these exemplars constitute an aristocracy. But surely Hauerwas does not suppose that they are to be found in a particular social class or that their spiritual gifts can be correlated with the titles, ranks, or offices of some existing institution, ecclesial or secular.

---

authority adequate to sustain the better social and institutional flowering that public theology fortifies, he is right that Hauerwas's work really does not help us identify what the structure of better societal institutions might be. Stackhouse is willing to appeal to *(a priori)* "natural law" in the form of divine grace manifested as a general revelation that transcends all particular cultures. I remain decidedly agnostic about this, choosing instead to cast my faith with history-bound revelation reflective of the divine that dwells "outside" history. All human truth-claims are tempered by the bone-deep historicity of all human knowledge.

The Bible says that such gifts might be found in any human being among us — old or young, male or female, free or enslaved (Joel 2:27-28, Acts 2:17-18). No idea is more central to modern democracy — or to "liberalism" in the best sense of the term — than this one. It is because Emerson, Whitman, and Thoreau were suspicious of institutional arrangements that might prevent inspirited speech or true prophecy from being heard that they affirmed the democratic ideal of equal voice.[88]

A basic theological translation that Christians can take from what Stout (an atheist) has said is that God's grace operates at a high level *in* the world. Even liberal democracy contains what Karl Barth termed "secular parables of the Kingdom" (or "Truth"). So Christians should feel free to acknowledge that God's grace could just as well have inspired a biblical passage like Psalm 72 as J. S. Mill's *On Liberty* with the command that the cause of the poor should be defended. And, conversely, an ecclesiastical organization's use of Scripture can be regarded as just as socially and politically dangerous as a secular humanist's citation of *On Liberty*.[89] Indeed, a self-described secular humanist like Richard Rorty is correct to note that while religious belief is not irrational or intrinsically wrong-headed, the ecclesiastical organizations that give religion its content and function aid exclusivism and "contempt for people who should be accorded the same respect as the rest of their fellow-citizens."[90] Rorty goes on to grant that ecclesiastical organizations are sometimes on the right side of social history, yet he maintains that the occasional Gustavo Guttiérez or Martin Luther King Jr. cannot compensate for the ubiquitous Jerry Falwells or Pat Robinsons. History suggests, according to Rorty, that ecclesiastical organizations "will always, on balance, do more harm than good."[91] Perhaps Rorty has offered Christians a secular parable of the truth.

Of course, liberal democracy in its contemporary incarnation does its fair share of harm as well. One sees this particularly in liberal democracy's ugly sidekick "late capitalism." Michael Quirk's summary of the faults of late

88. Jeffrey Stout, *Democracy and Tradition* (Princeton, N.J.: Princeton University Press, 2004), p. 167.

89. See and cf. Richard Rorty, "Religion in the Public Square: A Reconsideration," *Journal of Religious Ethics* 31, no. 1 (Spring 2003): 141-49; esp. 142-43.

90. Rorty, "Religion in the Public Square: A Reconsideration," p. 142.

91. Rorty, "Religion in the Public Square: A Reconsideration," p. 142.

capitalism, with its underlying "thin" notions of obligation, is essentially correct: "[late capitalism] deprives its citizens of any robust opportunities to debate and deliberate on the nature of the good, and in part because the noisy, relentless triumphalism of the liberal-democratic cheerleaders for 'globalism' has grown so tiresome, and is so transparently a front for American corporate interests to colonize and homogenize the world."[92] Angela Y. Davis (along with multitudes of others) has also been actively concerned with the contemporary "global assembly line, which links us in ways contingent on exploitive practices of production and consumption." Davis tells us for example, "In the Global North, we purchase the pain and exploitation of girls in the Global South, which we wear everyday on our bodies."[93] Indeed, to the extent that late capitalism (or global "neoliberalism")[94] represents the contemporary face of liberal democracy, Hauerwas's critique of liberalism is sound enough.

92. Michael J. Quirk, "Stanley Hauerwas: An Interview," *Cross Currents*, available online at http://www.crosscurrents.org/Hauerwasspring2002.htm.

93. Davis, *Abolition Democracy*, pp. 25-26.

94. I am employing the term "neoliberalism" (a.k.a. "Washington consensus") as descriptive of ways in which primary holders of worldwide wealth and power have come to dominate nation-state policy formation and the structures that manipulate consumption-oriented thought, opinion, and action. The primary holders of such wealth and power include huge, privately held, profit-oriented multinational corporations. Neoliberalism is a system of primarily economic (but also political, social, cultural, and psychological) principles whose basic rules, in brief, according to Noam Chomsky, are to, "liberalize trade and finance, let markets set price ('get prices right'), end inflation ('macroeconomic stability'), privatize." Chomsky asserts further that under neoliberalism, "[t]he government should 'get out of the way' — hence the population too, insofar as the government is democratic, the conclusion remains implicit." Under neoliberalism there are few, if any, governmental restrictions on industrialization, commerce, and there are no tariffs. This constitutes the basics of what is "liberal" about neoliberalism. Essentially, it is a return to the philosophy of "economic liberalism" advocated in Adam Smith's *The Wealth of Nations* published in 1776. The "neo" in neoliberalism has to do with a return to a policy of economic liberalism by highly developed nation states and multinational corporations. Additionally, and very critically, there is a concurrent volatization of capital that can be partly traced back to the (circa) 1973 decision to stop utilizing the gold standard as a measure to anchor, or stabilize, world currencies in relation to each other. Under neoliberalism, world currencies are valued and devalued against one another in the global marketplace, giving the currency of highly developed nations a devastating advantage over currencies from poorer nations. This advantage is intensified further by the instantaneous way that modern communication technologies, employed by wealthy nations, help to structure and restructure capital for maximum productivity and profits with little or no voice from the masses of people who will be negatively effected. And this is made all the easier now with the existence of just one world "super-

Yet Hauerwas is wrong to think that the contemporary manifestations of liberal democracy represent the best pragmatic "essence" of liberalism. Just as large numbers of Christians who favor capital punishment, the possession and use of nuclear weapons, and the establishment of the United States as world empire (the so-called Pax Americana) do not represent Hauerwas's ideal version of Christianity, nor does vulgar individualism and late capitalism/neoliberalism necessarily represent the ideal spirit of liberal democratic, or even secular humanist, traditions. Speaking more broadly, Michael Ignatieff is basically right to contend (even if he does so in too totalizing a fashion) that in the face of radical evil manifested throughout the span of human history, "both secular humanism and ancient [religious] belief have been utterly helpless victims or enthusiastic accomplices."[95]

I would suggest that there are correlations between the best of the peace church tradition and the best of the liberal democratic tradition (as well as the best of what might be viewed as more radical justice traditions challenging from outside the established order).[96] Such correlations can result in common understandings of the virtues adequate to establish a common good. Many sociopolitical traditions, be they based in a religious, liberal, democratic, or socialist sensibility (or combinations of these), have a deep and profound sense of a just common good to which they aim, however imperfectly. The distinctively Christian faith warrant for such a common good is revealed in the politics of Jesus, God's self-unveiled and love-soaked grace for the world. From the Christian perspective this grace constitutes the supreme model of the hope for ontological intimacy among all creation. Christian strivings toward a politics of ontological intimacy may well be "universal" for them while still affirming Hauerwas's rejection of the "idea of a 'universal reason' subsisting apart from particular practices and traditions. . . ."[97] This is so because no "universal reason" emerges traditionless. There is a bone-deep historicity that gives birth to

---

power" — the United States of America. See Noam Chomsky, *Profit Over People: Neoliberalism and the Global Order* (New York: Seven Stories Press, 1999), p. 20.

95. Michael Ignatieff, *Human Rights As Politics and Idolatry*, ed. Amy Gutmann (Princeton, N.J.: Princeton University Press, 2001), p. 86.

96. For good examples of correlations between Christian experiences of God and Jesus Christ with radical justice movements and traditions, see Taylor, *The Executed God*, pp. 127-54.

97. Michael J. Quirk, "Stanley Hauerwas: An Interview," *CrossCurrents*, http://www.crosscurrents.org/Hauerwasspring2002.htm.

every claim of "universal," "transcendent," "natural," and "eternal" truth, notwithstanding the Christian faith that our God is a gracious mystery both without and within time.

Both the Christian churches and liberal democracy (as traditions) can rehabilitate "thick" conceptions of the kinds of virtues that make common notions of the societal good possible. The Christian warrant for this possibility is the reconciling politics of Jesus Christ in history. In Christ there is justification for the Christian impulse to work alongside others for the common good. Achieving a common good, based on Jesus' own reconciling efforts, is always forged in the context of dialogue and struggle. In the work toward ontological intimacy, any agreements issuing from dialogue and struggle should always be negotiable and revisable because of the shifting realities of circumstances. Of course, secular humanists and others will not accept the theological assumptions underlying Christian points of view in order to work with Christians. Hopefully, though, they can affirm the existence of correlations between the best traditions of "secular" political philosophy and the best traditions of Christian faith for the establishment of a common and flourishing society and world. Given the interconnectedness and correlations between many sociopolitical goals in the basic service of a general pursuit of human rights and dignity, secularists, Christians, and others can contribute together to a critical celebration of plurality and improvisational resistance to human misery and domination.[98]

---

98. Cf., for example, Mark Lewis Taylor's critical retrieval of the notion of *(dynamically interrelated)* "correlation" which (1) analyzes social location (experience) through a practice of critical "reflexive analysis," (2) practices "portaiture," or interprets the wider corporate historical situation or tradition, and (3) practices "address," i.e., mining the richness of distinctively Christian narratives and practices; and engages situations that re/produce dominative movements and ideas with words and actions while also affirming/celebrating alternative ones. The core traits of Taylor's "postmodern trilemma" include a critical cultural-political correlation among tradition, the celebration of plurality, and resistance to domination. Taylor works to move beyond commonly understood methods of correlation, which tend to focus on reconciling two poles (e.g., experience and tradition) that are subject to correlation. His "cultural-political theology" is an effort to engage cultural-political threats to human dignity that emerge through "disciplined attention to the (nondialectical) 'theoretical practices' of reflexivity, portraiture, and address." The "trilemmic consciousness" of Taylor's cultural political theology "grants a significant privilege to the interpretive stance of the victims of [cultural-]political oppression." Sadly, this is something that most Christian theologians are apparently not about to consider, much less practice. See Mark Kline Taylor, *Remembering Esperanza*, pp. 23-45.

The power of God's grace is more than sufficient to allow for symbolic correspondences between church and society: Christians (and other religious moralists) could still believe in the reality of sin while secular humanists and others speak of the corresponding dangers of vice; Christians could vouch for the reality of grace while others vouch for the possibility of a virtuous life in trying circumstances; the church could continue to be embraced by Christians as the community of God's body in time while others "embrace philosophy, and its community of inquiry, as a vocation that makes one's life worthy and worthwhile."[99] Indeed, the church could embrace Jesus even while others might embrace corresponding exemplars in the persons of, say, Socrates, Buddha, or Mawu-Lisa. Christians could view all of this in the context of God's grace bestowed on humans in the form of an "analogical imagination" of correspondence sufficient to forge a consensus about what constitutes movement toward ontological intimacy.

Essentially, these concluding thoughts aim to free a Christian social ethics of good punishment from the prison of dogmatic illiberality. I, like so many others before me, work here to extend the moral reach of Christian social ethics in relation to an important contemporary social issue beyond where some Christians seem willing to go. I do this with the understanding that God's love-soaked grace is profoundly *for and against* "the world." God's grace works *against* the complex alienations that divide individuals, families, communities, churches, society, and world. Yet this same grace, this most profound love, is *for* these interlocking dimensions of life as humanity struggles (ironically) toward the kinds of restorative and flourishing social-political arrangements that have never truly been. To seek better interconnected human restoration and flourishing, to seek a politics of ontological intimacy for all of us who are society's victims and offenders, amounts to a pursuit of human participation in the Being of God — participation, indeed, in a Love Supreme.

99. Quirk, "Stanley Hauerwas: An Interview."

Index